5 STEPS TO A 5

AP English Language

2017

WITHDRAWN
From Toronto Public Library

Barbara L. Murphy
Estelle M. Rankin

McGraw Hill Education

New York Chicago San Francisco Athens London Madrid
Mexico City Milan New Delhi Singapore Sydney Toronto

D1247307

Copyright © 2016, 2015, 2014, 2013, 2011, 2010, 2007, 2002 by McGraw-Hill Education. All rights reserved. Printed in the United States of America. Except as permitted under the United States Copyright Act of 1976, no part of this publication may be reproduced or distributed in any form or by any means, or stored in a database or retrieval system, without the prior written permission of the publisher.

1 2 3 4 5 6 7 8 9   RHR   21 20 19 18 17 16 (book alone)
1 2 3 4 5 6 7 8 9   RHR   21 20 19 18 17 16 (Cross-Platform Prep Course)

ISBN   978-1-259-58652-1 (book alone)
MHID   1-259-58652-9
ISSN   2150-6302

ISBN   978-1-259-58344-5 (Cross-Platform Prep Course)
MHID   1-259-58344-9

e-ISBN 978-1-259-58653-8 (e-book alone)
e-MHID   1-259-58653-7

e-ISBN 978-1-259-58345-2 (Cross-Platform Prep Course)
e-MHID   1-259-58345-7

Trademarks: McGraw-Hill Education, the McGraw-Hill Education logo, *5 Steps to a 5* and related trade dress are trademarks or registered trademarks of McGraw-Hill Education and/or its affiliates in the United States and other countries and may not be used without written permission. All other trademarks are the property of their respective owners. McGraw-Hill Education is not associated with any product or vendor mentioned in this book.

The series editor for this book was Grace Freedson and the project editor was Del Franz.

AP, Advanced Placement Program, and *College Board* are registered trademarks of the College Board, which was not involved in the production of, and does not endorse, this product.

McGraw-Hill Education products are available at special quantity discounts to use as premiums and sales promotions or for use in corporate training programs. To contact a representative, please visit the Contact Us pages at www.mhprofessional.com.

ABOUT THE AUTHORS

Barbara L. Murphy taught AP Language and other college-level courses at Jericho High School for more than 26 years. She has been a reader of the AP Language and Composition exam since 1993 and is a consultant for the College Board's AP Language and Composition, for which she has conducted workshops, conferences, and Summer Institutes. She is currently on the faculty of Syracuse University's Project Advance in English.

After earning her B.A. from Duquesne University and her M.A. from the University of Pittsburgh, Ms. Murphy did her doctoral course work at Columbia University. She also holds professional certifications in still photography and motion picture production and is one of the founding members of the women's film company Ishtar Films.

Estelle M. Rankin taught AP Literature at Jericho High School for more than 25 years. She was honored with the AP Literature Teacher of the Year award by the College Board in 1996. She also received the Long Island Teacher of the Year award in 1990. She was the recipient of the Cornell University Presidential Scholars' Award and has been recognized by the C.W. Post Master Teachers Program.

Ms. Rankin earned her B.A. from Adelphi University and her M.A. from Hofstra University. She has pursued further graduate work in the field of creative studies at Queens College and Brooklyn College.

She has done extensive work in the research and development of film, drama, and creative writing curricula, SAT prep, and the new NYS Regents benchmarks for English, and has participated in numerous AP Literature conferences and workshops. Ms. Rankin is currently a College Board consultant for pre-AP and AP English. Her finest teachers were her parents, Edward and Sylvia Stern.

Ms. Murphy and Ms. Rankin are also the coauthors of McGraw-Hill's *5 Steps to a 5: AP English Literature*, *Writing the AP English Essay*, and *Writing an Outstanding College Application Essay*.

Cartoon by Jim Sizemore used with permission of Cartoon Stock Ltd. (www.Cartoon Stock.com).

Editorial cartoon by Chris Britt used with permission of the cartoonist.

Editorial cartoon by Clay Bennett © 2006 *The Christian Science Monitor* (www.csmonitor. com). All rights reserved.

Editorial cartoon by Jeff Koterba/*Omaha World-Herald*.

"Eminent Domain," excerpt from *60 Minutes*, July 4, 2004. Reprinted by permission of CBS News Archives.

From *In Cold Blood* by Truman Capote, copyright © by Truman Capote and renewed 1993 by Alan U. Schwartz. Used by permission of Random House, Inc.

From "Introduction," *The Best Essays of 1988*. Reprinted by permission of Russell & Volkening as agents for the author. Copyright © 1988 by Annie Dillard.

From "States Curbing Right to Seize Private Houses," by John Broder from the *New York Times* on the Web © The New York Times Company. Reprinted with permission.

From "The Case for Flag-Burning. . .," an editorial published June 27, 2006. Copyright © 2006 *Los Angeles Times*. Reprinted with permission.

From *What Is Marriage For?* by E. J. Graff. Copyright © 1999. Reprinted by permission of Beacon Press, Boston.

Jencks, Christopher. From a review and discussion of *American Dream: Three Women, Ten Kids, and a Nation's Drive to End Welfare* appearing in *The New York Review of Books*, December 15, 2005. Reprinted with permission from *The New York Review of Books*. Copyright © 2005 NYREV, Inc.

Lapham, Lewis. Excerpt from *Money and Class in America: Notes and Observations on Our Civil Religion*. Copyright © 1988 by Lewis Lapham. Reprinted by permission.

Lindberg, Todd. "The Star Spangled Banner." Copyright © 2006 The Washington Times LLC. This reprint does not constitute or imply any endorsement or sponsorship of any product, service, company or organization.

O'Neill, Jesse. From *The Golden Ghetto: The Psychology of Affluence*. Copyright © 1997 The Affluenza Project. Reprinted by permission.

Sekula, Allen. "Reading an Archive." From *Blasted Allegories*. Copyright © 1987 by MIT. Used by permission of the publisher, MIT Press.

"The Voice of the Story, the Story as Voice," an excerpt from "Reading Blind"; first appeared in *The Best American Short Stories 1989* © 1989 O.W. Toad, Ltd.

CONTENTS

Preface   ix
Acknowledgments   xi
Introduction: The Five-Step Program   xiii

STEP 1 Set Up Your Study Program

1 **What You Need to Know About the AP English Language and Composition Exam   3**
Background on the AP English Language and Composition Exam   3
Reasons for Taking the AP English Language and Composition Exam   4
What You Need to Know About the AP English Language and Composition Exam   5

2 **How to Plan Your Time   8**
Three Approaches to Prepare for the AP English Language and Composition Exam   8

STEP 2 Determine Your Test Readiness

3 A Walk Through the Diagnostic/Master Exam   17

STEP 3 Develop Strategies for Success

4 **Section I of the Exam—The Multiple-Choice Questions   41**
Introduction to the Multiple-Choice Section of the Exam   41
Types of Multiple-Choice Questions   44
Scoring the Multiple-Choice Section   46
Strategies for Answering the Multiple-Choice Questions   46
The Time Is at Hand   49
Answer Sheet for Diagnostic Multiple-Choice Questions   50
Diagnostic/Master Exam   51
Explanations of Answers to the Multiple-Choice Questions   62
Introduction to Chapters 5, 6, and 7   66

5 **Introduction to the Analysis Essay   67**
Some Basics   68
Types of Analysis Essay Prompts   69
Rating the Analysis Essay   69
Timing and Planning the Analysis Essay   70
Working the Prompt   71
Reading and Notating the Passage   72
Developing the Opening Paragraph   75
Writing the Body of the Essay   76
Sample Student Essays   78
Rating the Essays   81
Other Types of Analysis Essays   84
Writing the Body of the Essay   90
Rapid Review   95

6 Introduction to the Argumentative Essay   96
Some Basics   96
Timing and Planning the Essay   97
Working the Prompt   98
Developing the Opening Paragraph   99
Developing the Body of the Essay   100
Sample Student Essays   102
Rating the Essays   104
Rapid Review   105

7 Introduction to the Synthesis Essay   107
Some Basics   107
Timing and Planning the Synthesis Essay   109
Working the Prompt   110
Developing the Opening Paragraph   111
Developing the Body of the Essay   113
Writing the Conclusion   115
Sample Synthesis Essay from the Master Exam   116
Sample Student Essays   117
Rating the Essays   120
Rapid Review   121

STEP 4 Review the Knowledge You Need to Score High

8 Comprehensive Review—Analysis   125
Some Basics   125
Rhetorical Strategies   127
About Style   135
The "Connective Tissue" Issue   144
Voice: Pen, Paper, Action!   145
A Few Words About Coherence   148
An Essay Editing and Revision Template   148
Rapid Review   150

9 Comprehensive Review—Argument   153
Some Basics   153
The Argument   155
Reading the Argument   157
Writing the Argument   160
Rapid Review   161

10 Comprehensive Review—Synthesis   162
Some Basics   162
A Few Comments Before Beginning   163
Strategies   163
A Note About Summary, Paraphrase, and Inference   170
Final Comment   174
Rapid Review   174

STEP 5 Build Your Test-Taking Confidence

Practice Exam 1   177
Answer Sheet   177
Section I   179
Section II   190
Answer Key   196
Explanations of Answers to the Multiple-Choice Section   197
Sample Student Essays   200

Practice Exam 2   211
Answer Sheet   211
Section I   213
Section II   224
Answer Key   230
Explanations of Answers to the Multiple-Choice Section   231
Sample Student Essays   234

Appendixes

Glossary   247
Selected Bibliography   251
Websites   253

PREFACE

Welcome to our latest revised AP English Language class. As we said in the earlier versions of this book, we are, first and foremost, teachers who have taught Advanced Placement to literally thousands of students who successfully took the AP exam. With this guide, we hope to share with you what we know, as well as what we have learned from our own students.

We see you as a student in our class—only quieter! Our philosophy has always been NOT to teach only for the AP test. Instead, our goal is to develop those insights, appreciations, and skills that lead to advanced levels of facility with a wide range of texts. These are the same skills that will enable you to do well on the AP English Language exam. Our aim is to remove your anxiety and to improve your comfort level with the test. We believe that you are already motivated to succeed; otherwise, you would not have come this far. And, obviously, you would not have purchased this prep book.

Because you are already in an AP English class, this book is going to supplement your course readings, analysis, and writing. We are going to give you the opportunity to practice processes and techniques that we know from experience REALLY WORK! If you apply the techniques and processes presented in this book, we are confident you can succeed in both the course and on the exam.

We have listened to comments and suggestions from both instructors and students of AP English Language. Keeping their thoughts in mind, this revised text has more interactive activities and practice to help hone those skills needed to do well in class and on the AP English Language exam. In addition, there are special review questions and activities related to specific chapters that McGraw-Hill has available on its website devoted to the *5 Steps* series. There you can test how well you have internalized the material in the chapter.

Let's begin.

ACKNOWLEDGMENTS

Our love and appreciation to Leah and Allan for their constant support and encouragement. Special thanks to our professional mentors who have guided us throughout our careers: Steven Piorkowski and Howard Damon. To the following for their support and suggestions: Diane Antonucci, Jodi Rice, Margaret Cross Rice, Pat Kelley, Stephanie Tidwell, and Sandi Forsythe—thank you.

The authors want to acknowledge the participation, insights, and feedback provided us by the following colleagues and students:

East Islip High School:
    Teacher: Marge Grossgold
    Students: Kyle Hill, Jamie Ray

Garden City High School:
    Teachers: Mary Watts, Ed Schmeider
    Students: Alexandra Wertis, Michael Marino

Jericho High School:
    Teachers: Diane Antonucci, Patricia Gulitti
    Students: Vikas Anand, Jenna Butner, Shinae Lee, Josh Levine, Boyang Li, Anish
        Mashettiwar, Erica Ross, Sherli Yeroushalmi, Qi Yu

Kings Park High School:
    Teacher: Jeanne Palm
    Students: Fred Langer, Stephanie Kersling, Janet Lee

Moro Bay High School:
    Teacher: Michelle Dowell
    Students: Katey Maruska, Heather Spellacy

Roslyn High School:
    Student: Jenna Kahn

Wellington High School:
    Teacher: Margaret Cross Rice
    Student: Annaliesa Copan

Also, our thanks to Yale University students Danielle Tumminio and Jilian Cabot Fletcher. We'd also like to acknowledge the collaborative and inventive participants in the 2006–2015 AP English Language Institutes held at Goucher College, Molloy College, in Lewes, Delaware; and in Philadelphia, Pennsylvania, for their contributions and constructive comments.

INTRODUCTION: THE FIVE-STEP PROGRAM

Some Basics

Reading

We believe that reading should be an exciting interaction between you and the writer. You must bring your own context to the experience, and you must feel comfortable reaching for and exploring ideas. You are an adventurer on a journey of exploration, and we act as your guides. We set the itinerary, but you will set your own pace. You can feel free to "stop and smell the roses" or to explore new territory.

The Journey

On any journey, each traveler sees something different on new horizons. So, too, each student is free to personalize his or her own literary experience, provided he or she tries at all times to strive for excellence and accuracy.

Critical Thinking

There are no tricks to critical thinking. Those who claim to guarantee you a 5 by using gimmicks are doing you a disservice. No one can guarantee a 5. However, the reading and writing skills you will review, practice, and master will give you the very best chance to do your very best. You will have the opportunity to learn, to practice, and to master the critical thinking processes that can empower you to achieve your highest score.

Philosophy of This Book: In the Beginning . . .

This is an important concept for us, because we believe that if you focus on the beginning, the rest will fall into place. When you purchased this book and decided to work your way through it, you were beginning your journey to the AP English Language and Composition exam. We will be with you every step of the way.

Why This Book?

We believe we have something unique to offer you. For more than 25 years we have addressed the needs of AP students just like you, and we have been fortunate to learn from these students. Therefore, the contents of this book reflect genuine student concerns and needs. This is a student-oriented book. We will not overwhelm you with pompous language, mislead you with inaccurate information and tasks, or lull you into a false sense of confidence through cutesy shortcuts. We stand behind every suggestion, process, and question we present. There is no "busywork" in this book.

We know you will not do every activity we suggest. Therefore, think of this text as a resource and guide to accompany you on your AP English Language and Composition exam journey throughout the year. This book is designed to serve many purposes. It will:

- clarify requirements for the AP English Language and Composition exam;
- provide you with test practice;

- show you models and rubrics on which you can model and evaluate your own work;
- anticipate and answer your questions;
- enrich your understanding and appreciation of the writing process;
- help you pace yourself; and
- make you aware of the Five Steps to Mastering the AP English Language and Composition exam.

Organization of the Book

We know that your primary concern is information about the AP English Language and Composition exam; therefore, we begin at the beginning with an overview of the AP exam in general. We then introduce you to the Diagnostic/Master exam we use throughout the book to show you the "ins and outs" of an AP test. In separate chapters, you will become familiar with both sections of the exam. We lead you through the multiple-choice questions and how to go about answering them, and we take you through the essay questions and approaches to writing these essays.

Because you must be fluent in the language and the process of composition, synthesis, and analysis, we provide a full comprehensive review part in analysis, synthesis, and argument. This review is not a mere listing of terms and concepts. Rather, it is a series of practices that will hone your analytical and writing skills. However, do not fear. You will find terms and concepts clearly delineated within their contexts. We will also provide you with annotated suggestions for high-interest readings for analysis, synthesis, and argument.

After carefully working your way through Chapters 4 through 10, you may wish to go to McGraw-Hill's *5 Step* series website which provides review, reinforcement, and enrichment questions that refer to the skills covered in each chapter. You can compare your response(s) with what we provide on the website for this book. **www.mhpracticeplus.com**

A separate section of this book contains the practice exams. Here is where you will test your own skills. You may be sure that the selections included in each exam are on an AP level. The multiple-choice questions provide practice with types of questions asked on AP exams. The essay questions are designed to cover the techniques and terms required by the AP exam. The free-response essays are both challenging and specific, but broad enough to suit all curricula. After taking each exam, you can check yourself against the explanations of every multiple-choice question and the ratings of the sample student essays.

The final part is one you should not pass over. It contains a glossary of terms, a bibliography of works that may be of importance to you, and a list of websites related to the AP English Language and Composition exam.

Introduction to the Five-Step Preparation Program

The Five-Step Preparation Program is a powerful tool designed to provide you with the best possible skills, strategies, and practice to help lead you to that perfect 5 on the AP English Language and Composition exam administered each May to more than 250,000 high school students. Each of the five steps will provide you with the opportunity to get closer and closer to the 5, which is the "Holy Grail" to all AP students.

Step 1: Set Up Your Study Program
- Month-by-month: September through May
- The calendar year: January through May
- Basic training: the 4 to 6 weeks before the exam

Step 2: Determine Your Test Readiness

- A comprehensive review of the exam
- One "Diagnostic/Master exam" you will go through step by step and question by question to build your confidence level
- Explanation of multiple-choice answers

Step 3: Develop Strategies for Success

- Learn about the test itself
- Learn to read multiple-choice questions
- Learn how to answer multiple-choice questions, including whether or not to guess
- Learn how to deconstruct the essay prompts
- Learn how to plan the essay

Step 4: Review the Knowledge You Need to Score High

- A comprehensive review of analysis and argument
- Practice activities that will hone your skills in close reading
- Practice activities in critical thinking
- Practice activities in critical/analytical/argumentative writing

Step 5: Build Your Test-Taking Confidence

- The opportunity to take a Diagnostic/Master exam
- Time management techniques/skills
- Two practice exams that test how well-honed your skills are
- Rubrics for self-evaluation

Finally, at the back of the book you'll find additional resources to aid your preparation. These include:

- Glossary of terms
- Bibliography for further reading
- Websites related to the AP English Language exam

The Graphics Used in This Book

To emphasize particular skills and strategies, we use several icons throughout this book. An icon in the margin will alert you that you should pay particular attention to the accompanying text. We use three icons:

This icon points out a very important concept or fact that you should not pass over.

This icon calls your attention to a problem-solving strategy that you may want to try.

This icon indicates a tip that you might find useful.

In addition, **bold** and **<u>bold underlined</u>** words indicate terms included in the Glossary.

Scattered throughout the book are marginal notes and numerous shaded boxes. We urge you to pay close attention to them because they can provide tips, hints, strategies, and further explanations to help you reach your full potential.

STEP 1

Set Up Your Study Program

CHAPTER **1** What You Need to Know About the AP English Language and Composition Exam

CHAPTER **2** How to Plan Your Time

CHAPTER 1

What You Need to Know About the AP English Language and Composition Exam

IN THIS CHAPTER

Summary: Information about the AP English Language and Composition exam and its scoring.

Key Ideas
✪ Learn answers to frequently asked questions.
✪ Learn how your final score is calculated.
✪ Learn tips for successfully taking the exam.

Background on the AP English Language and Composition Exam

What Is the AP Program?

The Advanced Placement program was begun by the College Board in 1955 to construct standard achievement exams that would allow highly motivated high school students the opportunity to be awarded advanced placement as freshmen in colleges and universities in the United States. Today, there are more than 37 courses and exams with over two million students from every state in the nation, and from foreign countries, taking the annual exams in May.

As is obvious, the AP programs are designed for high school students who want to take college-level courses. In our case, the AP English Language and Composition course and exam are designed to involve high school students in college-level English studies in both the use and structure of language and composition.

Who Writes the AP English Language and Composition Exam?

According to the College Board, the AP Comp exam is created by a group of college and high school English instructors called the "AP Development Committee." Their job is to ensure that the annual AP Comp exam reflects what is being taught and studied in college-level English classes at the high schools.

This committee writes a large number of multiple-choice questions that are pretested and evaluated for clarity, appropriateness, and range of possible answers. The committee also generates a pool of essay questions, pretests them, and chooses those questions that best represent the full range of the scoring scale to allow the AP readers to evaluate the essays equitably.

It is important to remember that the AP English Language and Composition exam is thoroughly evaluated after it is administered each year. This way, the College Board can use the results to make course suggestions and to plan future tests.

What Are the AP Grades and Who Receives Them?

Once you have taken the exam and it has been scored, your test will be given one of five numbers by the College Board.

- 5 indicates you are extremely well qualified.
- 4 indicates you are well qualified.
- 3 indicates you are qualified.
- 2 indicates you are possibly qualified.
- 1 indicates you are not qualified to receive college credit.

Your grade is reported first to your college or university, second to your high school, and third to you. All the reporting is usually completed by the middle to end of July.

Reasons for Taking the AP English Language and Composition Exam

Why Would I Want to Take the AP English Language and Composition Exam?

Good question. Why put yourself through a year of intensive study, pressure, stress, and preparation? To be honest, only you can answer that question. However, over the years, our students have indicated to us that there are several reasons why they were willing to take the risk and to put in the effort.

- For personal satisfaction
- To compare themselves with other students across the nation
- Because colleges look favorably on the applications of students who elect to enroll in AP courses
- To receive college credit or advanced standing at their colleges or universities

- A love of the subject
- So the family will be proud of them

There are plenty of other reasons, but hopefully, no matter what the other reasons might be, the top reason for your enrolling in the AP English Language and Composition course and taking the exam in May is to feel good about yourself and the challenges you have met.

What You Need to Know About the AP English Language and Composition Exam

If I Don't Take an AP Composition Course, Can I Still Take the AP English Language and Composition Exam?

Yes. Although the AP English Language and Composition exam is designed for the student who has had a year's course in AP English Language and Composition, there are high schools that do not offer this type of course, and the students in these high schools have also done well on the exam. However, if your high school does offer an AP Composition course, by all means take advantage of it and the structured background it will provide you.

How Is the AP English Language and Composition Exam Organized?

The exam has two parts and is scheduled to last 3 hours and 15 minutes. The first section is a set of multiple-choice questions based on a series of prose passages. You will have 1 hour to complete this part of the test. The second section of the exam is a 2-hour and 15-minute essay writing segment consisting of three different essays: analysis, argument, and synthesis. According to the College Board's **AP English Language and Composition Exam Instructions**, the 15-minute reading period in Section II is recommended, not required. While students are strongly encouraged to use the reading period to read the questions and sources and plan their responses, they may begin writing their responses during that time if they choose to do so.

After you complete the multiple-choice section, you will hand in your test booklet and scan sheet, and you will be given a brief break. Note that you will not be able to return to the multiple-choice questions when you return to the examination room.

Must I Check the Box at the End of the Essay Booklet That Allows the AP People to Use My Essays as Samples for Research?

No. This is simply a way for the College Board to make certain that it has your permission if it decides to use one or more of your essays as a model. The readers of your essays pay no attention to whether or not that box is checked. Checking the box will not affect your grade either.

How Is My AP English Language and Composition Exam Scored?

Let's look at the basics first. The multiple-choice section counts for 45% of your total score, and the essay section counts for 55%. Next comes a four-part calculation: the raw scoring of the multiple-choice section, the raw scoring of the essay section, the calculation of the composite score, and the conversion of the composite score into the AP grade of 5, 4, 3, 2, or 1.

How Is the Multiple-Choice Section Scored?

The scan sheet with your answers is run through a computer that counts the number of correct answers. Questions left blank and questions answered incorrectly are treated the same and get no points. There is no longer a "guessing penalty," which formerly involved the deduction of a fraction of a point for answering a question but getting it wrong.

How Is My Essay Section Scored?

Each of your essays is read by a different, trained AP reader called a "faculty consultant." The AP/College Board people have developed a highly successful training program for its readers, together with many opportunities for checks and double checks of essays to ensure a fair and equitable reading of each essay.

The scoring guides are carefully developed by the chief faculty consultant, question leader, table leaders, and content experts. All faculty consultants are then trained to read and score just **one** essay question on the exam. They become experts in that one essay question. No one knows the identity of any writer. The identification numbers and names are covered, and the exam booklets are randomly distributed to the readers in packets of 25 randomly chosen essays. Table leaders and the question leader review samples of each reader's scores to ensure quality standards are constant.

Each essay is scored as 9, 8, 7, 6, 5, 4, 3, 2, or 1, plus 0, with 9 the highest possible score. Once your essay is rated from 9 to 1, the next set of calculations is completed. Here, if there are 27 possible points divided into 55% of the total possible score, each point awarded is given a value of 3.055. The formula would look something like this:

$$(\text{pts.} \times 3.055) + (\text{pts.} \times 3.055) + (\text{pts.} \times 3.055) = \text{essay raw score}$$

$$\text{Essay 1} \qquad\qquad \text{Essay 2} \qquad\qquad \text{Essay 3}$$

How Do They Calculate My Composite Score?

You need to do a little math here: 150 is the total composite score for the AP English Language and Composition test. Fifty-five percent of this score is the essay section; that equals 82.5 points. Forty-five percent of the composite score is the multiple-choice section, which equals 67.5 points. Each of your three essays is graded on a 9-point scale; therefore, each point is worth 3.055. You would divide the number of multiple-choice questions by 67.5. For example, if there were 55 questions, each point of the raw score would be multiplied by 1.227. If you add together the raw scores of each of the two sections, you will have a composite score. We provide a little practice with this process in the two practice exams in this book.

How Is My Composite Score Turned into the Grade Reported to My College?

Remember that the total composite scores needed to earn a 5, 4, 3, 2, or 1 differ each year. This is determined by a committee of AP/College Board/ETS directors, experts, and statisticians. The grading is based on such items as:

- AP distribution over the past three years
- Comparability studies
- Observations of the chief faculty consultant
- Frequency distributions of scores on each section and the essays
- Average scores on each exam section and essays

However, over the years a trend can be observed that indicates the number of points required to achieve a specific grade.

- 150–100 points = 5
- 99–86 = 4
- 85–67 = 3

2 and 1 fall below this range. You do not want to go there.

What Should I Bring to the Exam?

- Several pencils
- Several BLACK pens (black ink is easier on the eyes)
- A watch
- Something to drink—water is best
- A quiet snack, such as Life Savers
- Tissues

Are There Additional Recommendations?

- Allow plenty of time to get to the test site.
- Wear comfortable clothing.
- Eat a light breakfast or lunch.
- Remind yourself that you are well prepared and that the test is an enjoyable challenge and a chance to share your knowledge. Be proud of yourself! You worked hard all year. Now is your time to shine.

Is There Anything Special I Should Do the Night Before the Exam?

We certainly don't advocate last-minute cramming, and, if you've been following the guidelines, you won't have to. However, there may be a slight value to some last minute review. Spend the night before the exam relaxing with family or friends. Watch a movie; play a game; gab on the telephone, blog, or Twitter; and then find a quiet spot. While you're unwinding, flip through your own notebook and review sheets. By now, you're bound to be ready to drift off to sleep. Pleasant dreams.

CHAPTER > 2

How to Plan Your Time

IN THIS CHAPTER

Summary: Assess your own study patterns and preparation plans.

Key Ideas
✪ Explore three approaches.
✪ Choose a calendar that works for you.

Three Approaches to Prepare for the AP English Language and Composition Exam

No one knows your study habits, likes, and dislikes better than you. You are the only one who can decide which approach you want and/or need to adopt to prepare for the AP English Language and Composition exam. Look at the brief profiles below. These may help you to place yourself in a particular prep mode.

You are a full-year prep student (Approach A) if:

1. You like to plan for a vacation or the prom a year in advance.
2. You never think of missing a practice session, whether it's for your favorite sport, musical instrument, or activity.
3. You like detailed planning and everything in its place.
4. You feel you must be thoroughly prepared.
5. You hate surprises.
6. You are always early for appointments.

You are a one-semester prep student (Approach B) if:

1. You begin to plan for your vacation or the prom 4 to 5 months before the event.
2. You are willing to plan ahead to feel comfortable in stressful situations, but are okay with skipping some details.
3. You feel more comfortable when you know what to expect, but a surprise or two does not floor you.
4. You are always on time for appointments.

You are a 4- to 6-week prep student (Approach C) if:

1. You accept or find a date for the prom a week before the big day.
2. You work best under pressure and close deadlines.
3. You feel very confident with the skills and background you've learned in your AP English Language and Composition class.
4. You decided late in the year to take the exam.
5. You like surprises.
6. You feel okay if you arrive 10 to 15 minutes late for an appointment.

CALENDARS FOR PREPARING FOR THE AP ENGLISH LANGUAGE AND COMPOSITION EXAM

Calendar for Approach A:
Yearlong Preparation for the AP English Language and Composition Exam

Although its primary purpose is to prepare you for the AP English Language and Composition exam you will take in May, this book can enrich your study of language and composition, your analytical skills, and your writing skills.

SEPTEMBER–OCTOBER (Check off the activities as you complete them.)

_____ Determine into which student mode you would place yourself.

_____ Carefully read the Introduction and Chapter 1.

_____ Pay very close attention to the "Walk Through" the Diagnostic/Master exam.

_____ Get on the Web and take a look at the AP website(s).

_____ Skim the Comprehensive Review section. (These areas will be part of your yearlong preparation.)

_____ Buy a highlighter.

_____ Flip through the entire book. Break the book in. Write in it. Highlight it.

_____ Get a clear picture of what your own school's AP English Language curriculum is.

_____ Review the Bibliography and establish a pattern of outside reading.

_____ Begin to use this book as a resource.

NOVEMBER (The first 10 weeks have elapsed.)

_____ Write the argumentative essay in the Diagnostic/Master exam.

_____ Compare your essay with the sample student essays.

_____ Refer to Chapters 6 and 9 on the argumentative essay.

_____ Take five of our prompts and write solid opening paragraphs.

DECEMBER

_____ Maintain notes on literary works studied in and out of class.

_____ Refine analytical skills (see Chapters 5 and 8).

_____ Write one of the two analytical essays in the Diagnostic/Master exam. (This will depend on the organization of your own curriculum.)

_____ Compare your essay with the sample student essays.

JANUARY (20 weeks have now elapsed.)

_____ Write the synthesis essay in the Diagnostic/Master exam. (This will depend on your previous choice.)

_____ Compare your essay with the sample student essays.

_____ Refer to Chapters 7 and 10 on the synthesis essay.

FEBRUARY

_____ Take the multiple-choice section of the Diagnostic/Master exam.

_____ Carefully go over the explanations of the answers to the questions.

_____ Score yourself honestly.

_____ Make a note of terms and concepts and types of questions that give you trouble.

_____ Review troublesome terms by checking the Glossary.

MARCH (30 weeks have now elapsed.)

_____ Form a study group.

_____ Choose a selection you have studied in class and create an essay question to go with it, or you can use one of our suggested prompts.

_____ Choose a passage from a current editorial and create an essay question to go with it, or you can choose one of our suggested prompts.

_____ Write one of the analytical essays.

_____ Write one of the synthesis essays.

_____ Compare essays and rate them with your study group. (Use our rubrics.)

APRIL

_____ Take Practice Exam 1 in the first week of April.

_____ Evaluate your strengths and weaknesses.

_____ Study appropriate chapters to correct weaknesses.

_____ Practice creating multiple-choice questions of different types with your study group.

_____ Develop and review worksheets for and with your study group.

MAY—First two weeks (THIS IS IT!)

_____ Highlight only those things in the Glossary about which you are still unsure. Ask your teacher for clarification. Study!

_____ Write at least three times a week under timed conditions.

_____ Take Practice Exam 2.

_____ Score yourself.

_____ Give yourself a pat on the back for how much you have learned and improved over the past nine months.

_____ Go to the movies. Call a friend.

_____ Get a good night's sleep. Fall asleep knowing you are well prepared.

GOOD LUCK ON THE TEST!

Calendar for Approach B:
Semester-Long Preparation for the AP English Language and Composition Exam

The following calendar assumes that you have completed one semester of language and composition and will use those skills you have been practicing to prepare you for the May exam. You still have plenty of time to supplement your course work by taking our study recommendations, maintaining literary notations, doing outside readings, and so forth. We divide the next 16 weeks into a workable program of preparation for you.

JANUARY–FEBRUARY (Check off the activities as you complete them.)

_____ Carefully read the Introduction and Chapter 1.

_____ Write the three essays on the Diagnostic/Master exam.

_____ Compare your essays with the sample student essays.

_____ Complete the multiple-choice section of the Diagnostic/Master exam.

_____ Carefully go over the answers and explanations of the answers.

_____ Take a close look at the Bibliography for suggestions regarding possible outside readings.

MARCH (10 weeks to go)

_____ Form a study group.

_____ Choose a favorite essay or excerpt from a book and create an essay question to go with it, or you can use one of our suggested prompts.

_____ Choose a prose passage or essay and create an essay question to go with it, or you can choose one of our suggested prompts.

_____ Write one of the analytical essays.

_____ Write one of the synthesis essays.

_____ Compare essays and rate them with your study group. (Use our rubrics.)

APRIL

_____ Take Practice Exam 1 in the first week of April.

_____ Evaluate your strengths and weaknesses.

_____ Study appropriate chapters to correct weaknesses.

_____ Practice creating multiple-choice questions of different types with your study group.

_____ Develop and review worksheets for and with your study group.

MAY—First two weeks (THIS IS IT!)

_____ Highlight only those things in the Glossary about which you are still unsure. Ask your teacher for clarification. Study!

_____ Write at least three times a week under timed conditions.

_____ Take Practice Exam 2.

_____ Score yourself.

_____ Give yourself a pat on the back for how much you have learned and improved over the past nine months.

_____ Go to the movies. Call a friend.

_____ Get a good night's sleep. Fall asleep knowing you are well prepared.

GOOD LUCK ON THE TEST!

Calendar for Approach C:
4- to 6-Week Preparation for the AP English Language and Composition Exam

 At this point, we assume that you have been developing your argumentative, analytical, and writing skills in your English class for more than six months. You will, therefore, use this book primarily as a specific guide to the AP English Language and Composition exam. Remember, there is a solid review section in this book, to which you should refer.

Given the time constraints, now is not the time to try to expand your AP curriculum. Rather, it is the time to limit and refine what you already do know.

APRIL

_____ Skim the Introduction and Chapter 1.

_____ Carefully go over the "Rapid Review" sections of Chapters 5 through 10.

_____ Strengthen, clarify, and correct your weak areas after taking the Diagnostic/Master exam.

_____ Write a minimum of three sample opening paragraphs for each of the three types of essays.

_____ Write a minimum of two timed essays for each type of essay on the exam.

_____ Complete Practice Exam 1.

_____ Score yourself and analyze your errors.

_____ Refer to the appropriate chapters to correct weaknesses.

_____ Refer to the Bibliography.

_____ If you feel unfamiliar with specific forms of discourse, refer to the list of suggested appropriate works.

_____ Develop a weekly study group to hear each other's essays and discuss writing.

_____ Skim and highlight the Glossary.

MAY—First two weeks (THIS IS IT!)

_____ Complete Practice Exam 2.

_____ Score yourself and analyze your errors.

_____ Refer to the appropriate chapters to correct weaknesses.

_____ Go to the movies. Call a friend.

_____ Get a good night's sleep. Fall asleep knowing you are well prepared.

GOOD LUCK ON THE TEST!

"One of the first steps to success on the AP exam is knowing your own study habits."
—Margaret R., AP Language teacher

STEP 2

Determine Your Test Readiness

CHAPTER 3   A Walk Through the Diagnostic/Master Exam

CHAPTER 3

A Walk Through the Diagnostic/Master Exam

IN THIS CHAPTER

Summary: Familiarize yourself with the diagnostic exam.

Key Ideas

✪ Examine the multiple-choice section in Section I of the exam.
✪ Peruse the essay questions in Section II.

What follows is our version of an AP English Language and Composition exam we use throughout this book to demonstrate processes, examples, terms, and so forth. We call this our Diagnostic/Master exam. You will not be taking this exam at this point, but we would like you to "walk through" the exam with us, now.

The first part of this 3¼-hour exam is always going to be the multiple-choice section, which lasts 1 hour. It comprises both fiction and nonfiction. The multiple-choice section of the Diagnostic/Master exam contains several passages from different time periods and of different styles and purposes. It may include letters, essays, journal entries, editorials, speeches, and excerpts from longer works. The multiple-choice questions for each selection were developed to provide you with a wide range of question types and terminology that have been used in the actual AP English Language and Composition exams over the years.

To begin to know how the exam is structured, take some time now to look through the multiple-choice section of the Diagnostic/Master exam. Do not try to answer questions; just peruse the types of passages and questions.

- Review all of the pages of the test and familiarize yourself with their format.
- See where the long and short readings are.

"You know, from my experience with AP exams, I've learned never to assume anything."
— Jeremy G.,
   AP student

- Check the total number of questions and know what you are facing.
- Check out the essay prompts.

A Word About Our Sample Student Essays

We field-tested each of the essay questions in a variety of high schools, both public and private. We could have chosen to present essays that would have "knocked your socks off"; however, we chose to present samples we feel are truly representative of the essays usually written within the time constraints of the exam.

These essays are indicative of a wide range of styles and levels of acceptability. We want you to recognize that there is not one model to which all essays must conform.

"To Thine Own Self Be True" (Polonius–*Hamlet*)

This well-known caveat is always the very best advice and especially appropriate for the writer. Listen to your teacher's advice; listen to our advice; listen to your own voice. That's the voice we want to "hear" in your writing. Use natural vocabulary and present honest observations. It is wonderful to read professional criticism, but you cannot adopt another's ideas and remain true to your own thoughts. Trust your brain—if you've prepared well, you'll do well.

DIAGNOSTIC/MASTER EXAM
ADVANCED PLACEMENT ENGLISH LANGUAGE
AND COMPOSITION

Section I

Total Time—1 hour

Carefully read the following passages and answer the accompanying questions. Questions 1–12 are based on the following passage from "Samuel Johnson on Pope," which appeared in *The Lives of the English Poets* (1779–1781).

    The person of Pope is well known not to have been formed by the nicest model. He has compared himself to a spider and, by another, is described as protuberant behind and before. He is said to have been beautiful in his infancy, but he was of a constitution feeble and weak. As bodies of a tender frame are easily distorted, his deformity was probably in part the effect of his application. But his face was not displeasing, and his   5 eyes were animated and vivid.

    By natural deformity, or accidental distortion, his vital functions were so much disordered, that his life was a "long disease."

    He sometimes condescended to be jocular with servants or inferiors; but by no merriment, either of others or his own, was he ever seen excited to laughter.   10

    Of his domestic character frugality was a part eminently remarkable. Having determined not to be dependent, he determined not to be in want, and, therefore, wisely and magnanimously rejected all temptations to expense unsuitable to his fortune.

    The great topic of his ridicule is poverty; the crimes with which he reproaches his antagonists are their debts and their want of a dinner. He seems to be of an opinion not   15 very uncommon in the world, that to want money is to want everything.

    He professed to have learned his poetry from Dryden, whom he praised through his whole life with unvaried liberality; and perhaps his character may receive some illustration, if he be compared with his master.

    Integrity of understanding and nicety of discernment were not allotted in a less   20 proportion to Dryden than to Pope. But Dryden never desired to apply all the judgment that he had. He wrote merely for the people. When he pleased others, he contented himself. He never attempted to mend what he must have known to be faulty. He wrote with little consideration and, once it had passed the press, ejected it from his mind.

    Pope was not content to satisfy; he desired to excel, and, therefore, always endeavored   25 to do his best. Pope did not court the candor, but dared the judgment of his reader, and, expecting no indulgence from others, he showed none to himself. He examined lines and words with minute and punctilious observation, and he retouched every part with diligence, until he had nothing left to be forgiven.

    Poetry was not the sole praise of either; for both excelled likewise in prose. The   30 style of Dryden is capricious and varied; that of Pope is cautious and uniform. Dryden observes the motions of his own mind; Pope constrains his mind to his own rules of composition. Dryden's page is a natural field, diversified by the exuberance of abundant vegetation. Pope's is a velvet lawn, shaven by the scythe, and leveled by the roller.

    If the flights of Dryden are higher, Pope continues longer on the wing. If of Dryden's   35 fire the blaze is brighter, of Pope's the heat is more regular and constant. Dryden is read with frequent astonishment, and Pope with perpetual delight.

1. The passage is primarily a(n)
   A. character sketch of Pope
   B. discussion of poetic style
   C. criticism of Dryden
   D. model for future poets
   E. opportunity for the writer to show off his own skills

2. The passage discusses a contrast among all of the following <u>except</u>:
   A. prose and poetry
   B. Pope and Dryden
   C. body and mind
   D. poverty and wealth
   E. body and soul

3. "If the flights" (35) means
   A. Pope's writing will outlast Dryden's
   B. both Pope and Dryden are equal
   C. Pope is not idealistic
   D. Pope is more wordy
   E. Pope is not as bright as Dryden

4. The character of Pope is developed by all of the following <u>except</u>:
   A. examples
   B. comparison
   C. contrast
   D. satire
   E. description

5. According to the passage, Pope and Dryden are
   A. rivals
   B. equally intelligent
   C. outdated
   D. equally physically attractive
   E. in debt

6. From the passage, the reader may infer that Pope
   A. was extravagant
   B. was a man of the people
   C. was jealous of Dryden
   D. had a desire to be popular
   E. had a bitter, satirical nature

7. The tone of the passage is
   A. informal and affectionate
   B. formal and objective
   C. condescending and paternalistic
   D. laudatory and reverent
   E. critical and negative

8. Lines 20–24 indicate that Dryden was what type of writer?
   A. one who labored over his thoughts
   B. one who wrote only for himself
   C. one who wrote only for the critics
   D. one who wrote to please Pope
   E. one who did not revise

9. Using the context of lines 27–29, "punctilious" means
   A. precise
   B. timely
   C. cursory
   D. scholarly
   E. philosophical

10. In the context of the passage, "until he had nothing left to be forgiven" (29) means
    A. Pope outraged his readers
    B. Pope suffered from writer's block
    C. Pope exhausted his subject matter
    D. Pope's prose was revised to perfection
    E. Pope cared about the opinions of his readers

11. "Shaven" and "leveled" in line 34 indicate that Pope's style of writing was
    A. natural
    B. richly ornamented
    C. highly controlled
    D. mechanical
    E. analytical

12. Based on a close reading of the final paragraph of the passage, the reader could infer that the author
    A. looks on both writers equally
    B. prefers the work of Pope
    C. sees the two writers as inferior to his own writing style
    D. indicates no preference
    E. prefers the work of Dryden

Questions 13–23 are based on the following excerpt from Charlotte Perkins Gilman's "Politics and Warfare," which appears in *The Man-Made World: Our Androcentric Culture* (1911).

There are many today who hold that politics need not be at all connected with warfare; and others who hold that politics is warfare from start to finish.   1

The inextricable confusion of politics and warfare is part of the stumbling block   2
in the minds of men. As they see it, a nation is primarily a fighting organization; and its principal business is offensive and defensive warfare; therefore the ultimatum with which they oppose the demand for political equality—"women cannot fight, therefore they cannot vote."

Fighting, when all is said, is to them the real business of life; not to be able to fight   3
is to be quite out of the running; and ability to solve our growing mass of public problems; questions of health, of education, of morals, of economics; weighs naught against the ability to kill.

This naïve assumption of supreme value in a process never of the first importance;   4
and increasingly injurious as society progresses, would be laughable if it were not for its evil effects. It acts and reacts upon us to our hurt. Positively, we see the ill effects already touched on; the evils not only of active war, but of the spirit and methods of war; idealized, inculcated, and practiced in other social processes. It tends to make each man-managed nation an actual or potential fighting organization, and to give us, instead of civilized peace, that "balance of power" which is like the counted time in the prize ring—only a rest between combats.

It leaves the weaker nations to be "conquered" and "annexed" just as they used   5
to be; with "preferential tariffs" instead of tribute. It forces upon each the burden of armament; upon many the dreaded conscription; and continually lowers the world's resources in money and in life.

Similarly in politics, it adds to the legitimate expenses of governing the illegitimate   6
expenses of fighting; and must needs have a "spoils system" by which to pay its mercenaries.

In carrying out the public policies the wheels of state are continually clogged by the   7
"opposition"; always an opposition on one side or the other; and this slow wiggling uneven progress, through shorn victories and haggling concessions, is held to be the proper and only political method.

"Women do not understand politics," we are told; "Women do not care for politics";   8
"Women are unfitted for politics."

It is frankly inconceivable, from the androcentric viewpoint, that nations can live in   9
peace together, and be friendly and serviceable as persons are. It is inconceivable also, that, in the management of a nation, honesty, efficiency, wisdom, experience and love could work out good results without any element of combat.

The "ultimate resort" is still to arms. "The will of the majority" is only respected on   10
account of the guns of the majority. We have but a partial civilization, heavily modified to sex—the male sex.

13. The author's main purpose in the passage is to
    A. argue for women being drafted
    B. criticize colonialism
    C. present a pacifist philosophy
    D. criticize the male-dominated society
    E. protest tariffs

14. In paragraph 2, the author maintains that men support their position on equality for women based upon which of the following approaches?
    A. begging the question
    B. a syllogism using a faulty premise
    C. an appeal to emotion
    D. circular reasoning
    E. an *ad hoc* argument

15. Using textual clues, one can conclude that "androcentric" most probably means
    A. robot-centered
    B. world-centered
    C. female-centered
    D. self-centered
    E. male-centered

16. In addition to indicating a direct quotation, the author uses quotation marks to indicate
    A. the jargon of politics and warfare
    B. the coining of a phrase
    C. a definition
    D. the author's scholarship
    E. that the author does not take responsibility for her words

17. In paragraph 4, "increasingly injurious as society progresses" is reinforced by all of the following except:
    A. "ill effects already touched on" [paragraph 4]
    B. "active war" [paragraph 4]
    C. "weaker nations to be 'conquered' and 'annexed'" [paragraph 5]
    D. "illegitimate expenses of fighting" [paragraph 6]
    E. "Women do not understand politics" [paragraph 8]

18. According to the author, men view the primary purpose of government to be
    A. educating the people
    B. solving the "mass of public problems"
    C. obtaining as much power as possible
    D. economics
    E. health

19. The argument shifts from a discussion of warfare to a discussion of politics in the first lines of which of the following paragraphs?
    A. paragraph 4
    B. paragraph 5
    C. paragraph 6
    D. paragraph 7
    E. paragraph 9

20. The tone of the passage is best described as
    A. ambivalent
    B. reverent
    C. condescending
    D. accusatory
    E. indifferent

21. The style of the passage can best be described as
    A. poetic and emotional
    B. editorial and analytical
    C. mocking and self-serving
    D. preaching and moralistic
    E. authoritative and pretentious

22. To present her argument, Gilman primarily uses which of the following rhetorical strategies (techniques/modes of discourse)?
    A. process
    B. definition
    C. cause and effect
    D. narration
    E. description

23. "It," as used in paragraphs 4, 5, and 6, only refers to
    A. "Fighting is to them the real business of life" [paragraph 3]
    B. "evil effects" [paragraph 4]
    C. "man-managed nation" [paragraph 4]
    D. "preferential tariffs" [paragraph 5]
    E. "spoils system" [paragraph 6]

Questions 24–33 are based on the speech "On the Death of Martin Luther King, Jr." by Robert F. Kennedy.

I have bad news for you, for all of our fellow citizens, and people who love peace all over the world, and that is that Martin Luther King was shot and killed tonight. 1

Martin Luther King dedicated his life to love and to justice for his fellow human beings, and he died because of that effort. 2

In this difficult day, in this difficult time for the United States, it is perhaps well to ask what kind of a nation we are and what direction we want to move in, for those of you who are black—considering the evidence there evidently is that there were white people who were responsible—you can be filled with bitterness, with hatred, and a desire for revenge. We can move in that direction as a country, in great polarization—black people amongst black, white people amongst white, filled with hatred toward one another. 3

Or we can make an effort, as Martin Luther King did, to understand and to comprehend, and to replace that violence, that stain of bloodshed that has spread across our land, with an effort to understand with compassion and love. 4

For those of you who are black and are tempted to be filled with hatred and distrust at the injustice of such an act, against all white people, I can only say that I feel in my own heart the same kind of feeling. I had a member of my family killed, [and] he was killed by a white man. But we have to make an effort in the United States, we have to make an effort to understand, to go beyond these rather difficult times. 5

My favorite poet was Aeschylus. He wrote: "In our sleep, pain which cannot forget falls drop by drop upon the heart until, in our own despair, against our will, comes wisdom through the awful grace of God." 6

What we need in the United States is not division; what we need in the United States is not hatred; what we need in the United States is not violence or lawlessness but love and wisdom, and compassion toward one another and a feeling of justice toward those who still suffer within our country, whether they be white or black. 7

So I shall ask you tonight to return home, to say a prayer for the family of Martin Luther King, that's true, but more importantly to say a prayer for our own country, which all of us love—a prayer for understanding and that compassion of which I spoke. 8

We can do well in this country. We will have difficult times. We've had difficult times in the past. We will have difficult times in the future. It is not the end of violence; it is not the end of lawlessness; it is not the end of disorder. 9

But the vast majority of white people and the vast majority of black people in this country want to live together, want to improve the quality of our life, and want justice for all human beings who abide in our land. 10

Let us dedicate ourselves to what the Greeks wrote so many years ago: to tame the savageness of man and to make gentle the life of this world. 11

Let us dedicate ourselves to that, and say a prayer for our country and for our people. 12

24. The primary purpose of RFK's speech is most probably to
A. inform the people of the event
B. praise the accomplishments of Martin Luther King, Jr.
C. offer condolences to King's family
D. call for calm and unity between blacks and whites
E. offer condolences to the black community at large

25. Which of the following paragraphs does not contain examples of parallel structure?
    A. paragraph 3 beginning with "In this difficult . . ."
    B. paragraph 6 beginning with "My favorite poet . . ."
    C. paragraph 7 beginning with "What we need . . ."
    D. paragraph 9 beginning with "We can do well . . ."
    E. paragraph 10 beginning with "But the vast majority . . ."

26. Paragraph 5 contains an example of
    A. understatement
    B. figurative language
    C. sarcasm
    D. logical fallacy
    E. analogous example

27. The tone of the speech can best be described as
    A. elevated and conciliatory
    B. angry and inflammatory
    C. formal and detached
    D. informal and emotional
    E. accusatory and bitter

28. To keep his speech from leading to violence, RFK makes use of which of the following?
    I. constantly repeating King's name and his desire for unity between races
    II. an ethical appeal based on the power of religion
    III. emphasizing a common bond to show the connection between himself and his audience
    A. I
    B. II
    C. III
    D. I and III
    E. I, II, and III

29. All of the following paragraphs give support to the inference that RFK expected violence to follow the assassination except:
    A. paragraph 3 beginning with "In the beginning . . ."
    B. paragraph 4 beginning with "Or we can . . ."
    C. paragraph 6 beginning with "My favorite . . ."
    D. paragraph 7 beginning with "What we need . . ."
    E. paragraph 9 beginning with "We can do well . . ."

30. RFK most probably chose to refer to the Greeks in paragraph 11 for all of the following reasons except:
    A. to impress the audience with his scholarship
    B. to concisely restate the theme of the speech
    C. to provide a healing thought for the people to remember
    D. to elevate the level of discourse
    E. to reinforce the ideals of democracy with which the Greeks are associated

31. Paragraphs 7 and 8 are constructed around which of the following rhetorical strategies?
    A. analysis
    B. definition
    C. narration
    D. process
    E. cause and effect

32. The quotation given in paragraph 6 can best be restated as
    A. the process of healing is inevitable
    B. time heals all wounds
    C. sleep numbs those in pain
    D. God is the source of humankind's grief
    E. sleep is the only escape from pain

33. All of the following are effects of the repetition in paragraphs 11 and 12, except that it
    A. links the speaker with the audience
    B. refers to paragraph 2 and King's dedication
    C. emphasizes dedication so that the audience will remember it
    D. reinforces the tribute to Martin Luther King, Jr.
    E. elevates the occasion to one which is worthy of honor

Questions 34–44 are based on the following letter.

Albert Einstein
Old Grove Road
Nassau Point
Peconic, New York
August 2, 1939

F. D. Roosevelt,
President of the United States,
White House
Washington, D.C.

Sir:

1 Some recent work by E. Fermi and L. Szilard, which has been communicated to me in manuscript, leads me to expect that the element uranium may be turned into a new and important source of energy in the immediate future. Certain aspects of the situation which has [sic] arisen seem to call for watchfulness and, if necessary, quick action on the part of the Administration. I believe therefore that it is my duty to bring to your attention the following facts and recommendations:

2 In the course of the last four months it has been made probable—through the work of Joliot in France as well as Fermi and Szilard in America—that it may become possible to set up a new nuclear chain reaction in a large mass of uranium, by which vast amounts of power and large quantities of new radium-like elements would be generated. Now it appears almost certain that this could be achieved in the immediate future.

3 This new phenomenon would also lead to the construction of bombs, and it is conceivable—though much less certain—that extremely powerful bombs of a new type may thus be constructed. A single bomb of this type, carried by boat and exploded in a port, might very well destroy the whole port together with some of the surrounding territory. However, such bombs might very well prove to be too heavy for transportation by air.

4 The United States has only very poor ores of uranium in moderate quantities. There is some good ore in Canada and the former Czechoslovakia, while the most important source of uranium is Belgian Congo.

5 In view of this situation you may think it desirable to have some permanent contact maintained between the Administration and the group of physicists working on chain reactions in America. One possible way of achieving this might be for you to entrust with this task a person who has your confidence and who could perhaps serve in an official capacity. His task might comprise the following:

a) to approach Government Departments, keep them informed of the further development and put forward recommendations for Government action;

b) giving particular attention to the problem of securing a supply of uranium ore for the United States;

c) to speed up the experimental work, which is at present being carried on within the limits of the budgets of University laboratories, by providing funds, if such funds be required, through his contacts with private persons who are willing to make contributions for this cause, and perhaps also by obtaining the co-operation of industrial laboratories which have the necessary equipment.

I understand that Germany has actually stopped the sale of uranium from the   6
Czechoslovakian mines which she has taken over. That she should have taken such early
action might perhaps be understood on the ground that the son of the German Under-
Secretary of State, von Weizacker, is attached to the Kaiser-Wilhelm-Institut in Berlin
where some of the American work on uranium is now being repeated.

Yours very truly,
Albert Einstein

34. In both paragraphs 2 and 3, Einstein makes use of the dash
  A. to emphasize the words set off
  B. as an exception to the point immediately before it
  C. to sound more scholarly and formal
  D. as an informal aside to what was said previously
  E. to summarize

35. The omission of a cordial opening and identification of the credentials of the writer imply all of the following <u>except</u>:
  A. Einstein expects his name alone will identify him
  B. Einstein assumes that the information he presents is compelling enough to command a response
  C. Einstein believes himself too busy and important to waste time on pleasantries
  D. As a scientist, Einstein was accustomed to having the facts speak for themselves
  E. They've had previous contact

36. The purpose of the listing in paragraph 5 is to
  A. secure Einstein's role as Roosevelt's "permanent contact"
  B. suggest a plan of necessary action to ensure American security
  C. increase research funding for further nuclear experimentation
  D. end scientific research leading to the construction of nuclear bombs
  E. send a letter of warning to Germany

37. Einstein's attitude can best be described as
  A. confrontational
  B. deferential
  C. cautionary
  D. complacent
  E. antagonistic

38. Einstein's first paragraph suggests all of the following <u>except</u>:
  A. FDR is not staying abreast of important scientific developments
  B. Einstein is concerned about how the administration is handling the new developments in uranium research
  C. Einstein is concerned that the administration may be unaware of important developments in the scientific community
  D. Einstein is an authority in the use of uranium
  E. FDR is familiar with the work of Fermi and Szilard

39. Which of the following best identifies Einstein's primary mode of discourse in his letter to FDR?
  A. narration
  B. process
  C. analysis
  D. persuasion
  E. exposition

40. To illustrate the gravity of the situation, Einstein uses all of the following <u>except</u>:
  A. "call for watchfulness" [paragraph 1]
  B. "it is my duty" [paragraph 1]
  C. "appears almost certain" [paragraph 2]
  D. "in the immediate future" [paragraph 2]
  E. "obtaining the cooperation" [paragraph 7]

41. Einstein understates the urgency of developing "chain reactions" in America
  A. with the repetition of the words *might* and *may*
  B. by excluding a fatalistic prediction
  C. by mentioning "other countries repeating America's work"
  D. with the phrase "though much less certain"
  E. all of the above

42. To persuade Roosevelt to consider his recommendations, Einstein uses all of the following approaches <u>except</u>:
A. discussions with other members of the scientific community
B. appeals to fear
C. presentation of evidence
D. making predictions
E. offering a plan

43. In his letter, Einstein's own assumptions are all of the following <u>except</u>:
A. his interpretation of the manuscript is accessible
B. his reputation as a scientist lends weight to his opinion
C. his plan can be implemented quietly

D. his urgency concerning the situation is apparent
E. Germany recognizes the urgency of the situation

44. After a careful reading of the letter, which of the following inferences is <u>not</u> valid?
A. Einstein understood the urgency of addressing the nuclear problem.
B. Einstein assumed FDR would react to the letter.
C. Einstein viewed the private sector as a means of circumventing a possible governmental impasse.
D. The Germans could have possibly misunderstood the significance of this scientific discovery.
E. Einstein is suspicious of German espionage.

Questions 45–56 are based on the following passage entitled "Reading an Archive," by Allan Sekula, which appeared in *Blasted Allegories*, a collection of contemporary essays and short stories, published by MIT Press in 1987.

. . . The widespread use of photographs as historical illustrations suggests that significant events are those which can be pictured, and thus history takes on the character of *spectacle*.[7] But this pictorial spectacle is a kind of rerun, since it depends on prior spectacles for its supposedly "raw" material.[8] Since the 1920's, the picture press, along with the apparatuses of a corporate public relations, publicity, advertising, and government propaganda, have contributed to a regularized flow of images: of disasters, wars, revolutions, new products, celebrities, political leaders, official ceremonies, public appearances, and so on. For a historian to use such pictures without remarking on these initial uses is naïve at best, and cynical at worst. What would it mean to construct a pictorial history of postwar coal mining in Cape Breton by using pictures from a company public relations archive without calling attention to the bias inherent in that source? What present interests might be served by such an oversight?　　[10]

The viewer of standard historical histories loses any ground in the present from which to make critical evaluations. In retrieving a loose succession of fragmentary glimpses of the past, the spectator is flung into a condition of imaginary temporal and geographical mobility. In this dislocated and disoriented state, the only coherence offered is that provided by the constantly shifting position of the camera, which provides the spectator with a kind of powerless omniscience. Thus, the spectator comes to identify with the technical apparatus, with the authoritative institution of photography. In the face of this authority, all other forms of telling and remembering　　[20] begin to fade. But the machine establishes the truth, not by logical argument, but by providing an experience. This experience characteristically veers between nostalgia, horror, and an overriding sense of the exoticism of the past, its irretrievable otherness for the viewer in the present. Ultimately, then, when photographs are uncritically presented as historical documents, they are transformed into aesthetic objects. Accordingly, the　　[25]

pretense to historical understanding remains, although that understanding has been
replaced by aesthetic experience.[9]

But what of our second option? Suppose we abandoned all pretense to historical
explanation, and treated these photographs as artworks of one sort or another? This
book would then be an inventory of aesthetic achievement and/or an offering for   30
disinterested aesthetic perusal. The reader may well have been prepared for these
likelihoods by the simple fact that this book has been published by a press with a
history of exclusive concern with the contemporary vanguard art of the United States
and Western Europe (and, to a lesser extent, Canada). Further, as I've already suggested,
in a more fundamental way, the very removal of these photographs from their initial   35
contexts invites aestheticism.

I can imagine two ways of converting these photographs into "works of art," both
a bit absurd, but neither without ample precedent in the current fever to assimilate
photography into the discourse and market of the fine arts. The first path follows
the traditional logic of romanticism, in its incessant search for aesthetic origins in a   40
coherent and controlling authorial "voice." The second path might be labeled "post-
romantic" and privileges the subjectivity of the collector, connoisseur, and viewer over
that of any specific author. This latter mode of reception treats photographs as "found
objects." Both strategies can be found in current photographic discourse; often they
are intertwined in a single book, exhibition, or magazine or journal article. The former   45
tends to predominate, largely because of the continuing need to validate photography
as a fine art, which requires an incessant appeal to the myth of authorship in order
to wrest photography away from its reputation as a servile and mechanical medium.
Photography needs to be won and rewon repeatedly for the ideology of romanticism to
take hold.[10]   50

[7] See Guy DeBord, *La société du spectacle* (Paris: Editions Buchat-Chastel, 1967): unauthorized translation, *Society of the Spectacle* (Detroit: Black and Red, 1970: rev. ed. 1977).

[8] We might think here of the reliance, by the executive branch of the United States government, on "photo opportuni-ties." For a discussion of an unrelated example, see Susan Sontag's dissection of Leni Reifenstahl's alibi that *Triumph of the Will* was merely an innocent documentary of the orchestrated-for-cinema 1934 Nuremberg Rally of the National Socialists. Sontag quotes Reifenstahl: "Everything is genuine. . . . It is *history—pure history.*" Susan Sontag, "Fascinat-ing Fascism," *New York Review of Books* 22, no. 1 (February 1975); reprinted in *Under the Sign of Saturn* (New York: Farrar, Straus, & Giroux, 1980), p. 82.

[9] Two recent books counter this prevailing tendency in "visual history" by directing attention to the power relationships behind the making of pictures: Craig Heron, Shea Hoffmitz, Wayne Roberts, and Robert Storey, *All that Our Hands Have Done: A Pictorial History of the Hamilton Workers* (Oakville, Ontario: Mosaic Press, 1981), and Sarah Graham-Brown, *Palestinians and Their Society, 1880–1946* (London: Quartet Books, 1980).

[10] In the first category are books that discover unsung commercial photographers: e.g., Mike Disfarmer, *Disfarmer: The Heber Springs Portraits*, text by Julia Scully (Danbury, N.H.: Addison House, 1976). In the second category are books that testify to the aesthetic sense of the collector: e.g., Sam Wagstaff, *A Book of Photographs from the Collection of Sam Wagstaff* (New York: Gray Press, 1978).

45. The first sentence (lines 1–3) does all of the
following, except:
   A. to indicate that material appears in this
      essay prior to this section
   B. to indicate scholarly research
   C. to indicate a cause/effect relationship
   D. to state the thesis of the piece
   E. to establish that the essay is based on the
      opinion of the author

46. The word *oversight* in line 12 refers to
   A. "pictures from a company public relations
      archive" (10–11)
   B. "without calling attention to the bias" (11)
   C. "construct a pictorial history" (9–10)
   D. "coal mining in Cape Breton" (10)
   E. "present interests" (12)

47. An accurate reading of footnote 7 informs the reader that the author based his material on
A. *Society of the Spectacle*, rev. ed. 1977
B. *Society of the Spectacle*, 1970
C. *La société du spectacle*, 1967
D. The Black and Red, 1970
E. Buchat-Chastel, 1967

48. The author directly involves the reader using which of the following linguistic devices?
A. direct address
B. exhortation
C. metaphor
D. direct quotation
E. rhetorical question

49. "initial contexts" in lines 35–36 refers to
A. "our second option" (28)
B. "historical explanation" (28–29)
C. "inventory of aesthetic achievement" (30)
D. "contemporary vanguard art" (33)
E. "disinterested aesthetic perusal" (31)

50. The main concern of the passage is contained in which of the following lines?
A. "Since the 1920's . . . and so on." (4–8)
B. "The viewer . . . critical evaluations." (13–14)
C. "In retrieving . . . geographical mobility." (14–16)
D. "I can imagine . . . of the fine arts." (37–39)
E. "The former . . . mechanical medium." (45–48)

51. The most probable implication of this passage is that
A. historians are cynical
B. historians are naïve
C. readers/viewers must be aware of the bias inherent in source material
D. viewers/readers are ill equipped to make critical evaluations
E. dealing with photographs demands a combination of the mechanical and the aesthetic

52. The purpose of footnote 9 is to
A. enhance the reputation of the writer
B. cite a primary source
C. direct the reader to opposing positions
D. compare differing cultures
E. provide a historical context

53. The tone of the passage can best be described as
A. argumentative and scholarly
B. romantic and artistic
C. philosophical and didactic
D. informative and sarcastic
E. informal and playful

54. According to the author, the power of photography as historical illustration is found in the
A. historian
B. spectator
C. picture press
D. image itself
E. camera

55. The last paragraph is primarily developed using which of the following rhetorical strategies?
A. cause and effect
B. comparison and contrast
C. definition
D. description
E. narration

56. The reader may infer from the footnotes that the author is a(n)
A. photographer himself
B. journalist reporting on photography
C. fan of Leni Reifenstahl
D. established authority in this field
E. art critic

END OF SECTION I

The second part of the test is the 2¼-hour essay writing section. This is taken after the break following completion of the multiple-choice section of the exam. You will be required to write three different essays: analysis, synthesis, and argument.

Before you begin your essays, you will be given 15 minutes to read a packet containing all of the sources for the synthesis essay, plus each of the individual prompts. During this 15 minutes you can read and annotate the texts. You will not be permitted to begin writing the essays until the 15 minutes are up and you are told to open your test booklet.

Again, we do not want you to write any essays at this time; just take a careful look at each of the questions to get an idea of the types of writing assignments you are expected to produce. Essay questions are called **prompts** by the AP.

Section II

Total Time—2¼ hours

Question 1

(Suggested time—45 minutes. This question counts
as one-third of the total score for Section II.)

The following paragraphs are from the opening of Truman Capote's *In Cold Blood*. After carefully reading the excerpt, write a well-organized essay in which you characterize Capote's view of Holcomb, Kansas, and analyze how Capote conveys this view. Your analysis may consider such elements as diction, imagery, syntax, structure, tone, and selection of detail.

The village of Holcomb stands on the high wheat plains of western Kansas, a lonesome area that other Kansans call "out there." Some seventy miles east of the Colorado border, the countryside, with its hard blue skies and desert-clear air, has an atmosphere that is rather more Far Western than Middle West. The local accent is barbed with a prairie twang, a ranch-hand nasalness, and the men, many of them, wear narrow frontier trousers, Stetsons, and high-heeled boots with pointed toes. The land is flat, and the views are awesomely extensive; horses, herds of cattle, a white cluster of grain elevators rising as gracefully as Greek temples are visible long before a traveler reaches them. [1]

Holcomb, too, can be seen from great distances. Not that there is much to see— simply an aimless congregation of buildings divided in the center by the main-line tracks of the Santa Fe Railroad, a haphazard hamlet bounded on the south by a brown stretch of the Arkansas (pronounced "Ar-kan-sas") River, on the north by a highway, Route 50, and on the east and west by prairie lands and wheat fields. After rain, or when snowfalls thaw, the streets, unnamed, unshaded, unpaved, turn from the thickest dust into the direst mud. At one end of the town stands a stark old stucco structure, the roof of which supports an electric sign—Dance—but the dancing has ceased and the advertisement has been dark for several years. Nearby is another building with an irrelevant sign, this one in flaking gold on a dirty window—HOLCOMB BANK. The bank closed in 1933, and it is one of the town's two "apartment houses," the second being a ramshackle mansion known, because a good part of the local school's faculty lives there, as the Teacherage. But the majority of Holcomb's homes are one-story frame affairs, with front porches. [2]

Down by the depot, the postmistress, a gaunt woman who wears a rawhide jacket and denims and cowboy boots, presides over a falling-apart post office. The depot, itself, with its peeling sulphur-colored paint, is equally melancholy; the Chief, the Super Chief, the El Capitan go by every day, but these celebrated expresses never pause there. No passenger trains do—only an occasional freight. Up on the highway, there are two filling stations, one of which doubles as a meagerly supplied grocery store, while the other does extra duty as a cafe—Hartman's Cafe, where Mrs. Hartman, the proprietress, dispenses sandwiches, coffee, soft drinks, and 3.2 beer. (Holcomb, like all the rest of Kansas, is "dry.") 3

And that, really, is all. Unless you include, as one must, the Holcomb School, a good-looking establishment, which reveals a circumstance that the appearance of the community otherwise camouflages: that the parents who send their children to this modern and ably staffed "consolidated" school—the grades go from kindergarten through senior high, and a fleet of buses transport the students, of which there are usually around three hundred and sixty, from as far as sixteen miles away—are, in general, a prosperous people. . . . The farm ranchers in Finney County, of which Holcomb is a part, have done well; money has been made not from farming alone but also from the exploitation of plentiful natural-gas resources, and its acquisition is reflected in the new school, the comfortable interiors of the farmhouses, the steep and swollen grain elevators. 4

Until one morning in mid-November of 1959, few Americans—in fact, few Kansans—had ever heard of Holcomb. Like the waters of the river, like the motorists on the highway, and like the yellow trains streaking down the Santa Fe tracks, drama in the shape of exceptional happenings, had never stopped there. The inhabitants of the village, numbering two hundred and seventy, were satisfied that this should be so, quite content to exist inside ordinary life . . . 5

Question 2

(Suggested time—45 minutes. This question counts
as one-third of the total score for Section II.)

English Language and Composition

Reading Time: 15 minutes
Suggested Writing Time: 40 minutes

A recent Supreme Court decision has provoked much debate about private property rights. In it, the court ruled that the city of New London was within the bounds of the *U.S. Constitution* when it condemned private property for use in a redevelopment plan. This ruling is an example of the classic debate between individual rights versus the greater good.

Carefully read the following sources, including any introductory information. **Then, in an essay that synthesizes at least three of the sources for support, take a position that supports, opposes, or qualifies the claim that the governmental taking of property from one private owner to give to another to further economic development constitutes a permissible "public use" under the Fifth Amendment.**

Make certain that you take a position and that the essay centers on your argument. Use the sources to support your reasoning; avoid simply summarizing the sources. You may refer to the sources by their letters (Source A, Source B, etc.) or by the identifiers in the parentheses below.

Source A (*U.S. Constitution*)
Source B (*60 Minutes*)
Source C (*Kelo* decision)
Source D (Koterba, political cartoon)
Source E (Broder)
Source F (Britt, political cartoon)
Source G (CNN and American Survey)

Source A

"Amendments." The United States Constitution, 1787.
The following is a section from the Fifth Amendment to the *U.S. Constitution*.

> *"nor shall private property be taken for public use, without just compensation."*

Note: This is known as *eminent domain*, which refers to the power of government to take private property for "public use" if the owner is fairly compensated. Eminent domain has been used to build roads, schools, and utility lines. Cities also have used it to transfer property from unwilling sellers to developers who want to build shopping malls, offices, or other projects.

Source B

Adapted from the July 4, 2004, edition of *60 Minutes*. Available at http://www.cbsnews
.com/stories/2003/09/26/60minutes/main575343.shtml.
The following is part of an interview conducted for the CBS news magazine *60 Minutes*. In it, the audience is introduced to a couple whose house had been taken by the local government for development of condos.

> *Jim and Joanne Saleet are refusing to sell the home they've lived in for 38 years. They live in a quiet neighborhood of single-family houses in Lakewood, Ohio, just outside Cleveland. The City of Lakewood is trying to use eminent domain to force the Saleets out to make way for more expensive condominiums. But the Saleets are telling the town, "Hell no! They won't go."*
>
> *"The bottom line is this is morally wrong, what they're doing here. This is our home. And we're going to stay here. And I'm gonna fight them tooth and nail. I've just begun to fight," says Jim Saleet. "We talked about this when we were dating. I used to point to the houses and say, 'Joanne, one of these days, we're going to have one of these houses.' And I meant it. And I worked hard."*
>
> *Jim Saleet worked in the pharmaceutical industry, paid off his house, and then retired. Now, he and his wife plan to spend the rest of their days there, and pass their house on to their children.*
>
> *But Lakewood's mayor, Madeleine Cain, has other plans. She wants to tear down the Saleets' home, plus 55 homes around it, along with four apartment buildings and more than a dozen businesses.*
>
> *Why? So that private developers can build high-priced condos, and a high-end shopping mall, and, thus, raise Lakewood's property tax base.*
>
> *The mayor told* 60 Minutes *that she sought out a developer for the project because Lakewood's aging tax base has been shrinking, and the city simply needs more money.*
>
> *"This is about Lakewood's future. Lakewood cannot survive without a strengthened tax base. Is it right to consider this a public good? Absolutely," says the mayor, who admits that it's difficult and unfortunate that the Saleets are being asked to give up their home.*

The Saleets live in an area called Scenic Park, and because it is so scenic, it's a prime place to build upscale condominiums. With great views, over the Rocky River, those condos will be a cinch to sell. But the condos can't go up unless the city can remove the Saleets and their neighbors through eminent domain. And, to legally invoke eminent domain, the city had to certify that this scenic park area is, really, "blighted."

"We're not blighted. This is an area that we absolutely love. This is a close-knit, beautiful neighborhood. It's what America's all about," says Jim Saleet. "And, Mike, you don't know how humiliating this is to have people tell you, 'You live in a blighted area,' and how degrading this is."

"The term 'blighted' is a statutory word," says Mayor Cain. "It is, it really doesn't have a lot to do with whether or not your home is painted. . . . A statutory term is used to describe an area. The question is whether or not that area can be used for a higher and better use."

Source C

Kelo v. New London. U.S. Supreme Court 125 S. Ct. 2655.
The following is a brief overview of a decision by the U.S. Supreme Court in 2005.

Susette Kelo, et al. v. City of New London, et al., *125 S. Ct. 2655 (2005), more commonly* Kelo v. New London, *is a land-use law case argued before the United States Supreme Court on February 22, 2005. The case arose from a city's use of eminent domain to condemn privately owned real property so that it could be used as part of a comprehensive redevelopment plan.*

The owners sued the city in Connecticut courts, arguing that the city had misused its eminent domain power. The power of eminent domain is limited by the Fifth and Fourteenth Amendments to the United States Constitution. The Fifth Amendment, which restricts the actions of the federal government, says, in part, that "private property [shall not] be taken for public use, without just compensation"; under Section 1 of the Fourteenth Amendment, this limitation is also imposed on the actions of U.S. state and local governments. Kelo and the other appellants argued that economic development, the stated purpose of the Development Corporation, did not qualify as public use.

The Supreme Court's Ruling: This 5:4 decision holds that the governmental taking of property from one private owner to give to another in furtherance of economic development constitutes a permissible "public use" under the Fifth Amendment.

Source D

Koterba, Jeff, *Omaha World Herald*. Available at http://cagle.msnbc.com/news/
EminentDomain/4.asp.

The following political cartoon appeared in an Omaha, Nebraska, newspaper.

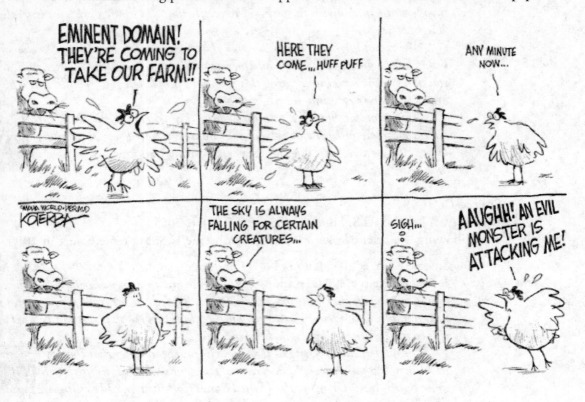

Jeff Koterba, *Omaha World Herald*, NE

Source E

Broder, John M, "States Curbing Right to Seize Private Homes." *New York Times*,
February 21, 2006.

The following passage is excerpted from an article published in the *New York Times*.

> *"Our opposition to eminent domain is not across the board," he [Scott G. Bullock of
> the Institute for Justice] said. "It has an important but limited role in government
> planning and the building of roads, parks, and public buildings. What we oppose is
> eminent domain abuse for private development, and we are encouraging legislators to
> curtail it."*
>
> *More neutral observers expressed concern that state officials, in their zeal to protect
> homeowners and small businesses, would handcuff local governments that are trying to
> revitalize dying cities and fill in blighted areas with projects that produce tax revenues
> and jobs.*
>
> *"It's fair to say that many states are on the verge of seriously overreacting to the
> Kelo decision," said John D. Echeverria, executive director of the Georgetown Envi-
> ronmental Law and Policy Institute and an authority on land-use policy. "The danger
> is that some legislators are going to attempt to destroy what is a significant and some-
> times painful but essential government power. The extremist position is a prescription
> for economic decline for many metropolitan areas around the country."*

Source F

Britt, Chris, *The State Journal-Register*. Available at http://cagle.msnbc.com/news/
EminentDomain/4.asp.

The following political cartoon appeared in a Springfield, Illinois, newspaper.

Chris Britt, Springfield, IL — *The State Journal-Register*

Source G

Andres, Gary J., "The Kelo Backlash." *Washington Times*, August 29, 2005.

CNN Pollserver, "Local governments should be able to seize homes and businesses."
Quick Vote, June 23, 2005. Available at http://www.cnn.com/POLLSERVER/
results/18442.exclude.html.

The following are the results of two surveys/polls. The first appeared in a *Washington Times*
article, and the second was commissioned by CNN.

American Survey | July 14–17, 2005

*An American Survey of 800 registered voters nationwide shows 68 percent favor-
ing legislative limits on the government's ability to take private property away from
owners, with 62 percent of Democrats, 74 percent of independents and 70 percent of
Republicans supporting such limits.*

Created: Thursday, June 23, 2005 at 11:48:12 EDT

Local governments should be able to seize homes and businesses:

For public use	33%	58481 votes
For private economic development	1%	2445 votes
Never	66%	117061 votes

Total: 177987 votes

This QuickVote is not scientific and reflects the opinions of only those Internet users who have chosen to participate. The results cannot be assumed to represent the opinions of Internet users in general, nor the public as a whole.

Question 3

(Suggested time—45 minutes. This question counts
as one-third of the total score for Section II.)

In his famous "Vast Wasteland" address to the National Association of Broadcasters in May of 1961, Newton Minow, the Chairman of the Federal Communications Commission, spoke about the power of television to influence the taste, knowledge, and opinions of its viewers around the world. Carefully read the following, paying close attention to how timely it is today, especially in light of the worldwide Internet. 1

Minow ended his speech warning that "The power of instantaneous sight and sound is without precedent in mankind's history. This is an awesome power. It has limitless capabilities for good—and for evil. And it carries with it awesome responsibilities— responsibilities which you and [the government] cannot escape . . ." 2

Using your own knowledge and your own experiences or reading, write a carefully constructed essay that defends, challenges, or qualifies Minow's ideas. 3

END OF SECTION II

"Even though I was 'turned off' by the thought of having to read old-fashioned writing, I was really proud of myself once I found out that I could make sense out of it when I concentrated and focused the way my teacher showed us."
—Sean V.S.,
　AP student

So, that's what the Advanced Placement English Language exam looks like.

If you're being honest with yourself, you're probably feeling a bit overwhelmed at this point. GOOD! This is primarily why we are going to deconstruct this entire Diagnostic/Master exam for you and with you throughout this book. By the time you reach Practice Exams 1 and 2, you should be feeling much more confident and comfortable about doing well on the AP English Language and Composition exam.

As you progress through this book, you will:

- take each section of the Diagnostic/Master exam;
- read the explanations for the answers to the multiple-choice questions;
- read sample student essays written in response to each of the three prompts;
- read the rubrics and ratings of the student essays; and
- evaluate your own performance in light of this information.

STEP **3**

Develop Strategies for Success

CHAPTER **4** Section I of the Exam—The Multiple-Choice Questions
CHAPTER **5** Introduction to the Analysis Essay
CHAPTER **6** Introduction to the Argumentative Essay
CHAPTER **7** Introduction to the Synthesis Essay

CHAPTER 4

Section I of the Exam—
The Multiple-Choice Questions

IN THIS CHAPTER

Summary: Become comfortable with the multiple-choice section of the exam. If you know what to expect, you can prepare.

Key Ideas

✪ Prepare yourself for the multiple-choice section of the exam.
✪ Review the types of multiple-choice questions asked on the exam.
✪ Learn strategies for approaching the multiple-choice questions.
✪ Score yourself by checking the answer key and explanations for the multiple-choice section of the Diagnostic/Master exam.

Introduction to the Multiple-Choice Section of the Exam

Multiple choice? Multiple guess? Multiple anxiety? It's been our experience that the day after the exam finds students bemoaning the difficulties and uncertainties of Section I of the AP English Language and Composition exam.

"It's unfair."

"I didn't understand a word of the third reading."

"Was that in English?"

"Did you get four Ds in a row for the last reading?"

"I just closed my eyes and pointed."

Is it really possible to avoid these and other exam woes? We hope that by following along with us in this chapter, you will begin to feel a bit more familiar with the world of multiple-choice questions and, thereby, become a little more comfortable with the multiple-choice section of the exam.

What Is It About the Multiple-Choice Questions That Causes Such Anxiety?

Basically, a multiple-choice literature question is a flawed method of gauging understanding. Why? Because, by its very nature, a multiple-choice question forces you to play a cat-and-mouse game with the test maker, who demands that you concentrate on items that are incorrect before you can choose what is correct. We know, however, that complex literary works have a richness that allows for ambiguity. In the exam mode, you are expected to match someone else's reading of a work with your choice of answers. This is what often causes the student to feel that the multiple-choice section is unfair. And, perhaps, to a degree, it is. But, get with the program! It's a necessary evil. So, our advice to you is to accept the difficulties and limitations of Section I and to move on.

This said, it's wise to develop a strategy for success. Once again, practice is the key to this success.

You've answered all types of multiple-choice questions during your career as a student. The test-taking skills you have learned in your social studies, math, and science classes may also apply to this specific situation.

A word in defense of the test makers is in order here. The test is designed to allow you to shine, NOT to be humiliated. To that end, the people who design the multiple-choice questions take their job seriously and take pride in their product. You will not find "cutesy" questions, and they will not play games with you. What they will do is present several valid options in response to a challenging and appropriate question. These questions are designed to separate the knowledgeable, perceptive, and thoughtful reader from the superficial and impulsive one.

"You know, when my teacher required us to make up multiple-choice questions that came from the AP prompts we wrote essays on, I really became more confident about how to answer these types of questions on the exam."
—Samantha T., AP student

What Should I Expect in Section I?

For this first section of the AP English Language and Composition exam, you are allotted 1 hour to answer between 45 and 60 objective questions on four to five prose passages. The selections may come from works of fiction or nonfiction and be from different time periods, of different styles, and of different purposes. In other words, you will not find two essays by Thoreau in the multiple-choice section of the same test.

At least one of the readings will contain some type of citation, attribution, footnote, and so on. You will be expected to be able to determine HOW this citation, etc., is employed by the author to further his purpose. You will NOT be asked about specific formats such as MLA or APA.

These are NOT easy readings. They are representative of the college-level work you have been doing throughout the year. You will be expected to:

- follow sophisticated syntax;
- respond to diction;
- be comfortable with upper-level vocabulary;
- be familiar with rhetorical terminology;
- make inferences;
- be sensitive to irony and tone;
- recognize components of organization and style;
- be familiar with modes of discourse and rhetorical strategies; and
- recognize how information contained in citations contributes to the author's purpose.

THE GOOD NEWS IS . . . the selection is self-contained. If it is about the Irish Potato Famine, you will NOT be at a disadvantage if you know nothing about Irish history. Frequently, there will be biblical references in a selection. This is especially true of works from an earlier time period. You are expected to be aware of basic allusions to biblical and mythological works often found in literary texts, but the passage will never require you to have any particular religious background.

DO NOT LET THE SUBJECT MATTER OF A PASSAGE THROW YOU. Strong analytical skills will work on any passage.

How Should I Begin to Work with Section I?

Take no more than a minute and thumb through the exam, looking for the following:

- The length of the selections
- The time periods or writing styles, if you can recognize them
- The number of questions asked
- A quick idea of the type of questions

This brief skimming of the test will put your mind into gear, because you will be aware of what is expected of you.

How Should I Proceed Through This Section of the Exam?

Timing is important. Always maintain an awareness of the time. Wear a watch. (Some students like to put it directly in front of them on the desk.) Remember, this is not your first encounter with the multiple-choice section of the test. You've probably been practicing timed exams in class; in addition, this book provides you with three timed experiences. We're sure you will notice improvements as you progress through the timed practice activities.

Although the test naturally breaks into 15-minute sections, you may take less or more time on a particular passage, but know when to move on. The test DOES NOT become more difficult as it progresses; therefore, you will want to give yourself the opportunity to answer each set of questions.

Work at a pace of about one question per minute. Every question is worth the same number of points, so don't get bogged down on those that involve multiple tasks. Don't panic if a question is beyond you. Remember, it will probably be beyond a great number of the other students taking the exam. There has to be a bar that determines the 5's and 4's for this exam. Just do your best.

Reading the text carefully is a must. Begin at the beginning and work your way through.

Most people read just with their eyes. We want you to slow down and to read with your senses of sight, sound, and touch.

- Underline, circle, and annotate the text.
- Read closely, paying attention to punctuation, syntax, diction, pacing, and organization.
- Read as if you were reading the passage aloud to an audience, emphasizing meaning and intent.
- As corny as it may seem, hear those words in your head.
- This technique may seem childish, but it works. Using your finger as a pointer, underscore the line as you are reading it aloud in your head. This forces you to slow down and to really notice the text. This will be helpful when you have to refer to the passage.
- Use all of the information given to you about the passage, such as title, author, date of publication, and footnotes.
- Be aware of organizational and rhetorical devices and techniques.

"Even though it's time-consuming, I find it invaluable to take class time to accurately simulate exam conditions."
—Cynthia N., AP teacher

- Be aware of thematic lines and be sensitive to details that will obviously be material for multiple-choice questions.
- Quickly skim the questions, ignoring the choices. This will give you an idea as to what is expected of you as a reader of the given text.

> You can practice these techniques anytime. Take any work and read it aloud. Time yourself. A good rate is about 1½ minutes per page.

Types of Multiple-Choice Questions

Is the Structure the Same for All of the Multiple-Choice Questions?

No. There are several basic patterns that the AP test makers employ. These include:

1. The *straightforward question*.
    - The passage is an example of
      C. a contrast/comparison essay
    - The pronoun "it" refers to
      B. his gait

2. The question that refers you to specific lines and asks you to *draw a conclusion* or *interpret*.
    - Lines 52–57 serve to
      A. reinforce the author's thesis

3. The ALL . . . <u>EXCEPT</u> *question* requires more time, because it demands that you consider every possibility.
    - The AP English Language and Composition exam is all of the following except
      A. It is given in May of each year.
      B. It is open to high school seniors.
      C. It is published in the *New York Times*.
      D. It is used as a qualifier for college credit.
      E. It is a 3-hour test.

4. The question that asks you to *make an inference or to abstract a concept not directly stated in the passage*.
    - In "Letter from a Birmingham Jail," the reader can infer that the speaker is
      E. religious

5. Here is the killer question. It even uses *Roman numerals!* This question is problematic and time consuming. You can be certain that each exam will have a couple of these questions lurking within it.
    - In the passage, "night" refers to
      I. the death of the young woman
      II. a pun on Sir William's title
      III. the end of the affair
      A. I only
      B. I and II
      C. I and III
      D. II and III
      E. I, II, and III

    This is the type of question to skip if it causes you problems and/or you are short on time.

6. The footnote question: This is the question that requires you to abstract, interpret, or apply information contained in footnotes attached to passages.
  • The purpose of the footnote is to
    A. cite a primary source
    B. verify the writer's assertions
    C. direct the reader to other sources
    D. cite a secondary source
    E. provide the writer's additional commentary

What Kinds of Questions Should I Expect on the Exam?

The multiple-choice questions center on form and content. Naturally, the test makers are assessing your understanding of the meaning of the selection as well as your ability to draw inferences and perceive implications based on the given work. They also want to know if you understand HOW an author develops his or her ideas.

The questions, therefore, will be *factual*, *technical*, *analytical*, and *inferential*. The brief chart below illustrates the types of key words/phrases in these four categories you can expect to encounter.

Note: DO NOT MEMORIZE THESE TABLES. Likewise, do not panic if a word or phrase is not familiar to you. You may or may not encounter any or all of these words or phrases on any given exam. You can, however, count on meeting up with many of these in our practice exams in this book.

FACTUAL	TECHNICAL	ANALYTICAL	INFERENTIAL
Words refer to	Sentence structure	Rhetorical strategy	Effect of diction
Allusions	Style	Shift in development	Tone
Antecedents	Grammatical purpose	Rhetorical stance	Inferences
Pronoun referents	Dominant technique	Style	Effect of description
	Imagery	Metaphor	Effect of last paragraph
	Point of view	Contrast	Effect on reader
	Organization of passage	Comparison	Narrator's attitude
		Cause/effect	Image suggests
	Narrative progress of passage	Argument	Effect of detail
		Description	Author implies
	Conflict	Narration	Author most concerned with
	Irony	Specific–general	Symbol
	Function of . . .	General–specific	
		How something is characterized	
		Imagery	
		Passage is primarily concerned with	
		Function of . . .	

> A WORD ABOUT JARGON: Jargon refers to words unique to a specific subject. A common language is important for communication, and there must be agreement on the basic meanings of terms. Although it is important to know the universal language of a subject, it is also important that you NOT limit the scope of your thinking to a brief definition. All of the terms used in the above chart are categorized only for easy reference. They also work in many other contexts. In other words, THINK OUTSIDE OF THE BOX.

Scoring the Multiple-Choice Section

How Does the Scoring of the Multiple-Choice Section Work?

The College Board has implemented a new scoring process for the multiple-choice section of the AP English Language and Composition exam. No longer are points deducted for incorrect responses, so there is no longer a penalty for guessing incorrectly. **Multiple-choice scores are based solely on the number of questions answered correctly.** Therefore, it is to your advantage to answer ALL of the multiple-choice questions. Your chances of guessing the correct answer improve if you skillfully apply the process of elimination to narrow the choices.

Strategies for Answering the Multiple-Choice Questions

As observed earlier, you've been answering multiple-choice questions most of your academic life, and you've probably figured out ways to deal with them. There may, however, be some points you have not considered that will be helpful for this particular exam.

General Guidelines

"One of my biggest challenges in preparing for the exam was to learn not to jump to conclusions when I was doing the multiple-choice questions."
—Samantha S., AP student

- Work in order. We like this approach for several reasons:
  — It's clear.
  — You will not lose your place on the scan sheet.
  — There may be a logic to working sequentially which will help you to answer previous questions. BUT, this is your call. If you are more comfortable moving around the exam, do so.
- Write on the exam booklet. Mark it up. Make it yours. Interact with the test.
- Do not spend too much time on any one question.
- Do not be misled by the length or appearance of a selection. There is no correlation between this and the difficulty of the questions.
- Don't fight the question or the passage. You may know other information about the subject of the text or a question. It's irrelevant. Work within the given context.
- Consider all the choices in a given question. This will guard against your jumping to a false conclusion. It helps you to slow down and to look closely at each possibility. You may find that your first choice was not the best or most appropriate one.
- Maintain an open mind as you answer subsequent questions in a series. Sometimes a later question will contradict an answer to a previous one. Reconsider both. Likewise, even the phrasing of a question may point to an answer in a previous question.
- Remember that all parts of an answer must be correct.
- When in doubt, go back to the text.

Specific Techniques

- <u>Process of Elimination</u>—This is the primary tool, except for direct knowledge of the answer.
  1. Read the five choices.
  2. If no choice immediately strikes you as correct, you can
     — eliminate any which are obviously wrong;
     — eliminate those choices which are too narrow or too broad;
     — eliminate illogical choices;
     — eliminate answers which are synonymous;
     — eliminate answers which cancel each other out.
  3. If two answers are close,
     — find the one general enough to contain all aspects of the question

     OR

     — find the one limited enough to be the detail the question is seeking.

- <u>Substitution/Fill In the Blank</u>
  1. Rephrase the question, leaving a blank where the answer should go.
  2. Use each of the choices to fill in the blank until you find the one that is the best fit.

- <u>Using Context</u>
  1. Use this technique when the question directs you to specific lines, words, or phrases.
  2. Locate the given word, phrase, or sentence and read the sentence before and after the section of the text to which the question refers. Often this provides the information or clues you need to make your choice.

- <u>Anticipation</u>
  As you read the passage for the first time, mark any details and ideas that you would ask a question about. You may second-guess the test makers this way.

- <u>Intuition/The Educated Guess</u>
  You have a wealth of skills and knowledge in your language and composition subconscious. A question or a choice may trigger a "remembrance of things past." This can be the basis for your educated guess. Have the confidence to use the educated guess as a valid technique. Trust your own resources.

A Survival Plan

If time is running out and you haven't finished the last selection,

1. Scan the remaining questions and look for:
   — the shortest questions; and/or
   — the questions that point you to a line.

These two types of questions are relatively easy to work with and to verify.

2. Look for specific detail/definition questions.

3. Look for self-contained questions.
   "The jail sentence was a bitter winter for his plan" is an example of
   C. an analogy.

You did not have to go to the passage to answer this question.

Some Thoughts About Guessing

You can't be hurt by making educated guesses based on a careful reading of the selection. Be smart. Understand that you need to come to this exam well prepared. You must have a foundation of knowledge and skills. You cannot guess through the entire exam and expect to do well.

This is not Lotto. This book is not about how to "beat the exam." We want to maximize the skills you already have. There is an inherent integrity in this exam and your participation in it. With this in mind, when there is no other direction open to you, it is perfectly fine to make an educated guess.

Is There Anything Special I Should Know About Preparing for the Multiple-Choice Questions?

After you have finished with the Diagnostic/Master exam, you will be familiar with the format and types of questions asked on the AP English Language and Composition exam. However, just practicing answering multiple-choice questions on specific works will not give you a complete understanding of this questioning process. We suggest the following to hone your multiple-choice skills with prose multiple-choice questions.

- Choose a challenging passage from a full-length prose work or a self-contained essay, plus choose another that contains documentation/citations. (Take a close look at your science and social studies texts for examples.)
- Read the selection a couple of times and create several multiple-choice questions about specific sections of the selection.
  — Make certain the section is self-contained and complex.
  — Choose a speech, a philosophical passage, an essay, an editorial, a letter, a preface or epilogue, a significant passage from a chapter, or a news article.
- Refer to the chart given earlier in this chapter for suggested language and type.
- Administer your miniquiz to a classmate, study group, or class.
- Evaluate your results.
- Repeat this process through several different works during your preparation for the exam. The selections can certainly come from those you are studying in class.
- Create a variety of question types.

Here's What Should Happen as a Result of Your Using This Process

- Your expectation level for the selections in the actual test will be more realistic.
- You will become familiar with the language of multiple-choice questions.
- Your understanding of the process of choosing answers will be heightened.
- Questions you write that you find less than satisfactory will trigger your analytical skills as you attempt to figure out "what went wrong."
- Your understanding of terminology will become more accurate.
- BONUS: If you continue to do this work throughout your preparation for the AP exam, you will have created a mental storehouse of literary and analytical information. So, when you are presented with an analytical or argumentative essay in Section II, you will have an extra resource at your disposal.

> You might want to utilize this process throughout the year with selections studied in and out of class and keep track of your progress. See the Bibliography at the back of this book.

The Time Is at Hand

It is now your turn to try the Diagnostic/Master exam, Section I.

Do this section in ONE sitting. Time yourself!

Be honest with yourself when you score your answers.

Note: If the 1 hour passes before you have a chance to finish all of the questions, stop where you are and score what you have done up to this point. Afterward, complete the remaining parts of the section, but do not count it as part of your score.

When you have completed all of the multiple-choice questions in this diagnostic exam, carefully look at the explanations of the answers. Spend time here and assess which types of questions are giving you trouble. Use this book to learn from your mistakes.

ANSWER SHEET FOR DIAGNOSTIC MULTIPLE-CHOICE QUESTIONS

1. _____	15. _____	29. _____	43. _____
2. _____	16. _____	30. _____	44. _____
3. _____	17. _____	31. _____	45. _____
4. _____	18. _____	32. _____	46. _____
5. _____	19. _____	33. _____	47. _____
6. _____	20. _____	34. _____	48. _____
7. _____	21. _____	35. _____	49. _____
8. _____	22. _____	36. _____	50. _____
9. _____	23. _____	37. _____	51. _____
10. _____	24. _____	38. _____	52. _____
11. _____	25. _____	39. _____	53. _____
12. _____	26. _____	40. _____	54. _____
13. _____	27. _____	41. _____	55. _____
14. _____	28. _____	42. _____	56. _____

I _____ did _____ did not finish all the questions in the allotted 1 hour.

I had _____ correct answers. I had _____ incorrect answers. I left _____ blank.

I have carefully reviewed the explanations of the answers, and I think I need to work on the following types of questions:

DIAGNOSTIC/MASTER EXAM
ADVANCED PLACEMENT ENGLISH LANGUAGE
AND COMPOSITION

Section I

Total Time–1 hour

Carefully read the following passages and answer the accompanying questions.

Questions 1–12 are based on the following passage from "Samuel Johnson on Pope," which appeared in *The Lives of the English Poets* (1779–1781).

The person of Pope is well known not to have been formed by the nicest model. He has compared himself to a spider and, by another, is described as protuberant behind and before. He is said to have been beautiful in his infancy, but he was of a constitution feeble and weak. As bodies of a tender frame are easily distorted, his deformity was probably in part the effect of his application. But his face was not displeasing, and his eyes were animated and vivid.   5

By natural deformity, or accidental distortion, his vital functions were so much disordered, that his life was a "long disease."

He sometimes condescended to be jocular with servants or inferiors; but by no merriment, either of others or his own, was he ever seen excited to laughter.   10

Of his domestic character frugality was a part eminently remarkable. Having determined not to be dependent, he determined not to be in want, and, therefore, wisely and magnanimously rejected all temptations to expense unsuitable to his fortune.

The great topic of his ridicule is poverty; the crimes with which he reproaches his antagonists are their debts and their want of a dinner. He seems to be of an opinion not   15
very uncommon in the world, that to want money is to want everything.

He professed to have learned his poetry from Dryden, whom he praised through his whole life with unvaried liberality; and perhaps his character may receive some illustration, if he be compared with his master.

Integrity of understanding and nicety of discernment were not allotted in a less   20
proportion to Dryden than to Pope. But Dryden never desired to apply all the judgment that he had. He wrote merely for the people. When he pleased others, he contented himself. He never attempted to mend what he must have known to be faulty. He wrote with little consideration and, once it had passed the press, ejected it from his mind.

Pope was not content to satisfy; he desired to excel, and, therefore, always endeavored   25
to do his best. Pope did not court the candor, but dared the judgment of his reader, and, expecting no indulgence from others, he showed none to himself. He examined lines and words with minute and punctilious observation, and he retouched every part with diligence, until he had nothing left to be forgiven.

Poetry was not the sole praise of either; for both excelled likewise in prose. The   30
style of Dryden is capricious and varied; that of Pope is cautious and uniform. Dryden observes the motions of his own mind; Pope constrains his mind to his own rules of composition. Dryden's page is a natural field, diversified by the exuberance of abundant vegetation. Pope's is a velvet lawn, shaven by the scythe, and leveled by the roller.

If the flights of Dryden are higher, Pope continues longer on the wing. If of Dryden's   35
fire the blaze is brighter, of Pope's the heat is more regular and constant. Dryden is read with frequent astonishment, and Pope with perpetual delight.

1. The passage is primarily a(n)
   A. character sketch of Pope
   B. discussion of poetic style
   C. criticism of Dryden
   D. model for future poets
   E. opportunity for the writer to show off his own skills

2. The passage discusses a contrast among all of the following except
   A. prose and poetry
   B. Pope and Dryden
   C. body and mind
   D. poverty and wealth
   E. body and soul

3. "If the flights" (35) means
   A. Pope's writing will outlast Dryden's
   B. both Pope and Dryden are equal
   C. Pope is not idealistic
   D. Pope is more wordy
   E. Pope is not as bright as Dryden

4. The character of Pope is developed by all of the following except:
   A. examples
   B. comparison
   C. contrast
   D. satire
   E. description

5. According to the passage, Pope and Dryden are
   A. rivals
   B. equally intelligent
   C. outdated
   D. equally physically attractive
   E. in debt

6. From the passage, the reader may infer that Pope
   A. was extravagant
   B. was a man of the people
   C. was jealous of Dryden
   D. had a desire to be popular
   E. had a bitter, satirical nature

7. The tone of the passage is
   A. informal and affectionate
   B. formal and objective
   C. condescending and paternalistic
   D. laudatory and reverent
   E. critical and negative

8. Lines 20–24 indicate that Dryden was what type of writer?
   A. one who labored over his thoughts
   B. one who wrote only for himself
   C. one who wrote only for the critics
   D. one who wrote to please Pope
   E. one who did not revise

9. Using the context of lines 27–29, "punctilious" means
   A. precise
   B. timely
   C. cursory
   D. scholarly
   E. philosophical

10. In the context of the passage, "until he had nothing left to be forgiven" (29) means
    A. Pope outraged his readers
    B. Pope suffered from writer's block
    C. Pope exhausted his subject matter
    D. Pope's prose was revised to perfection
    E. Pope cared about the opinions of his readers

11. "Shaven" and "leveled" in line 34 indicate that Pope's style of writing was
    A. natural
    B. richly ornamented
    C. highly controlled
    D. mechanical
    E. analytical

12. Based on a close reading of the final paragraph of the passage, the reader could infer that the author
    A. looks on both writers equally
    B. prefers the work of Pope
    C. sees the two writers as inferior to his own writing style
    D. indicates no preference
    E. prefers the work of Dryden

Questions 13–23 are based on the following excerpt from Charlotte Perkins Gilman's "Politics and Warfare," which appears in *The Man-Made World: Our Androcentric Culture* (1911).

There are many today who hold that politics need not be at all connected with warfare; and others who hold that politics is warfare from start to finish. 1

The inextricable confusion of politics and warfare is part of the stumbling block 2 in the minds of men. As they see it, a nation is primarily a fighting organization; and its principal business is offensive and defensive warfare; therefore the ultimatum with which they oppose the demand for political equality—"women cannot fight, therefore they cannot vote."

Fighting, when all is said, is to them the real business of life; not to be able to fight 3 is to be quite out of the running; and ability to solve our growing mass of public problems; questions of health, of education, of morals, of economics; weighs naught against the ability to kill.

This naïve assumption of supreme value in a process never of the first importance; 4 and increasingly injurious as society progresses, would be laughable if it were not for its evil effects. It acts and reacts upon us to our hurt. Positively, we see the ill effects already touched on; the evils not only of active war, but of the spirit and methods of war; idealized, inculcated, and practiced in other social processes. It tends to make each man-managed nation an actual or potential fighting organization, and to give us, instead of civilized peace, that "balance of power" which is like the counted time in the prize ring—only a rest between combats.

It leaves the weaker nations to be "conquered" and "annexed" just as they used 5 to be; with "preferential tariffs" instead of tribute. It forces upon each the burden of armament; upon many the dreaded conscription; and continually lowers the world's resources in money and in life.

Similarly in politics, it adds to the legitimate expenses of governing the illegitimate 6 expenses of fighting; and must needs have a "spoils system" by which to pay its mercenaries.

In carrying out the public policies the wheels of state are continually clogged by the 7 "opposition"; always an opposition on one side or the other; and this slow wiggling uneven progress, through shorn victories and haggling concessions, is held to be the proper and only political method.

"Women do not understand politics," we are told; "Women do not care for politics"; 8 "Women are unfitted for politics."

It is frankly inconceivable, from the androcentric viewpoint, that nations can live in 9 peace together, and be friendly and serviceable as persons are. It is inconceivable also, that, in the management of a nation, honesty, efficiency, wisdom, experience and love could work out good results without any element of combat.

The "ultimate resort" is still to arms. "The will of the majority" is only respected on 10 account of the guns of the majority. We have but a partial civilization, heavily modified to sex—the male sex.

13. The author's main purpose in the passage is to
A. argue for women being drafted
B. criticize colonialism
C. present a pacifist philosophy
D. criticize the male-dominated society
E. protest tariffs

14. In paragraph 2, the author maintains that men support their position on equality for women based upon which of the following approaches?
    A. begging the question
    B. a syllogism using a faulty premise
    C. an appeal to emotion
    D. circular reasoning
    E. an *ad hoc* argument

15. Using textual clues, one can conclude that "androcentric" most probably means
    A. robot-centered
    B. world-centered
    C. female-centered
    D. self-centered
    E. male-centered

16. In addition to indicating a direct quotation, the author uses quotation marks to indicate
    A. the jargon of politics and warfare
    B. the coining of a phrase
    C. a definition
    D. the author's scholarship
    E. that the author does not take responsibility for her words

17. In paragraph 4, "increasingly injurious as society progresses" is reinforced by all of the following except:
    A. "ill effects already touched on" [paragraph 4]
    B. "active war" [paragraph 4]
    C. "weaker nations to be 'conquered' and 'annexed'" [paragraph 5]
    D. "illegitimate expenses of fighting" [paragraph 6]
    E. "Women do not understand politics" [paragraph 8]

18. According to the author, men view the primary purpose of government to be
    A. educating the people
    B. solving the "mass of public problems"
    C. obtaining as much power as possible
    D. economics
    E. health

19. The argument shifts from a discussion of warfare to a discussion of politics in the first sentence of which of the following paragraphs?
    A. paragraph 4
    B. paragraph 5
    C. paragraph 6
    D. paragraph 7
    E. paragraph 9

20. The tone of the passage is best described as
    A. ambivalent
    B. reverent
    C. condescending
    D. accusatory
    E. indifferent

21. The style of the passage can best be described as
    A. poetic and emotional
    B. editorial and analytical
    C. mocking and self-serving
    D. preaching and moralistic
    E. authoritative and pretentious

22. To present her argument, Gilman primarily uses which of the following rhetorical strategies?
    A. process
    B. definition
    C. cause and effect
    D. narration
    E. description

23. "It," as used in paragraphs 4, 5, and 6, only refers to
    A. "Fighting is to them the real business of life" [paragraph 3]
    B. "evil effects" [paragraph 4]
    C. "man-managed nation" [paragraph 4]
    D. "preferential tariffs" [paragraph 5]
    E. "spoils system" [paragraph 6]

Questions 24–33 are based on the following speech, "On the Death of Martin Luther King, Jr." by Robert F. Kennedy.

I have bad news for you, for all of our fellow citizens, and people who love peace all over the world, and that is that Martin Luther King was shot and killed tonight. 1

Martin Luther King dedicated his life to love and to justice for his fellow human beings, and he died because of that effort. 2

In this difficult day, in this difficult time for the United States, it is perhaps well to ask what kind of a nation we are and what direction we want to move in, for those of you who are black—considering the evidence there evidently is that there were white people who were responsible—you can be filled with bitterness, with hatred, and a desire for revenge. We can move in that direction as a country, in great polarization—black people amongst black, white people amongst white, filled with hatred toward one another. 3

Or we can make an effort, as Martin Luther King did, to understand and to comprehend, and to replace that violence, that stain of bloodshed that has spread across our land, with an effort to understand with compassion and love. 4

For those of you who are black and are tempted to be filled with hatred and distrust at the injustice of such an act, against all white people, I can only say that I feel in my own heart the same kind of feeling. I had a member of my family killed, [and] he was killed by a white man. But we have to make an effort in the United States, we have to make an effort to understand, to go beyond these rather difficult times. 5

My favorite poet was Aeschylus. He wrote: "In our sleep, pain which cannot forget falls drop by drop upon the heart until, in our own despair, against our will, comes wisdom through the awful grace of God." 6

What we need in the United States is not division; what we need in the United States is not hatred; what we need in the United States is not violence or lawlessness but love and wisdom, and compassion toward one another and a feeling of justice toward those who still suffer within our country, whether they be white or black. 7

So I shall ask you tonight to return home, to say a prayer for the family of Martin Luther King, that's true, but more importantly to say a prayer for our own country, which all of us love—a prayer for understanding and that compassion of which I spoke. 8

We can do well in this country. We will have difficult times. We've had difficult times in the past. We will have difficult times in the future. It is not the end of violence; it is not the end of lawlessness; it is not the end of disorder. 9

But the vast majority of white people and the vast majority of black people in this country want to live together, want to improve the quality of our life, and want justice for all human beings who abide in our land. 10

Let us dedicate ourselves to what the Greeks wrote so many years ago: to tame the savageness of man and to make gentle the life of this world. 11

Let us dedicate ourselves to that, and say a prayer for our country and for our people. 12

24. The primary purpose of RFK's speech is most probably to
A. inform the people of the event
B. praise the accomplishments of Martin Luther King, Jr.
C. offer condolences to King's family
D. call for calm and unity between blacks and whites
E. offer condolences to the black community at large

25. Which of the following paragraphs does not contain examples of parallel structure?
A. paragraph 3 beginning with "In this difficult . . ."
B. paragraph 6 beginning with "My favorite poet . . ."
C. paragraph 7 beginning with "What we need . . ."
D. paragraph 9 beginning with "We can do well . . ."
E. paragraph 10 beginning with "But the vast majority . . ."

26. Paragraph 5 contains an example of
A. understatement
B. figurative language
C. sarcasm
D. logical fallacy
E. analogous example

27. The tone of the speech can best be described as
A. elevated and conciliatory
B. angry and inflammatory
C. formal and detached
D. informal and emotional
E. accusatory and bitter

28. To keep his speech from leading to violence, RFK makes use of which of the following?
  I. constantly repeating King's name and his desire for unity between races
  II. an ethical appeal based on the power of religion
  III. emphasizing a common bond to show the connection between himself and his audience
    A. I
    B. II
    C. III
    D. I and III
    E. I, II, and III

29. All of the following paragraphs give support to the inference that RFK expected violence to follow the assassination except:
A. paragraph 3 beginning with "In the beginning . . ."
B. paragraph 4 beginning with "Or we can . . ."
C. paragraph 6 beginning with "My favorite . . ."

D. paragraph 7 beginning with "What we need . . ."
E. paragraph 9 beginning with "We can do well . . ."

30. RFK most probably chose to refer to the Greeks in paragraph 11 for all of the following reasons except:
A. to impress the audience with his scholarship
B. to concisely restate the theme of the speech
C. to provide a healing thought for the people to remember
D. to elevate the level of discourse
E. to reinforce the ideals of democracy with which the Greeks are associated

31. Paragraphs 7 and 8 are constructed around which of the following rhetorical strategies?
A. analysis
B. definition
C. narration
D. process
E. cause and effect

32. The quotation given in paragraph 6 can best be restated as
A. the process of healing is inevitable
B. time heals all wounds
C. sleep numbs those in pain
D. God is the source of humankind's grief
E. sleep is the only escape from pain

33. All of the following are effects of the repetition in paragraphs 11 and 12 except that it
A. links the speaker with the audience
B. refers to paragraph 2 and King's dedication
C. emphasizes dedication so that the audience will remember it
D. reinforces the tribute to Martin Luther King, Jr.
E. elevates the occasion to one which is worthy of honor

Questions 34–44 are based on the following letter.

Albert Einstein
Old Grove Road
Nassau Point
Peconic, New York
August 2, 1939

F. D. Roosevelt,
President of the United States,
White House
Washington, D.C.

Sir:

Some recent work by E. Fermi and L. Szilard, which has been communicated to   1
me in manuscript, leads me to expect that the element uranium may be turned into
a new and important source of energy in the immediate future. Certain aspects of
the situation which has [*sic*] arisen seem to call for watchfulness and, if necessary,
quick action on the part of the Administration. I believe therefore that it is my duty
to bring to your attention the following facts and recommendations:

In the course of the last four months it has been made probable—through the   2
work of Joliot in France as well as Fermi and Szilard in America—that it may become
possible to set up a new nuclear chain reaction in a large mass of uranium, by which
vast amounts of power and large quantities of new radium-like elements would be
generated. Now it appears almost certain that this could be achieved in the immediate
future.

This new phenomenon would also lead to the construction of bombs, and it is   3
conceivable—though much less certain—that extremely powerful bombs of a new type
may thus be constructed. A single bomb of this type, carried by boat and exploded in
a port, might very well destroy the whole port together with some of the surrounding
territory. However, such bombs might very well prove to be too heavy for transportation
by air.

The United States has only very poor ores of uranium in moderate quantities. There   4
is some good ore in Canada and the former Czechoslovakia, while the most important
source of uranium is Belgian Congo.

In view of this situation you may think it desirable to have some permanent contact   5
maintained between the Administration and the group of physicists working on chain
reactions in America. One possible way of achieving this might be for you to entrust
with this task a person who has your confidence and who could perhaps serve in an
official capacity. His task might comprise the following:

a) to approach Government Departments, keep them informed of the further
    development and put forward recommendations for Government action;

b) giving particular attention to the problem of securing a supply of uranium ore for
    the United States;

c) to speed up the experimental work, which is at present being carried on within
    the limits of the budgets of University laboratories, by providing funds, if such
    funds be required, through his contacts with private persons who are willing to

make contributions for this cause, and perhaps also by obtaining the co-operation of industrial laboratories which have the necessary equipment.

I understand that Germany has actually stopped the sale of uranium from the Czechoslovakian mines which she has taken over. That she should have taken such early action might perhaps be understood on the ground that the son of the German Under-Secretary of State, von Weizacker, is attached to the Kaiser-Wilhelm-Institut in Berlin where some of the American work on uranium is now being repeated.

Yours very truly,
Albert Einstein

34. In both paragraphs 2 and 3, Einstein makes use of the dash
A. to emphasize the words set off
B. as an exception to the point immediately before it
C. to sound more scholarly and formal
D. as an informal aside to what was said previously
E. to summarize

35. The omission of a cordial opening and identification of the credentials of the writer imply all of the following except:
A. Einstein expects his name alone will identify him
B. Einstein assumes that the information he presents is compelling enough to command a response
C. Einstein believes himself too busy and important to waste time on pleasantries
D. As a scientist, Einstein was accustomed to having the facts speak for themselves
E. They've had previous contact

36. The purpose of the listing in paragraph 5 is to
A. secure Einstein's role as Roosevelt's "permanent contact"
B. suggest a plan of necessary action to ensure American security
C. increase research funding for further nuclear experimentation
D. end scientific research leading to the construction of nuclear bombs
E. send a letter of warning to Germany

37. Einstein's attitude can best be described as
A. confrontational
B. deferential
C. cautionary
D. complacent
E. antagonistic

38. Einstein's first paragraph suggests all of the following except:
A. FDR is not staying abreast of important scientific developments
B. Einstein is concerned about how the administration is handling the new developments in uranium research
C. Einstein is concerned that the administration may be unaware of important developments in the scientific community
D. Einstein is an authority in the use of uranium
E. FDR is familiar with the work of Fermi and Szilard

39. Which of the following best identifies Einstein's primary mode of discourse in his letter to FDR?
A. narration
B. process
C. analysis
D. persuasion
E. exposition

40. To illustrate the gravity of the situation, Einstein uses all of the following except:
A. "call for watchfulness" [paragraph 1]
B. "it is my duty" [paragraph 1]
C. "appears almost certain" [paragraph 2]
D. "in the immediate future" [paragraph 2]
E. "obtaining the co-operation" [paragraph 5]

41. Einstein understates the urgency of developing "chain reactions" in America
A. with the repetition of the words *might* and *may*
B. by excluding a fatalistic prediction
C. by mentioning "other countries repeating America's work"
D. with the phrase "though much less certain"
E. all of the above

42. To persuade Roosevelt to consider his recommendations, Einstein uses all of the following approaches <u>except</u>:

A. discussions with other members of the scientific community

B. appeals to fear

C. presentation of evidence

D. making predictions

E. offering a plan

43. In his letter, Einstein's own assumptions are all of the following <u>except</u>:

A. his interpretation of the manuscript is accessible

B. his reputation as a scientist lends weight to his opinion

C. his plan can be implemented quietly

D. his urgency concerning the situation is apparent

E. Germany recognizes the urgency of the situation

44. After a careful reading of the letter, which of the following inferences is *not* <u>valid</u>?

A. Einstein understood the urgency of addressing the nuclear problem.

B. Einstein assumed FDR would react to the letter.

C. Einstein viewed the private sector as a means of circumventing a possible governmental impasse.

D. The Germans could have possibly misunderstood the significance of this scientific discovery.

E. Einstein is suspicious of German espionage.

Questions 45–56 are based on the following passage entitled "Reading an Archive," by Allan Sekula, which appeared in *Blasted Allegories*, a collection of contemporary essays and short stories, published by MIT Press in 1987.

. . . The widespread use of photographs as historical illustrations suggests that significant events are those which can be pictured, and thus history takes on the character of *spectacle*.[7] But this pictorial spectacle is a kind of rerun, since it depends on prior spectacles for its supposedly "raw" material.[8] Since the 1920's, the picture press, along with the apparatuses of a corporate public relations, publicity, advertising, and   5
government propaganda, have contributed to a regularized flow of images: of disasters, wars, revolutions, new products, celebrities, political leaders, official ceremonies, public appearances, and so on. For a historian to use such pictures without remarking on these initial uses is naïve at best, and cynical at worst. What would it mean to construct a pictorial history of postwar coal mining in Cape Breton by using pictures from a   10
company public relations archive without calling attention to the bias inherent in that source? What present interests might be served by such an oversight?

The viewer of standard historical histories loses any ground in the present from which to make critical evaluations. In retrieving a loose succession of fragmentary glimpses of the past, the spectator is flung into a condition of imaginary temporal   15
and geographical mobility. In this dislocated and disoriented state, the only coherence offered is that provided by the constantly shifting position of the camera, which provides the spectator with a kind of powerless omniscience. Thus, the spectator comes to identify with the technical apparatus, with the authoritative institution of photography. In the face of this authority, all other forms of telling and remembering   20
begin to fade. But the machine establishes the truth, not by logical argument, but by providing an experience. This experience characteristically veers between nostalgia, horror, and an overriding sense of the exoticism of the past, its irretrievable otherness for the viewer in the present. Ultimately, then, when photographs are uncritically presented as historical documents, they are transformed into aesthetic objects. Accordingly, the   25

pretense to historical understanding remains, although that understanding has been replaced by aesthetic experience.[9]

But what of our second option? Suppose we abandoned all pretense to historical explanation, and treated these photographs as artworks of one sort or another? This book would then be an inventory of aesthetic achievement and/or an offering for disinterested aesthetic perusal. The reader may well have been prepared for these likelihoods by the simple fact that this book has been published by a press with a history of exclusive concern with the contemporary vanguard art of the United States and Western Europe (and, to a lesser extent, Canada). Further, as I've already suggested, in a more fundamental way, the very removal of these photographs from their initial contexts invites aestheticism. {.right-margin 30} {.right-margin 35}

I can imagine two ways of converting these photographs into "works of art," both a bit absurd, but neither without ample precedent in the current fever to assimilate photography into the discourse and market of the fine arts. The first path follows the traditional logic of romanticism, in its incessant search for aesthetic origins in a coherent and controlling authorial "voice." The second path might be labeled "post-romantic" and privileges the subjectivity of the collector, connoisseur, and viewer over that of any specific author. This latter mode of reception treats photographs as "found objects." Both strategies can be found in current photographic discourse; often they are intertwined in a single book, exhibition, or magazine or journal article. The former tends to predominate, largely because of the continuing need to validate photography as a fine art, which requires an incessant appeal to the myth of authorship in order to wrest photography away from its reputation as a servile and mechanical medium. Photography needs to be won and rewon repeatedly for the ideology of romanticism to take hold.[10] {.right-margin 40} {.right-margin 45} {.right-margin 50}

---

[7] See Guy DeBord, *La société du spectacle* (Paris: Editions Buchat-Chastel, 1967): unauthorized translation, *Society of the Spectacle* (Detroit: Black and Red, 1970: rev. ed. 1977).

[8] We might think here of the reliance, by the executive branch of the United States government, on "photo opportunities." For a discussion of an unrelated example, see Susan Sontag's dissection of Leni Reifenstahl's alibi that *Triumph of the Will* was merely an innocent documentary of the orchestrated-for-cinema 1934 Nuremberg Rally of the National Socialists. Sontag quotes Reifenstahl: "Everything is genuine. . . . It is *history—pure history*." Susan Sontag, "Fascinating Fascism," *New York Review of Books* 22, no. 1 (February 1975); reprinted in *Under the Sign of Saturn* (New York: Farrar, Straus, & Giroux, 1980), p. 82.

[9] Two recent books counter this prevailing tendency in "visual history" by directing attention to the power relationships behind the making of pictures: Craig Heron, Shea Hoffmitz, Wayne Roberts, and Robert Storey, *All that Our Hands Have Done: A Pictorial History of the Hamilton Workers* (Oakville, Ontario: Mosaic Press, 1981), and Sarah Graham-Brown, *Palestinians and Their Society, 1880–1946* (London: Quartet Books, 1980).

[10] In the first category are books that discover unsung commercial photographers: e.g., Mike Disfarmer, *Disfarmer: The Heber Springs Portraits*, text by Julia Scully (Danbury, N.H.: Addison House, 1976). In the second category are books that testify to the aesthetic sense of the collector: e.g., Sam Wagstaff, *A Book of Photographs from the Collection of Sam Wagstaff* (New York: Gray Press, 1978).

---

45. The first sentence (lines 1–3) does all of the following, <u>except</u>

  A. to indicate that material appears in this essay prior to this section

  B. to indicate scholarly research

  C. to indicate a cause/effect relationship

  D. to state the thesis of the piece

  E. to establish that the essay is based on the opinion of the author

46. The word *oversight* in line 12 refers to

  A. "pictures from a company public relations archive" (10–11)

  B. "without calling attention to the bias" (11)

  C. "construct a pictorial history" (9–10)

  D. "coal mining in Cape Breton" (10)

  E. "present interests" (12)

47. An accurate reading of footnote 7 informs the reader that the author based his material on
    A. *Society of the Spectacle*, rev. ed. 1977
    B. *Society of the Spectacle*, 1970
    C. *La société du spectacle*, 1967
    D. The Black and Red, 1970
    E. Buchat-Chastel, 1967

48. The author directly involves the reader using which of the following linguistic devices?
    A. direct address
    B. exhortation
    C. metaphor
    D. direct quotation
    E. rhetorical question

49. "initial contexts" in line 35–36 refers to
    A. "our second option" (28)
    B. "historical explanation" (28–29)
    C. "inventory of aesthetic achievement" (30)
    D. "contemporary vanguard art" (33)
    E. "disinterested aesthetic perusal" (31)

50. The main concern of the passage is contained in which of the following lines?
    A. "Since the 1920's . . . and so on." (4–8)
    B. "The viewer . . . critical evaluations." (13–14)
    C. "In retrieving . . . geographical mobility." (14–16)
    D. "I can imagine . . . of the fine arts." (37–39)
    E. "The former . . . mechanical medium." (46–49)

51. The most probable implication of this passage is that
    A. historians are cynical
    B. historians are naïve
    C. readers/viewers must be aware of the bias inherent in source material
    D. viewers/readers are ill equipped to make critical evaluations
    E. dealing with photographs demands a combination of the mechanical and the aesthetic

52. The purpose of footnote 9 is to
    A. enhance the reputation of the writer
    B. cite a primary source
    C. direct the reader to opposing positions
    D. compare differing cultures
    E. provide a historical context

53. The tone of the passage can best be described as
    A. argumentative and scholarly
    B. romantic and artistic
    C. philosophical and didactic
    D. informative and sarcastic
    E. informal and playful

54. According to the author, the power of photography as historical illustration is found in the
    A. historian
    B. spectator
    C. picture press
    D. image itself
    E. camera

55. The last paragraph is primarily developed using which of the following rhetorical strategies?
    A. cause and effect
    B. comparison and contrast
    C. definition
    D. description
    E. narration

56. The reader may infer from the footnotes that the author is a(n)
    A. photographer himself
    B. journalist reporting on photography
    C. fan of Leni Reifenstahl
    D. established authority in this field
    E. art critic

Explanations of Answers to the Multiple-Choice Questions

Explanations to the Samuel Johnson Essay

1. **A.** Although references to poetic style and to Dryden are contained in the passage, they are included to illuminate the character of Pope.
2. **E.** No references to body versus soul are in the passage. We do find references to both the prose and the poetry of Pope and Dryden. We are told of Pope's monetary concerns, and we can infer the contrast between Pope's broken body and healthy mind.
3. **A.** This is a fairly straightforward interpretation of a figurative line. The idea of "long on the wing" naturally leads the reader to think of endurance.
4. **D.** A careful reading of this passage allows you to locate each of the devices, except satire.
5. **B.** Lines 20–21 clearly state that the two men were equally gifted.
6. **E.** Lines 9 and 10 tell the reader that Pope's humor was condescending. Lines 14–15 allude to his use of ridicule, and the reader may infer that these characteristics were carried over into Pope's writing.
7. **B.** The author never interjects his own feelings, and the diction and syntax remain on a scholarly, elevated level.
8. **E.** Carefully read lines 23 and 24 and you will see a direct correlation between those lines and choice E.
9. **A.** This is strictly a vocabulary question. You should be able to use the context clues of "minute" and "diligent" to lead you to choose A.
10. **D.** If you go to lines 25–29, you will see that Pope demanded perfection of himself and his writing. This characteristic is further extended with the clause in line 29.
11. **C.** Both words indicate a practiced, continuous, and extreme control of the work at hand. Even the "velvet of the lawn" indicates a tightness, a smoothness, and a richness of form and content.
12. **B.** If it were a contest, Pope would be declared the winner by Johnson. A close reading of both the structure and the content of the paragraph leads the reader to Pope. When discussing Dryden and Pope, Pope has the last work. This allows Pope to linger in the reader's mind. "Frequent" with Dryden and "perpetual" with Pope is another indication of Samuel Johnson's preference.

Explanations to the Gilman Essay

13. **D.** Although Gilman touches upon each of the choices in the passage, A, B, C, and E are details used to support her argument that a man-managed nation is an imperfect culture.
14. **B.** The question requires the student to be familiar with methods of logical reasoning and logical fallacies. Gilman presents the syllogism men use to deny women the right to vote:
    Those who fight may vote.
    Women do not fight.
    Therefore, women may not vote.
    "Those" is understood to be men. The first premise is incorrect, as is the second premise. This being the case, the conclusion is invalid.
15. **E.** This question depends upon both vocabulary and careful reading. Paragraph 8 points to a philosophy that desires to exclude women from politics. Therefore, any political involvement must be male-centered.
16. **A.** Most readers expect quotations to be used to indicate a direct quotation or specific titles of works. However, there are other uses for these bits of punctuation. One is to set off specific words or phrases used by others in a given context. Here, Gilman is making direct reference to the words employed by society's male leadership.
17. **E.** Because the argument of the passage is to criticize the aggressive nature of politics in a male-managed society and to point out the results of combining politics and warfare, the question demands details that support the idea of aggression being detrimental to society. The only choice that does not reflect this idea is E.

18. **C.** Look carefully at the second paragraph to see the ranking Gilman sets up as the male-centered priorities. The only one ranked over the others is fighting and the ability to kill. Therefore, the only appropriate choice is C.

19. **C.** Syntactically, the phrase, "Similarly in politics" is an indicator that a comparison is being drawn between what came before and what comes after. No other phrase does this.

20. **D.** Because this is an argumentative selection, the author is expected to take a position on an issue. Because of this, the choices of "ambivalent" and "indifferent" are immediately eliminated. Keeping in mind the diction of the piece, you can see that "reverent" and "condescending" are also inappropriate.

21. **B.** Remember, all parts of your answer must be correct. The only choice that presents two correct descriptions of the style is B.

22. **C.** If you read the passage carefully, you cannot avoid the cause-and-effect sequencing throughout the excerpt. Look at paragraphs 2, 3, 4, 6, and the last. Remember that an author can use many different techniques in the same work, but only one will be predominant, and that strategy is what reinforces the author's purpose.

23. **A.** It is interesting to look at the singular use of this pronoun. In every instance, "it" refers to "fighting," while reinforcing the author's relentless focus on the essential problem.

Explanation of the Answers to the RFK Speech

24. **D.** Although RFK tells the audience of the death of Martin Luther King, Jr., and although he briefly asks the audience to pray for King's family, condolences are NOT the focus of the speech. No real listing or praise of King's accomplishments is given. Throughout his speech, Kennedy continually stresses the need for unity, wisdom, and compassion.

25. **B.** Every AP Comp student must be familiar with parallel structure and must be able to recognize it in writing. A close examination of paragraph 6 will reveal that no repetition of structure and/or diction is present.

26. **E.** RFK's comparison of his similar situation with regard to the assassination of his brother, John F. Kennedy, is the framework for this paragraph. No other choice is present.

27. **A.** Keeping in mind that both parts of the answer must be supported in the text, A is the only appropriate choice. All other choices are either unsupported or contradictory to the purpose of the speech.

28. **E.** This is a question that is helped by your close attention to the previous questions. In them you will see that ALL of the choices were referred to.

29. **C.** The paragraph is only concerned with the words of Aeschylus that are centered on the results of loss. The other paragraphs realistically acknowledge the violent history of this nation.

30. **A.** It is obvious that RFK does NOT want to separate himself from his audience. The hope is to take the emotions of his audience and to lift them out of the realm of emotional, violent responses and to provide an avenue for peaceful and positive outlets for their grief.

31. **E.** If you are familiar with rhetorical strategies, this question would be an easy one for you. The word "so" in the first line of paragraph 8 is your obvious indicator of cause and effect.

32. **A.** At first glance, this quotation seems quite obvious. However, careful consideration of its meaning is rather more difficult. Although each of the other choices contains words or an idea that is a single part of the quotation, none other than A takes into consideration sleep, time, pain, wisdom, and God.

33. **D.** There is nothing in the last two paragraphs that indicates that the purpose is to pay tribute to Martin Luther King, Jr. Therefore, D is the appropriate choice.

Explanations to the Questions Related to the Einstein Letter

34. **D.** This question requires your knowing the uses of the dash and your ability to recognize how it is actually used in a given text. Here, you should see that Einstein is making a statement that could have also been set off

with commas or parentheses. It is a more informal device.

35. **C.** This is a rather obvious answer to a question that many would be tempted to "over-read." Don't try to make things more complicated. You should also be aware of the conventions of the letter form.

36. **B.** This is a process of elimination question. Checking for evidence to support each of the choices eliminates A, C, D, and E. Those who would point to C must look again at both paragraphs 6 and 7. Here, it becomes obvious that paragraph 6 does not contain any reference to funding. Remember, all parts of the answer must be supported by the text.

37. **C.** This is a diction and tone question. If you look carefully at Einstein's choice of words and phrases in paragraphs 3 and 6 and his selection of supporting details, you can only conclude correctly that he is being cautionary.

38. **A.** The very fact that Einstein does not include any introductory information about Fermi or Szilard indicates that FDR *is* cognizant of current scientific endeavors. Moreover, there is no evidence of neglect on the part of the President. Therefore, A is your correct choice.

39. **D.** An AP Comp student needs to be familiar with the modes of discourse and must be able to recognize them. This question asks the reader to note the persuasive nature of Einstein's letter. There is no storytelling, no directions, and no exposition or analysis.

40. **E.** If you know the meaning of gravity as used in this selection, you are led to look for words that are indicative of a seriousness of purpose. This is also a question that can be answered without necessarily returning to the text. A, B, C, and D contain a common urgency and a seriousness lacking in choice E.

41. **E.** Understatement, which Einstein uses because of his unwillingness to become an alarmist, is shown by his use of qualifying words and phrases rather than direct statements. Each of the choices provides room for Presidential ambivalence.

42. **A.** Einstein appeals to fear (paragraph 3), presents evidence (paragraph 4, line 1), makes predictions (paragraph 2), and offers a plan [paragraph 5, (a), (b), and (c)]. However, he does NOT discuss anything with members of the scientific community in this letter.

43. **D.** Assumptions are tricky questions to work with because they demand your own thoughts and conclusions from the piece. Read each choice carefully, making certain that nothing in a choice is contradictory or invalid. In this question, choice D is the only assumption NOT supported by the text. (*Note:* Information contained in previous questions could have been helpful in selecting your answer.)

44. **D.** Inferences are NOT the same as assumptions. To infer is to reach a conclusion based on facts or observations. To assume is to take something for granted, although it is not proved. In other words, if I see you carrying an opened, wet umbrella and wearing a wet raincoat, I can *infer* that it is rainy outside. I could *assume* that you are a person who listens to the weather forecasts. For this question involving an inference, the reader cannot find proof in the letter to support the conclusion that the Germans may have misunderstood the significance of the scientific discovery.

Explanations of the Photography Passage

45. **D.** This selection is not totally focused on the subject of history being spectacle. The ellipsis indicates that material preceded this given piece. The use of footnote 7 is indicative of previous research. The word *this* establishes the relationship between cause and effect. The word *suggests* and the phrase "takes on the characteristics of spectacle" are indications of opinion.

46. **B.** This is a close-reading question in which the student MUST be able to recognize antecedents.

47. **A.** A close reading of the footnote will reveal that the last edition was 1977. The date would not be listed if the earlier version had been used.

48. **E.** Each of the rhetorical questions (lines 1–12 and 28–29) asks for the reader's input.

49. B. The "initial context" is that photographs are, by their very nature, historical.

50. E. These several lines present to the reader the double-edged debate. Is photography only objective or only subjective, or is it a combination of the two?

51. E. Choices A, B, C, and D are all directly stated by the author in the passage.

52. C. This footnote directs the reader to other sources that present differing opinions on the subject of "visual history."

53. A. Every point, including the footnotes, supports the author's position, which is clearly stated in this excerpt.

54. E. The evidence for this response is found in lines 21–22: ". . . machine establishes the truth. . . ."

55. B. If you look closely at the paragraph, you will see multiple indications of comparison and contrast: *both*, *first path*, and *second path*, *former*, and *latter*.

56. D. Footnotes 8, 9, and 10 indicate the breadth of knowledge and confidence of the author. This is obvious from his sources and his recommendations to the reader.

Introduction to Chapters 5, 6, and 7

The essay part of the AP Language and Composition exam emphasizes three major skills:

- Analysis
- Argument
- Synthesis

The analysis prompt asks the student to analyze the author's purpose and how he achieves it. The argument prompt requires the student to take a position on an issue and develop it with appropriate evidence. The synthesis prompt directs the student to carefully read several sources related to a specific topic and to cite at least three of these sources to support his argument or analysis.

Because of the need to carefully read the prompt related to a given subject for the synthesis essay, Section II has an additional 15 minutes.

You will be able to read all three of the essay questions during this 15-minute period.

But, you will NOT be permitted to open and write in the actual test booklet. Once the close reading time has elapsed, you will be directed to open the test booklet and begin to write your three essays.

The heading of Section II looks something like this:

Section II

Number of questions—3

Percent of total grade—55

Each question counts one-third of the total section score.

You will have a total of 2 hours to write, which you may divide any way you choose. Because each essay carries the same weight, do NOT spend an inappropriate amount of time on any one question.

Chapters 5, 6, and 7 of this book introduce you to each of the three essay types.

BEFORE BEGINNING TO WORK WITH ANY OF THE ACTUAL ESSAY PROMPTS IN THIS BOOK, READ THE REVIEW OF THE PROCESSES AND TERMS IN THE COMPREHENSIVE REVIEW SECTION. ALSO, COMPLETE SOME OF THE ACTIVITIES RELATED TO EACH OF THE SPECIFIC ESSAY TYPES.

CHAPTER 5

Introduction to the Analysis Essay

IN THIS CHAPTER

Summary: Complete explanation of the analysis essay and its purpose as it is presented on the AP English Language exam.

Key Ideas

✪ Learn the types of analysis prompts you might encounter on the AP English Language exam.

✪ Learn about the rubrics and rating of the AP English Language essay.

✪ Learn the basics of reading and notating a given passage.

✪ Learn the basics of constructing your response to the prompt.

✪ Examine student models that respond to the diagnostic exam's analysis essay prompt.

✪ Learn how the rubrics were used to rate the student sample essays.

After your brief break, you will be given a packet that contains all three essay prompts and several texts that are specifically related to the synthesis essay. You will have 15 minutes to read the prompts and the texts. During this time period, the essay test booklet must remain sealed. After the initial 15 minutes have elapsed, you will be directed to open the test booklet and begin to write your three essays. You will have 2 hours to write your essays.

On the cover of the booklet you will find the breakdown of the three essays and the time suggested for each.

Section II

Total Time—2¼ hours

Number of questions—3

Percent of total grade—55

Each question counts one-third of the total section score.

Note: You will have a total of 2 hours to write, which you may divide any way you choose. However, each essay carries the same weight, so do <u>NOT</u> spend an inappropriate amount of time on any one question.

The next step is to quickly turn the pages of the packet and skim the given selections. This should take you less than a minute.

Some Basics

Just What Is an AP English Language Analysis Essay?

Generally, the student is presented with a prose passage that can be drawn from various genres and time periods. Although the specific tasks asked of the student may vary from year to year, they almost always involve the analysis of language, including **rhetorical strategies** and **stylistic elements**. (If you are in doubt about the meaning of the underlined terms, make certain to refer to the Glossary and the Comprehensive Review section.)

> You may be extremely lucky and find a familiar piece by a familiar author. This certainly can enhance your comfort level. But, don't try to plug into the question everything you know about that author or selection if it does not exactly fit the prompt. Likewise, do not be rattled if you are unfamiliar with the work. <u>You will be familiar with the approaches necessary to analyze it</u>. Remember, this exam reaches thousands of students, many of whom will be in a similar situation and equally anxious. Be confident that you are thoroughly prepared to tackle these tasks and have fun doing so.

What Is the Purpose of the Analysis Essay?

The College Board wants to determine your facility with reading, understanding, and analyzing challenging texts. They also want to assess how well you manipulate language to communicate your written analysis of a specific topic to a mature audience. **The level of your writing should be a direct reflection of your critical thinking.**

AP is looking for connections between analysis and the passage. For example, when you find an image, identify it and connect it to the prompt. Don't just list items as you locate them.

"Doing close readings of editorial columns in newspapers and magazines is a real help to my students as they prepare to attack both multiple-choice questions and analysis essays."
—Chris S.,
   AP teacher

Types of Analysis Essay Prompts

What Kinds of Questions Are Asked in the Analysis Essay?

Let's look at a few of the TYPES of questions that have been asked on the AP English Language and Composition exam in the past. These types may seem more familiar to you if you see them in the form of prompts.

- Analyze an author's view on a specific subject.
- Analyze rhetorical devices used by an author to achieve his or her purpose.
- Analyze stylistic elements in a passage and their effects.
- Analyze the author's tone and how the author conveys this tone.
- Compare and/or contrast two passages with regard to style, purpose, or tone.
- Analyze the author's purpose and how he or she achieves it.
- Analyze some of the ways an author re-creates a real or imagined experience.
- Analyze how an author presents him- or herself in the passage.
- Discuss the intended and/or probable effect of a passage.

You should be prepared to write an essay based on any of these prompts. Practice. Practice. Practice. Anticipate questions. Keep a running list of the kinds of questions your teacher asks.

It's good to remember that the tasks demanded of you by the question remain constant. What changes is the source material on which you base your response to the question. Therefore, your familiarity with the terms and processes related to the types of questions is crucial.

Don't be thrown by the complexity of the passage. *You* choose the references you want to incorporate into your essay. So, even if you haven't understood everything, you *can* write an intelligent essay—AS LONG AS YOU ADDRESS THE PROMPT and refer to the parts of the passage you do understand.

Watch for overconfidence when you see what you believe to be an easy question with an easy passage. You are going to have to work harder to find the nuances in the text that will allow you to write a mature essay.

Rating the Analysis Essay

How Do the AP Readers Rate My Essay?

It's important to understand just what it is that goes into rating your essay. This is called a **rubric**, but don't let that word frighten you. A rubric is just a fancy, professional word that simply means the **rating standards that are set and used by the people who read the essays**. These standards are fairly consistent, no matter what the given prompt might be. The only primary change is in the citing of the specifics in a particular prompt.

As experienced readers of AP exams, let us assure you that the readers are trained to *reward* those things you do well in addressing the question. They are NOT looking to punish you. They are aware of the time constraints and read your essay just as your own instructor would read the first draft of an essay you wrote on a 40-minute exam. <u>These readers do look forward to reading an interesting, insightful, and well-constructed essay.</u>

So, let's take a look at these rubrics.

Remember: PROMPT is another word for QUESTION.

A **9** essay has all the qualities of an 8 essay, and the writing style is especially <u>impressive</u>, as is the analysis of the specifics related to the prompt and the text.

An **8** essay will <u>effectively</u> and <u>cohesively</u> address the prompt. It will analyze and/or argue the elements called for in the question. In addition, it will do so using appropriate evidence from the given text. The essay will also show the writer's ability to control language well.

A **7** essay has all the properties of a 6, only with a <u>more complete</u>, well-developed analysis/argument or a more mature writing style.

A **6** essay <u>adequately</u> addresses the prompt. The analysis and/or argument is on target and makes use of appropriate specifics from the text. However, these elements are less fully developed than scores in the 7, 8, and 9 range. The writer's ideas are expressed with clarity, but the writing may have a few errors in syntax and/or diction.

A **5** essay demonstrates that the writer <u>understands the prompt</u>. The analysis/argument is generally understandable but is limited or uneven. The writer's ideas are expressed clearly with a few errors in syntax or diction.

A **4** essay is <u>not an adequate response</u> to the prompt. The writer's analysis/argument of the text indicates a misunderstanding, an oversimplification, or a misrepresentation of the given passage. The writer may use evidence which is inappropriate or insufficient to support the analysis/argument.

A **3** essay is a lower 4, because it is <u>even less effective</u> in addressing the prompt. It is also less mature in its syntax and organization.

A **2** essay indicates <u>little success in speaking to the prompt</u>. The writer may misread the question, only summarize the passage, fail to develop the required analysis/argument, or simply ignore the prompt and write about another topic. The writing may also lack organization and control of language and syntax. (**Note: No matter how good the summary, it will never rate more than a 2.**)

A **1** essay is a lower 2, because it is even <u>more simplistic, disorganized</u>, and <u>lacking in control of language</u>.

"Throughout the year, I have students mimic the styles of various authors. We, then, present the pieces to the class, which tries to identify the author being imitated. Through this process, the students become more cognizant of what makes up style, tone, syntax, and diction."
—Denise C., AP teacher

> REMEMBER, THIS ESSAY IS REALLY A FIRST DRAFT. THE READERS KNOW THIS AND APPROACH EACH ESSAY KEEPING THIS IN MIND.

Timing and Planning the Analysis Essay

Just How Should I Plan to Spend My Time Writing This Type of Essay?

Remember, timing is crucial. With that in mind, here's a workable strategy:

- 1–3 minutes reading and working the prompt.
- 5 minutes reading and making marginal notes regarding the passage.
  - Try to isolate two references that strike you. This may give you your opening and closing.
- 10 minutes preparing to write. (Choose one or two of these methods with which you're comfortable.)
  - Highlighting
  - Marginal mapping
  - Charts or key word/one word/line number outlining
- 20 minutes writing your essay, based on your preparation.
- 3 minutes proofreading.

Working the Prompt

> For the purposes of this text, highlighting refers to any annotative technique, including underlining, circling, marginal notes, or using colored markers. The AP exam does NOT permit the use of highlighters, but this technique is valuable in other circumstances.

How Should I Go About Reading the Prompt?

To really bring the answer home to you, we are going to deconstruct a prompt for you right now. (This is the same question that is in the Diagnostic/Master exam you first saw in the introduction to this book.)

You should plan to spend 1–3 minutes <u>carefully</u> reading the question. This gives you time to really digest what the question is asking you to do.

Here's the prompt:

The following paragraphs are from the opening of Truman Capote's _In Cold Blood_. After carefully reading the excerpt, write a well-organized essay in which you characterize Capote's view of Holcomb, Kansas, and analyze how Capote conveys this view. Your analysis may consider such stylistic elements as diction, imagery, syntax, structure, tone, and selection of detail.

> In the margin, note what time you should be finished with this essay. For example, the test starts at 1:00. You write 1:40 in the margin. Time to move on.

Here are three reasons why you do a 1–3-minute careful analysis of the prompt.

1. Once you know what is expected, you will read in a more directed manner.
2. Once you internalize the question, you will be sensitive to those details that will apply.
3. Once you know all the facets that must be addressed, you will be able to write a complete essay demonstrating adherence to the topic.

> TOPIC ADHERENCE, WHICH MEANS STICKING TO THE QUESTION, IS A KEY STRATEGY FOR ACHIEVING A HIGH SCORE.

DO THIS NOW.
Highlight, circle, or underline the essential terms and elements in the prompt.

(Time yourself) How long did it take you? _____

(Don't worry if it took you longer than 1–3 minutes with this first attempt. You will be practicing this technique throughout this review, and it will become almost second nature to you.)

Compare our highlighting of the prompt with yours.

The following paragraphs are from the **<u>opening</u>** of **<u>Truman Capote's _In Cold Blood_</u>**. After carefully reading the excerpt, write a well-organized essay in which you **<u>characterize Capote's view of Holcomb, Kansas</u>**, and **<u>analyze how Capote conveys this view</u>**. Your analysis may **<u>consider such stylistic elements as diction, imagery, syntax, structure, tone, and selection of detail</u>**.

In this prompt, anything else you may have highlighted is extraneous.

Note: When the question reads *such as*, you are not required to use only those ideas presented; you are free to use your own selection of techniques, strategies, and devices. Notice the prompt requires more than one element. You MUST use more than one. Sorry, one will not be enough. No matter how well-presented, your essay will be incomplete.

Review terms related to elements of style and techniques and methods of analysis.

> Sometimes the incidental data given in the prompt, such as the title of the work, the author, the date of publication, the genre, etc., can prove helpful.

Reading and Notating the Passage

Finally, READ THE PASSAGE. Depending on your style and comfort level, choose one of these approaches to your **close reading**.

1. A. Read quickly to get the gist of the passage.
   B. Reread, using the highlighting and marginal notes approach discussed in this chapter.

2. A. Read slowly, using highlighting and marginal notes.
   B. Reread to confirm that you have caught the full impact of the passage.

Note: In both approaches, you MUST highlight and make marginal notes. There is no way to avoid this. Ignore what you don't immediately understand. It may become clear to you after reading the passage. Practice. Practice. Concentrate on those parts of the passage that apply to what you highlighted in the prompt.

There are many ways to read and analyze any given passage. You have to choose what to use and which specifics to include for support.

Don't be rattled if there is leftover material.

We've reproduced the passage for you below so that you can practice both the reading and the process of deconstructing the text. Use highlighting, arrows, circles, underlining, notes, numbers, whatever you need to make the connections clear to you.

DO THIS NOW.
Spend between 8 and 10 minutes "working the material."
   DO NOT SKIP THIS STEP. It is time well spent and is a key to the high score essay.

Excerpt from the opening of *In Cold Blood*

The village of Holcomb stands on the high wheat plains of western Kansas, a lonesome area that other Kansans call "out there." Some seventy miles east of the Colorado border, the countryside, with its hard blue skies and desert-clear air, has an atmosphere that is rather more Far Western than Middle West. The local accent is barbed with a prairie twang, a ranch-hand nasalness, and the men, many of them, wear narrow frontier trousers, Stetsons, and high-heeled boots with pointed toes. The land is flat, and the views are awesomely extensive; horses, herds of cattle, a white cluster of grain elevators rising as gracefully as Greek temples are visible long before a traveler reaches them.

Holcomb, too, can be seen from great distances. Not that there is much to see—simply an aimless congregation of buildings divided in the center by the main-line tracks of the Santa Fe Railroad, a haphazard hamlet bounded on the south by a brown stretch of the Arkansas (pronounced "Ar-kan-sas") River, on the north by a highway, Route 50, and on the east and west by prairie lands and wheat fields. After rain, or when snowfalls thaw, the streets, unnamed, unshaded, unpaved, turn from the thickest dust into the direst mud. At one end of the town stands a stark old stucco structure, the roof of which supports an electric sign—Dance—but the dancing has ceased and the advertisement has been dark for several years. Nearby is another building with an irrelevant sign, this one in flaking gold on a dirty window—HOLCOMB BANK. The bank closed in 1933, and it is one of the town's two "apartment houses," the second being a ramshackle mansion known, because a good part of the local school's faculty lives there, as the Teacherage. But the majority of Holcomb's homes are one-story frame affairs, with front porches.

Down by the depot, the postmistress, a gaunt woman who wears a rawhide jacket and denims and cowboy boots, presides over a falling-apart post office. The depot, itself, with its peeling sulphur-colored paint, is equally melancholy; the Chief, the Super Chief, the El Capitan go by every day, but these celebrated expresses never pause there. No passenger trains do—only an occasional freight. Up on the highway, there are two filling stations, one of which doubles as a meagerly supplied grocery store, while the other does extra duty as a cafe—Hartman's Cafe, where Mrs. Hartman, the proprietress, dispenses sandwiches, coffee, soft drinks, and 3.2 beer. (Holcomb, like all the rest of Kansas, is "dry.")

And that, really, is all. Unless you include, as one must, the Holcomb School, a good-looking establishment, which reveals a circumstance that the appearance of the community otherwise camouflages: that the parents who send their children to this modern and ably staffed "consolidated" school—the grades go from kindergarten through senior high, and a fleet of buses transport the students, of which there are usually around three hundred and sixty, from as far as sixteen miles away—are, in general, a prosperous people. . . . The farm ranchers in Finney County, of which Holcomb is a part, have done well; money has been made not from farming alone but also from the exploitation of plentiful natural-gas resources, and its acquisition is reflected in the new school, the comfortable interiors of the farmhouses, the steep and swollen grain elevators.

Until one morning in mid-November of 1959, few Americans—in fact, few Kansans—had ever heard of Holcomb. Like the waters of the river, like the motorists on the highway, and like the yellow trains streaking down the Santa Fe tracks, drama in the shape of exceptional happenings, had never stopped there. The inhabitants of the village, numbering two hundred and seventy, were satisfied that this should be so, quite content to exist inside ordinary life . . .

Now, compare your reading notes with what we've done. Yours may vary from ours, but the results of your note taking should be similar in scope.

Notice that, in the sample, we have used a kind of shorthand for our notations. Rather than repeating the specific elements or points each time they are found in the text, we have numbered the major points.

1 = Something old West and insignificant about Holcomb
2 = The starkness of the town
3 = People reflecting the setting
4 = Contrast between first three paragraphs and the last two

This saves precious time. All you need do is list the categories and number each. Then, as you go through the text, number specifics that support these categories.

Excerpt from the opening of *In Cold Blood*

The village of Holcomb stands on the high wheat plains of western Kansas, a lonesome area that other Kansans call "out there." Some seventy miles east of the Colorado border, the countryside, with its hard blue skies and desert-clear air, has an atmosphere that is rather more Far Western than Middle West. The local accent is barbed with a prairie twang, a ranch-hand nasalness, and the men, many of them, wear narrow frontier trousers, Stetsons, and high-heeled boots with pointed toes. The land is flat, and the views are awesomely extensive; horses, herds of cattle, a white cluster of grain elevators rising as gracefully as Greek temples are visible long before a traveler reaches them.

Holcomb, too, can be seen from great distances. Not that there is much to see—simply an aimless congregation of buildings divided in the center by the main-line tracks of the Santa Fe Railroad, a haphazard hamlet bounded on the south by a brown stretch of the Arkansas (pronounced "Ar-kan-sas") River, on the north by a highway, Route 50, and on the east and west by prairie lands and wheat fields. After rain, or when snowfalls thaw, the streets, unnamed, unshaded, unpaved, turn from the thickest dust into the direst mud. At one end of the town stands a stark old stucco structure, the roof of which supports an electric sign—Dance—but the dancing has ceased and the advertisement has been dark for several years. Nearby is another building with an irrelevant sign, this one in flaking gold on a dirty window—HOLCOMB BANK. The bank closed in 1933, and it is one of the town's two "apartment houses," the second being a ramshackle mansion known, because a good part of the local school's faculty lives there, as the Teacherage. But the majority of Holcomb's homes are one-story frame affairs, with front porches.

Down by the depot, the postmistress, a gaunt woman who wears a rawhide jacket and denims and cowboy boots, presides over a falling-apart post office. The depot, itself, with its peeling sulphur-colored paint, is equally melancholy; the Chief, the Super Chief, the El Capitan go by every day, but these celebrated expresses never pause there. No passenger trains do—only an occasional freight. Up on the highway, there are two filling stations, one of which doubles as a meagerly supplied grocery store, while the other does extra duty as a cafe—Hartman's Cafe, where Mrs. Hartman, the proprietress, dispenses sandwiches, coffee, soft drinks, and 3.2 beer. (Holcomb, like all the rest of Kansas, is "dry.")

And that, really, is all. Unless you include, as one must, the Holcomb School, a good-looking establishment, which reveals a circumstance that the appearance of the community otherwise camouflages: that the parents who send their children to this modern and ably staffed "consolidated" school—the grades go from kindergarten through senior high, and a fleet of buses transport the students, of which there are usually around three hundred and sixty, from as far as sixteen miles away—are, in general, a prosperous people. . . . The farm ranchers in Finney County, of which Holcomb is a part, have done well; money has been made not from farming alone but also from the exploitation of plentiful natural-gas resources, and its acquisition is reflected in the new school, the comfortable interiors of the farmhouses, the steep and swollen grain elevators.

Until one morning in mid-November of 1959, few Americans—in fact, few Kansans—had ever heard of Holcomb. Like the waters of the river, like the motorists on the highway, and like the yellow trains streaking down the Sante Fe tracks, drama in the shape of exceptional happenings, had never stopped there. The inhabitants of the village, numbering two hundred and seventy, were satisfied that this should be so, quite content to exist inside ordinary life . . .

Developing the Opening Paragraph

After you have marked your passage, review the prompt. Now, choose the elements you are able to identify and analyze those that support Capote's view. To demonstrate, we have chosen structure, tone, and selection of detail.

Now, it's time to write. Your opening statement is the one that catches the eye of the reader and sets the expectation and tone of your essay. Spend time on your first paragraph to maximize your score. A suggested approach is to relate a direct reference from the passage to the topic. Make certain that the topic is very clear to the reader. This reinforces the idea that you fully understand what is expected of you and what you will communicate to the reader. As always, identify both the text and its author in this first paragraph.

Now, you try it. Write your own first paragraph for this prompt. Write quickly, referring to your notes. Let's check what you've written:

- Have you included author, title?
- Have you addressed "Capote's view of Holcomb"?
- Have you specifically mentioned the elements you will refer to in your essay?

Here are four sample opening paragraphs that address each of the above criteria:

A

In the opening of *In Cold Blood*, Truman Capote presents a picture of the town of Holcomb, Kansas. Through structure, selection of detail, and a detached tone, he makes it clear that he views Holcomb as dull and ordinary.

B

Holcomb, Kansas. Holcomb, Kansas. Even the sound of the place is boring and uninteresting. Moreover, Truman Capote seems to agree with this in his opening to *In Cold Blood*. I, too, would be inclined to pass by this sleepy, bland, and undistinguished hamlet. This view is developed through the author's tone, structure, and selection of detail.

C

"Like the waters of the river, like the motorists on the highway, and like the yellow trains streaking down the Sante Fe tracks, drama in the shape of exceptional happenings, had never stopped here." This is the town of Holcomb, Kansas. Using a reportorial tone, specific structure, and selection of detail, Capote introduces the reader to this unremarkable town in the opening of *In Cold Blood*.

D

In Cold Blood is a very appropriate title, because Capote presents a cold and unemotional view of Holcomb, Kansas. His tone, structure, and selection of detail create a distant and detached picture of this desolate farm community.

Each of these opening paragraphs is an acceptable beginning to this AP English Language and Composition exam essay. Look at what each of the paragraphs has in common:

- Each has identified the title and author.
- Each has stated which stylistic elements will be used.
- Each has stated the purpose of analyzing these elements.

However, observe what is different about the opening paragraphs.

- **Sample A** restates the question without elaborating. It is to the point and correct, but it does not really pique the reader's interest. (Use this type of opening if you feel unsure or uncomfortable with the prompt.)
- **Sample B** reflects a writer who really has a voice. He or she has already determined Capote's view and indicates that he or she understands how this view is created.
- **Sample C** immediately places the reader into the passage by referring specifically to it.
- **Sample D** reveals a mature, confident writer who is unafraid to make his or her own voice heard.

Note: There are many other types of opening paragraphs that could also do the job. Into which of the above samples could your opening paragraph be classified?

Writing the Body of the Essay

What Should I Include in the Body of This Analysis Essay?

1. Obviously, this is where you present *your* analysis and the points you want to make that are related to the prompt.

2. Adhere to the question.

3. Use specific references and details from the passage.
   - Don't always paraphrase the original. Refer directly to it.
   - Place quotation marks around those words/phrases you extract from the passage.

4. Use "connective tissue" in your essay to establish adherence to the question.
- Use the repetition of key ideas in the prompt and in your opening paragraph.
- Try using "echo words" (that is, synonyms: *town/village/hamlet; bland/ordinary/ undistinguished*).
- Use transitions between paragraphs (see Chapter 8).

To understand the process, carefully read the sample paragraphs below. Each develops one of the elements asked for in the prompt. Notice the specific references and the "connective tissue." Details that do not apply to the prompt are ignored.

A
This paragraph develops **tone.**

Throughout the passage, Capote maintains a tone that resembles a detached reporter who is an observer of a scene. Although the impact of the passage is seeing Holcomb in a less than positive light, the author rarely uses judgmental terminology or statements. In describing the town, he uses words such as "float," "haphazard," "unnamed," "unshaded," "unpaved." Individuals are painted with an objective brush showing them in "denim," "Stetsons," and "cowboy boots." Capote maintains his panning camera angle when he writes of the buildings and the surrounding farmland. This matter-of-fact approach is slightly altered when he begins to portray the townspeople as a whole when he uses such words as "prosperous people," "comfortable interiors," and "have done well." His objective tone, interestingly enough, does exactly what he says the folks of Holcomb do. He "camouflages" his attitude toward the reality of the place and time.

B
This paragraph develops **structure.**

Capote organizes his passage spatially. He brings his reader from "great distances" to the periphery of the village with its borders of "main-line tracks" and roads, river and fields, to the heart of the town and its "unnamed, unshaded, unpaved" streets. As the reader journeys through the stark village, he or she is led eventually from the outskirts to the town's seemingly one bright spot—the prosperous Holcomb school. Capote develops our interest in the school by contrasting it with the bleak and lonely aspects of the first three paragraphs. He shifts our view with the word "unless" and focuses on the positive aspects of the town. Holcomb "has done well" despite its forbidding description. The passage could end now, except that Capote chooses to develop his next paragraph with the words, "until one morning," thus taking the reader on another journey, one of foreshadowing and implication. Something other than wheat is on the horizon.

C
This paragraph develops selection of **detail.**

In selecting his details, Capote presents a multilayered Holcomb, Kansas. The town is first presented as stark and ordinary. It is a "lonesome area" with "hard blue skies," where "the land is flat" and the buildings are an "aimless congregation." The ordinary qualities of the village are reinforced by his references to the "unnamed" streets, "one-story frame" houses, and the fact that "celebrated expresses never pause there" (i.e., the "Chief, the Super Chief, the El Capitan"). Details portray the citizens of Holcomb in the same light. Ranch hands speak with "barbed" and nasal "twangs." They wear the stereotypical "cowboy" uniform and so does the "gaunt" postmistress in her "rawhide jacket." Once this description is established, the author contrasts it with an unexpected view of the town. He now deals with the appearance of Holcomb's "camouflages," the "modern" school, the "prosperous people," the "comfortable interiors," and the "swollen grain elevators." If Capote chooses to illuminate this contrast, does it indicate more to come?

Study Group: Approach a subject in a joint manner. After you've deconstructed the prompt, have each person write a paragraph on a separate area of the question. Come together and discuss. You'll be amazed how much fun this is, because the work will carry you away. This is a chance to explore very exciting ideas.

We urge you to spend more time developing the body paragraphs rather than worrying about a concluding paragraph, especially one beginning with *"In conclusion,"* or *"In summary."* To be honest, in such a brief essay, the reader can remember what you have already stated. It is not necessary to repeat yourself in a summary final paragraph.

If you want to make a final statement, try to link your ideas to a particularly effective line or image from the passage. (It's a good thing.)

Look at the last line of Sample **B** on structure.

Something other than wheat is on the horizon.

Or, look at the last line of Sample **C** on selection of detail.

If Capote chooses to illuminate this contrast, does it indicate more to come?

Each of these two final sentences would be just fine as conclusions to the essay. A conclusion does not have to be a paragraph. It can be the writer's final remark/observation in a sentence or two.

DO THIS NOW.

Write the body of your essay. Time yourself.

When you write the body of your essay, take only 15–20 minutes.

Find a way to time yourself, and try your best to finish within that time frame.

Because this is practice, don't panic if you can't complete your essay within the given 20 minutes. You will become more and more comfortable with the tasks presented to you as you gain more experience with this type of question.

Refer to the Comprehensive Review section of this book on developing the body of an AP Language and Composition essay.

NOTE: Sharing your writing with members of your class or study group will allow you and all of the participants to gain more experience and more of a comfort zone with requirements and possibilities.

Sample Student Essays

Here are two actual student essays with comments on each.

Student Sample A

Truly successful authors have the ability to convey their view of a place without
actually saying it, to portray a landscape in a certain light simply by describing it. In
the provided excerpt taken from the opening paragraphs of <u>In Cold Blood</u>, Truman

1

Capote does just this. Through his use of stylistic elements such as selection of detail, imagery, and figurative language, Capote reveals his own solemn and mysterious view of Holcomb, Kansas, while setting the stage for an imminent change.

Beginning in the first line of the passage, Capote selects the most boring details of life in the small town in order to portray its solemnity. He draws attention to the physical isolation of Holcomb by referring to it as the place that "other Kansans call 'out there.'" In addition, he speaks of the parameters of the small town, pointing out that it is enclosed on all sides by rivers, prairies, and wheat fields. He describes the town as remote and unaffected, desolate and boring, continually mentioning the old, peeling paint and "irrelevant signs" that dot the landscape. Capote also gives the village a feeling of laziness in his writing, describing it as an "aimless congregation of buildings" and a "haphazard hamlet." He obviously feels that the town lacks liveliness, that it is bland and unchanging, simple and average. Almost looking down on the village and its inhabitants, the author characterizes the people in broad categories and focuses on their outward appearances and superficial similarities instead of delving more deeply into their abilities or livelihoods. This reveals that he views the people and their surroundings as one-dimensional and simplistic. The idea that he may summarize an entire town, generalize about its people and not be far from the truth, contributes greatly to Capote's solemn view of Holcomb. One gets the feelings from the author's selection of detail that he wishes there was something more interesting, deeper, to share with his audience, and is disappointed by the cursory nature in which he must approach the description of such a melancholy place.

In addition to including the most boring of details, Capote uses a great deal of imagery to describe the town and its residents. Focusing mostly on visual appeal, he describes the "sulphur-colored paint" and "flaking gold" to reveal the town's atrophying appearance and has-been status. Portraying the area as one that has seen better days, Capote writes about the "old stucco structure" that no longer holds dances, the crumbling post office, and the bank that now fails to serve its original purpose. Combining visual imagery with hints of desolation and obsoleteness, Capote attempts to reveal the gray and boring nature of the town through its appearance. He does not, however, rely only on visual details; in describing the local accent as "barbed with a prairie twang," he uses both auditory and visual appeal to make one imagine a ranch-hand's tone of voice and pattern of speech as he describes the monotonous events of his farming days. The "hard blue skies and desert-clear air" contribute to a feeling of emptiness, an emotional vacancy that seems omnipresent in the small town. Finally, even "the steep and swollen grain elevators" that represent the town's prosperity are seen in a solemn and mysterious light, as Capote makes certain to mention that the townspeople camouflage this abundance without explaining why they choose to do so.

Capote also uses a great deal of figurative language and contrasts to portray the small town as solemn and dead, yet somewhat mysterious. The area's intrigue lies more in its paradoxes than in its appearance, more in what Capote fails to explain than what he discusses. With the simile, "a white cluster of grain elevators rising as gracefully as

Greek temples," he almost points toward a happy, prosperous side of the town for the first and perhaps only time in this passage. Not long after this sentence, however, the author describes the streets as "unnamed, unshaded, unpaved," returning to his description of the village as desolate and empty, so destroyed that it is almost primitive.

This is not the only contrast of Capote's opening paragraphs; it seems the entire passage paints the town as quiet and simple only so that it may shock us with what is to come. The author uses personification at the end of the passage, stating that "drama . . . had never stopped there." The position of these words, just after he discusses the positive aspects of the school and its students' families, results in yet another contrast, another mysterious solemnity. Finally, in the last paragraph of this excerpt, when Capote writes "until one morning . . . few . . . had ever heard of Holcomb," the reader becomes aware that the solemn nature of this town is about to change. It becomes clear that the reader has been somewhat set up by Capote, made to view the town in the same way the author does, so that we may then realize the shock of the approaching aberration.

Through his use of stylistic elements, Capote builds the perfect scenery for the setting of a murder, the perfect simple town waiting for a complicated twist, a faded flower or ghost town that has surely seen better days. By the end of the passage, he has already warned the reader that everything he has stated about Holcomb is about to change, that the quiet and solitude, the blandness of the small town, may soon be replaced by very different descriptions.

Student Sample B

Holcomb, Kansas, a village containing two hundred and seventy inhabitants, has skipped over the drama of life, according to Truman Capote. The square town is described spatially with houses, rivers, fields of wheat, stations, a bank, and a school. In Truman Capote's <u>In Cold Blood</u>, an image of the town of Holcomb is presented through precise types of diction, syntax, imagery, and tone.

In order to convey a Western dialect used in Holcomb, Capote refers to the town as, "out there," and addresses the pronunciation of the Arkansas River with an informative, "Ar-kan-sas." Throughout the town there are quite a few signs which transmit the ghostliness present there. For example, "—Dance—but the dancing has ceased and the advertisement has been dark for several years," and "HOLCOMB BANK," which is later on discussed as being closed down, demonstrate the vacantness of the town. To create a better concept of the land itself, Capote uses alliterative devices and an allusion when he states, "horses, herds of cattle, a white cluster of grain elevators rising as gracefully as Greek temples are visible long before a traveler reaches them." This magnifies the field-like setting, and some of the town's old remnants of massive buildings. Altogether, the author's utilization of diction devices greatly personifies the town.

Although not a glaring feature of the excerpt, the sentence structure plays an important role in developing the author's viewpoint. He predominantly utilizes compound sentences, and complex with some prepositional phrases. The use of parallel structures such as, "Like the waters of the river, like the motorists on the highway, and like the yellow trains streaking down the Sante Fe tracks . . ." greatly adds to the monotony of the town. "(Holcomb, like all the rest of Kansas, is 'dry'.)" is one of the numerous similes found throughout the passage that create a sense of vacancy within the town.

Capote's use of all of these literary devices envelope the reader into picturing what   4
Holcomb looks like, a worn out, rustic town filled with "grain elevators," or fields and fields of wheat. The reference to the grain and wheat exemplifies the daily activities that occur in the town. After all of the rural descriptions, a vision of the school is given, as it "camouflages" into the mix. Reading about all of the emptiness of the town, then envisioning a school that is the pride of the town provides insight into the type of people the inhabitants of Holcomb are. For example, they are described as, "in general, a prosperous people." Overall, a precise and objective image of the town, along with the townspeople is certainly focused on in the passage.

Encompassing all of the author's literary, stylistic approaches, one is able to "hear" a   5
voice or tone in the reading. A feeling of desolation, weariness, and loneliness should be derived from reading about this town, and a sense of rejuvenation is experienced toward the closing of the excerpt due to descriptions of the school. In exemplifying that the town has pride in one area, which is education, it leaves the reader with a sense of hope in the town and in its inhabitants. A strong voice toward Holcomb of its rugged, run down, and exhausted institutions is present.

Truman Capote's excerpt from <u>In Cold Blood</u>, which objectively describes   6
Holcomb, a town in Kansas, is profoundly written because of its abundance of allusions, alliteration, imagery, and particular syntax utilized. Capote's detailing enables one to envision what the town looks like because of spatial and in-depth descriptions.

Rating the Essays

Let's Take a Look at a Set of Rubrics for This Analysis Essay

By the way, if you want to see actual AP rubrics as used in a recent AP English Language and Composition exam, log onto the College Board website at www.collegeboard.org/ap.

As you probably know, essays are rated on a 9–1 scale, with 9 being the highest and 1 the lowest. Because we are not there with you to rate your essay personally and to respond to your style and approach, we are going to list the criteria for high-, middle-, and low-range papers. These criteria are based on our experience with rubrics and reading AP Literature essays.

A **HIGH** range essay can be a 9, an 8, or a high-end 7. **MIDDLE** refers to essays in the 7 to 5 range, and the **LOW** scoring essays are rated 4 to 1.

> Let's be honest with each other. You and I both can recognize a 9 essay. It sings, and we wish we could have written it. And, it's wonderful that the essays don't all have to sing the same song with the same words and rhythm. Conversely, we can, unfortunately, recognize the 1 or 2 paper, which is off-key; and we are relieved not to have written it.

High-Range Essay (9, 8, 7)

- Indicates complete understanding of the prompt
- Integrates the analysis of Capote's view of Holcomb with his tone
- Explores the implications of the contrasts within the excerpt
- Identifies and analyzes stylistic elements, such as imagery, diction, structure, selection of detail
- Cites specific references to the passage
- Illustrates and supports the points being made
- Is clear, well-organized, and coherent
- Reflects the ability to manipulate language at an advanced level
- Contains, if any, only minor errors/flaws

Note: A 7 essay rated in the high range makes the jump from the middle range because of its more mature style and perception.

Mid-Range Essay (7, 6, 5)

- Refers accurately to the prompt
- Refers accurately to the stylistic elements used by Capote
- Provides a less thorough analysis of the development of Capote's view of Holcomb than the higher-rated paper
- Is less adept at linking techniques to the purpose of the passage
- Demonstrates writing that is adequate to convey the writer's intent
- May not be sensitive to the contrasts in the excerpts and their implications

Note:
- The 7 paper demonstrates a more consistent command of college-level writing than does the 5 or 6 essay.
- A 5 paper does the minimum required by the prompt. It relies on generalizations and sketchy analysis. It is often sidetracked by plot and the references may be limited or simplistic.

Low-Range Essay (4, 3, 2, 1)

- Does not respond adequately to the prompt
- Demonstrates insufficient and/or inaccurate understanding of the passage
- Does not link stylistic elements to Capote's view of Holcomb
- Underdevelops and/or inaccurately analyzes the development of Capote's view of Holcomb
- Fails to demonstrate an understanding of Capote's tone
- Demonstrates weak control of the elements of diction, syntax, and organization

Note:
- A 4 or 3 essay may do no more than paraphrase sections of the passage rather than analyze Capote's view of Holcomb.
- A 2 essay may merely summarize the passage.
  (NO MATTER HOW WELL WRITTEN, A SUMMARY CAN NEVER EARN MORE THAN A 2.)
- A 1–2 essay indicates a major lack of understanding and control. It fails to comprehend the prompt and/or the passage. It may also indicate severe writing problems.

Student Essay A

This is a **high-range** paper for the following reasons:

- It is on task.
- It indicates complete understanding of the prompt and the passage.
- It uses mature diction [paragraph 1: "Capote reveals . . . imminent change"], [paragraph 2: "Capote also gives . . . simplistic"], [paragraph 3: "the hard blue skies . . . to do so"].
- It integrates references to support the thesis of the essay [paragraph 2: "Capote also gives . . . hamlet"], [paragraph 3: "Focusing . . . has-been status"], [paragraph 4: "with the simile . . . passage"].
- It grasps subtleties and implications [paragraph 1: "Capote reveals . . . change"], [paragraph 2: "One gets . . . place"], [paragraph 4: "The area's . . . discusses"], [paragraph 6: "By the end . . . descriptions"].
- It introduces specifics in a sophisticated manner [paragraph 3: "He does not . . . farming days"], [paragraph 5: "The author . . . solemnity"].
- It uses good "connective tissue" [paragraphs 2 and 3: "in addition"], [paragraph 4: "Capote also uses . . ."], [paragraph 5: "This is not the only contrast . . ."].
- It creates original and insightful comments [paragraph 2: "one gets . . . melancholy place"], [paragraph 3: "He does not . . . farming days"].
- It presents a conclusion that introduces unique observations and brings the reader directly to what may follow this passage.

This is a high-range essay that indicates a writer who "gets it"—who clearly understands the passage and the prompt and who can present ideas in a mature, controlled voice.

Student Essay B

This is a **mid-range** essay for the following reasons:

- It sets up an introduction that indicates the writer's understanding of the prompt.
- It cites appropriate specifics, but often does not adequately integrate these into the analysis [paragraph 2: "In order . . . present there"], [paragraph 3, sentence 2].
- It uses frequently awkward diction and syntax [first line of paragraph 2], [last sentence of paragraph 2], [all of paragraph 5].
- It demonstrates good topic adherence.
- It reveals a facility with stylistic analysis [paragraph 2: "To create . . . reaches them"], [paragraph 3, sentence 3].
- It presents a conclusion that does not add anything to the impact of the essay.

This mid-range paper indicates a writer who understands both the prompt and the process of analysis. However, the essay does not address the subtle, underlying purpose of the passage and ignores the foreshadowing and contrast. The writer's frequently awkward and disconnected diction and syntax prevent it from achieving the level of the high-range essays.

Now It's Your Turn

1. Try a little reverse psychology. Now that you are thoroughly familiar with this passage, construct two or three alternate AP level prompts. (Walk a little in the examiner's shoes.) This will help you gain insight into the very process of test-making.

2. Find other examples of descriptions of setting you can analyze in the same way as you did with the Capote excerpt. You might want to investigate works by John Steinbeck, Joan Didion, Peter Matthiessen, and, certainly, Sebastian Jung's *The Perfect Storm*.

Other Types of Analysis Essays

Are There Other Types of Analysis Questions on the Exam?

You bet. Another analysis prompt you can expect on the exam asks the student to <u>analyze the author's intended effect on the reader and how the author re-creates an experience. Still another type is comparison and contrast.</u> This prompt can be based on either a fiction or a nonfiction passage.

What Am I Expected to Do When Asked to Identify the Author's Intended Effect on the Reader?

No one can ever know what an author intended, unless you could personally approach the writer and ask, "Tell me, just exactly what did you intend the effect to be on your reader when you wrote this passage?" And, we all know that this is not a possibility for 999 out of 1,000 authors. This said, keep the following in mind.

The AP Comp test makers obviously believe that there is a clear, definite effect on the reader; otherwise, they would not be asking you to identify it. When writing about effect, think about your *personal* reaction to the text. While reading it, or as a result of reading it, how do you *feel* (happy, sad, angry, amused, perplexed, uplifted, motivated, informed, inspired, "connected"—you get the idea)?

What Should I Try to Include in My Essay When I'm Asked to Analyze How an Author Re-creates an Experience?

Think about this. Have you ever tried to re-create your own personal experience for your friends, your family, or your teacher? Ask yourself what you did to ensure that your listeners would really feel as if they were actually there. Were you trying to be humorous or serious? You chose what you would say to introduce this experience, didn't you? Did you set up the scene with descriptions of the setting, the people? Did you tell them why you were there? What kind of details did you choose to include? Why those, and not others? What kind of language did you use? (You were quite aware that your audience responds to certain kinds of language manipulation.) Did you center the tale on yourself, the action, a person, or group of people? Did you emphasize actions, reactions, dialog? Did you tell the story in chronological order, or did you move back and forth in time? Did you interject personal comments? Did you tell the story so that the listeners felt a part of the experience or set apart from it? Did you emote or try to remain aloof?

Get the picture? This is the type of questioning that should be part of your process of analysis when asked how an author re-creates an experience.

What Do I Do About the Comparison and Contrast Essay?

The comparison and contrast essay is not difficult, but it demands that you have organizational control over your material. First, carefully read the prompt and understand what you are being asked to compare and contrast. With this in mind, carefully read and annotate each of the given texts, looking for major points to support and illustrate your thesis. Next, decide on the structure you want to use to present your points:

- Point by point
- Subject by subject
- A combination of both of the preceding

"Working the Prompt"

As you did with the previous essay, the very first thing you must do is to read and deconstruct the prompt carefully. What follows is a sample prompt that you could find in the essay section of the exam.

- Plan to spend 1–3 minutes carefully reading the question.
- After this initial reading, highlight the essential terms and elements of the prompt.

> **Carefully read the following excerpt from Louisa May Alcott's nonfiction narrative _Hospital Sketches_ (1863). In a carefully constructed essay, identify the author's intended effect on the reader and the ways in which the author re-creates her experience as a nurse in a U.S. Army hospital during the Civil War. Consider such elements as pacing, diction, imagery, selection of detail, and tone.**

Time yourself. How long did it take you? _____
Compare your highlighting of the prompt with ours.

> Carefully read the following excerpt from **Louisa May Alcott's nonfiction narrative _Hospital Sketches_ (1863)**. In a carefully constructed essay, **identify the author's intended effect on the reader** and the **ways** in which the **author re-creates her experience as a nurse in a U.S. Army hospital during the Civil War.** Consider **such** elements **as pacing, diction, imagery, selection of detail**, and **tone.**

As before, anything else you may have highlighted is extraneous. Notice that the prompt asks you to do TWO things. You must both identify the effect on the audience and analyze how the author re-creates her experience. If you address only one of these areas, your essay will be incomplete, no matter how well written it is.

> **Review terms and strategies related to purpose, effect, organization.**

Follow the process for reading the passage we illustrated for you in the first section of this chapter. Remember, you are going to do a close reading that requires you to highlight and make marginal notes (glosses) that refer you to the section of the prompt that this citation illustrates.

DO THIS NOW.
Spend between 8 and 10 minutes "working the material."
Do not skip this step. It is key to scoring well on the essay.

"Death of a Soldier"

As I went on my hospital rounds with Dr. P., I happened to ask which man in the room suffered most. He glanced at John. "Every breath he draws is like a stab; for the ball pierced the left lung and broke a rib. The poor lad must lie on his wounded back or suffocate."   1

"You don't mean he must die, doctor?"   2

"There's not the slightest hope for him."   3

I could have sat down on the spot and cried heartily, if I had not learned the wisdom of bottling up one's tears for leisure moments. The army needed men like John, earnest, brave, and faithful; fighting for liberty and justice with both heart and hand.   4

John sat with bent head, hands folded on his knee, and no outward sign of suffering, till, looking nearer, I saw great tears roll down and drop upon the floor. It was a new sight there; for, though I had seen many suffer, some swore, some groaned, most endured silently, but none wept. Yet it did not seem weak, only very touching, and straightway my fear vanished, my heart opened wide and took him in. Gathering the bent head in my arms, as freely as if he had been a little child, I said, "Let me help you bear it, John."   5

Never, on any human countenance, have I seen so swift and beautiful a look of gratitude, surprise and comfort. He whispered, "Thank you, m'am, this is right good! I didn't like to be a trouble; you seemed so busy . . ."   6

I bathed his face, brushed his bonny brown hair, set all things smooth about him. While doing this, he watched me with the satisfied expression I so liked to see. He spoke so hopefully when there was no hope. "This is my first battle; do they think it's going to be my last?"   7

It was the hardest question I had ever been called upon to answer; doubly hard with those clear eyes fixed upon mine. "I'm afraid they do, John."   8

He seemed a little startled at first, pondered over the fateful fact a moment, then shook his head. "I'm afraid, but it's difficult to believe all at once. I'm so strong it don't seem possible for such a little wound to kill me." And then he said, "I'm a little sorry I wasn't wounded in front; it looks cowardly to be hit in the back, but I obeyed orders."   9

John was dying. Even while he spoke, over his face I saw a gray veil falling that no human hand can lift. I sat down by him, wiped drops from his forehead, stirred the air about him with a slow wave of a fan, and waited to help him die. For hours he suffered dumbly, without a moment's murmuring: his limbs grew cold, his face damp, his lips white, and again and again he tore the covering off his breast, as if the lightest weight added to his agony.   10

One by one, the other men woke, and round the room appeared a circle of pale faces and watchful eyes, full of awe and pity; for, though a stranger, John was beloved by all. "Old boy, how are you?" faltered one. "Can I say or do anything for you anywheres?" whispered another.   11

"Take my things home, and tell them that I did my best."   12

He died then; though the heavy breaths still tore their way up for a little longer, short they were but the waves of an ebbing tide that beat unfelt against the wreck. He never spoke again, but to the end held my hand close, so close that when he was asleep at last, I could not draw it away. Dan, another patient, helped me, warning me as he did so that it was unsafe for dead and living flesh to lie so long together. But though my hand was strangely cold and stiff, and four white marks remained across its back, even when warmth and color had returned elsewhere, I could not but be glad that, through its touch, the presence of human sympathy, perhaps had lightened that hard hour.   13

When they had made him ready for the grave, I stood looking at him. The lovely expression which so often beautifies dead faces soon replaced marks of pain. The ward master handed me a letter, saying it had come the night before but was forgot. It was John's letter, come just an hour too late to gladden the eyes that had longed for it so eagerly.   14

After I had cut some brown locks for his mother, and taken off the ring to send her, I kissed this good son for her sake, and laid the letter in his hand. Then I left him, glad to have known so genuine a man, and carrying with me an enduring memory of a brave Virginia blacksmith, as he lay serenely waiting for the dawn of that long day which knows no night.   15

Now, compare your reading notes with ours. As we said earlier, your notes may vary from ours, but the results should be similar in scope.

"**Death** of a **Soldier**"

focus/subject?

simile
details
As I went on my **hospital** rounds with Dr. P., I happened to ask which man in the room **suffered most**. He glanced at John. "Every **breath** he draws **is like a stab**; for the ball **pierced** the left lung and **broke** a rib. The poor lad **must** lie on his **wounded back** or **suffocate**."   1

dialog
"You don't mean he must die, doctor?"   2

Pity/inevitable death
"There's not the slightest hope for him."   3

too busy to cry
I **could have** sat down on the spot and **cried** heartily, if I had not learned the wisdom of **bottling up one's tears for leisure moments**.   4

(emotional appeal to Americans who can empathize with John)
The army needed men **like John, earnest, brave, and faithful; fighting for liberty and justice with both heart and hand**.

prayer?
He has time to cry; she not
//
John sat with **bent head**, **hands folded** on his knee, and no outward sign of suffering, till, looking nearer, **I saw great tears** roll down and drop upon the floor. It was a new sight there; for, though I had seen **many suffer, some swore, some groaned, most endured silently, but none wept**. Yet it did not seem weak, only **very touching**, and straightway my fear vanished, my heart opened wide and took him in.   5

simile
Dialog—begin to identify with nurse
Gathering the **bent head** in my arms, as freely **as if he had been a little child,** I said, "**Let me help you bear it, John**."

Never, on any human countenance, have I seen so swift and beautiful a look of gratitude, surprise and comfort. He whispered,   6

dialog = real John
//
"Thank you, m'am, this is right good! I didn't like to be a trouble; you seemed so busy . . ."

I bathed his face, brushed his bonny brown hair, set all things smooth about him. While doing this, he watched me with the satisfied expression I so liked to see. He spoke so hopefully when there was no   7

dialog
hope. "This is my first battle; do they think it's going to be my last?"

It was the hardest question I had ever been called upon to answer; doubly hard with those **clear eyes fixed upon mine**. "I'm afraid they   8

dialog
do, John."

He seemed a little startled at first, pondered over the fateful fact a moment, then shook his head. "I'm afraid, but it's difficult to believe all at once. I'm so strong it don't seem possible for such a little wound to kill me." And then he said, "I'm a little sorry I wasn't wounded in front; it looks cowardly to be hit in the back, but I obeyed orders." 9

(Dialog—real insight into character)

short metaphor

imagery

[**John was dying.**] Even while he spoke, over his face I saw a gray veil falling that no human hand can lift. I sat down by him, **wiped drops** from his forehead, stirred the air about him with a **slow wave of a fan**, and waited to help him die. For hours he suffered dumbly, without a moment's murmuring: his **limbs grew cold**, **his face damp**, his **lips white**, and again and again he **tore the covering off his breast**, as if the lightest weight added to his agony. 10

imagery

how to think

One by one, the other men woke, and round the room appeared a **circle of pale faces and watchful eyes**, **full of awe and pity**; for, though a stranger, **John was beloved** by all. "Old boy, how are you?" faltered one. "Can I say or do anything for you anywheres?" whispered another. 11

dialog

dialog-character

"Take my things home, and tell them that I did my best." 12

obj. short

[**He died then**]; though the heavy breaths still tore their way up for a little longer, short they were but the **waves of an ebbing tide that beat unfelt against the wreck**. He never spoke again, but to the end held my hand close, so close that when he was asleep at last, I could not draw it away. Dan, another patient, helped me, warning me as he did so that it was unsafe for dead and living flesh to lie so long together. But though my hand was strangely cold and stiff, and four white marks remained across its back, even when warmth and color had returned elsewhere, I could not but be glad that, through its touch, the presence of human sympathy, **perhaps had lightened that hard hour**. 13

metaphor

lasting physical effect

(reinforces her purpose as a nurse)

When they had made him ready for the grave, I stood looking at him. The lovely expression which so often beautifies dead faces soon replaced marks of pain. The ward master handed me a letter, saying it had come the night before but was forgot. **It was John's letter, come just an hour too late to gladden the eyes that had longed for it so eagerly.** 14

(ironic detail—sentimental)

nurse's role
how to think
of John

After I had cut some brown locks for his mother, and taken off the ring to send her, I kissed this good son for her sake, and laid the letter in his hand. Then I left him, glad to have known **so genuine a man**, and carrying with me an enduring memory of a brave Virginia blacksmith, as he lay serenely **waiting for the dawn of that long day which knows no night**. 15

beautiful metaphor

The Opening Paragraph

Remember, your opening paragraph is going to set the subject and tone of your entire essay. Make certain that your reader knows precisely where you intend to take him or her. This clarity of purpose will give your reader confidence in what you have to present. Some of the questions you should ask yourself about your opening paragraph include.

- Have you cited the author and title?
- Have you identified the author's intended effect on the reader?
- Have you specifically mentioned which strategies, devices, or elements you will consider in your analysis of Alcott's re-creation of her experience?

Remember, this information can be provided to your reader in may different ways. You can be direct or inventive. Whatever you choose to do, be confident and clear.

Below are four sample opening paragraphs that address the prompt for the Louisa May Alcott analysis essay.

We recognized many areas we could develop in this analysis essay. Pacing is obvious in this brief narrative. Alcott tells of her experience in chronological order and uses a combination of short, direct sentences to balance longer, figurative ones. We could have just concentrated on dialog, but we chose to include it with our discussion of selection of detail, diction, imagery, and tone.

Sample A

In Hospital Sketches, Louisa May Alcott presents a sentimental retelling of an episode she experienced as a Civil War nurse. As she tells of her encounter with a dying soldier, Alcott uses details, imagery, and diction to make her reader emotionally identify with her and her subject. These strategies and devices evoke a sentimental and sorrowful response in the reader.

Sample B

"John was dying." Such a direct statement for such a tragic and moving event. But, Louisa May Alcott does more than just objectively present a medical report of the death of a Civil War soldier in Hospital Sketches. Rather, through diction, selection of details, imagery, and tone, Alcott emotionally involves her reader in this sentimental re-creation of one young blacksmith's death.

Sample C

War is hell. But, occasionally an angel of mercy on a mission braves the horror to save a lost soul. Louisa May Alcott, a Civil War nurse, was such an angel—and perhaps her presence helped the troubled soul of a dying blacksmith reach the rewards of heaven he so deserved. Through imagery, diction, selection of detail, and tone, Alcott allows her readers to join her in this sentimental and awe-inspiring narrative from Hospital Sketches.

Sample D

My only previous connection with Louisa May Alcott was with Little Women. What a very different scene she presents in her story from Hospital Sketches. The reader is made to come face to face with the death of a wounded Civil War soldier as he is tended by a most caring nurse. This moving and sentimental narrative is developed through imagery, diction, selection of detail, and tone.

Although each of these opening paragraphs is different, each does the expected job of an introductory AP Comp analysis essay.

- Each cites the author and title.
- Each identifies the author's intended effect on the reader.
- Each states which strategies/devices will be discussed in the analysis of Alcott's narrative.

Let's take a look at what is different about each of these introductory paragraphs.

- **Sample A** restates the prompt directly. It is to the point without elaboration, but it enables the reader to immediately know the focus of the essay.
- **Sample B** uses a direct quotation from the text to grab the reader's attention. It is obvious that this is a writer who understands how language operates.
- **Sample C** imposes a personal viewpoint immediately and establishes a metaphor that will most likely be the unifying structure of the essay.
- **Sample D** makes reference to one of Alcott's other works as the scene is being set. The writer does not spend any additional time referring to the other work. It merely provides a kind of "stepping-stone" for both the writer and the reader.

Into which of the above samples could your opening paragraph be classified?

Writing the Body of the Essay

What Should I Include in the Body of This Analysis Essay?

Your strategy here should be the same as on the previous essay:

1. Present *your* analysis and your prompt-related points.
2. Adhere to the question.
3. Use specific references and details from the passage.
4. Use connective tissue—repetition, "echo words," and transitions—to establish coherence.

For more detail, refer back to the first discussion of this subject, earlier in this chapter.

To understand the process, carefully read the sample paragraphs below. Each develops one of the elements asked for in the prompt and cited in the introductory paragraph. Notice the specific references and the "connective tissue." Also notice that details that do not apply to the Alcott prompt are ignored.

This Paragraph Develops Diction

Throughout her account, Alcott's diction manipulates emotional responses in her readers. Words such as "earnest," "brave" and "faithful" establish John as a soldier worthy of sympathy, while "liberty and justice" rally the reader to his side with their patriotic connotations. Once the reader is involved, Alcott directs the tragic scene with words intended to bring forth more negative emotional responses: "suffering, tears, groans, and wept" emphasize John's pain. Yet, when the author says, "very touching," "fear vanished," and "my heart opened wide," the reader also wants to help John bear his pain. Alcott balances the negative side of death by using words that will make the reader more at ease during this uncomfortable passage. "Beautiful, gratitude and comfort" relax the reader and allow him to feel good about Alcott and her caregiving. Then, her direction changes as the young man is dying. He is now "cold, damp, white, and in agony." When the reader's heart is breaking, Alcott chooses words to lift the moment. The other men are "full of awe and pity," like the reader. In this way, the diction unites the reader, John, and Alcott. She makes certain that her concluding choices are comforting and positive. The "hard hour" has been "lightened." His expression is now "lovely and beautiful."

This Paragraph Develops Selection of Details

Louisa May Alcott chooses very special details to include in her development of scene and character. Dialog is one of these details which provides tangible insights into the character of John. The immediacy and reality of John's inevitable death is brought straightforwardly home to the reader in paragraphs 2 and 3. "You don't mean he must die, doctor?" "There's not the slightest hope for him." John's politeness and unassuming personality are observed when we hear him respond to the nurse in paragraph 6. And, his youth and sense of honor are heartbreakingly presented in the dialog in paragraph 7 and the end of paragraph 9. This sense of duty and honor is reinforced with his last words, ". . . tell them that I did my best." Selection of details also help the reader to understand and feel the horror of war and its casualties. The pain and coldness of death is almost brutally punctuated in paragraph 5, where Alcott chooses to emphasize others not crying while John does. Alcott chooses to tell us about the letter from John's mother that was not delivered until after his death to add more pathos and irony to an already tragic scene. And, to select the detail of her placing this letter into the dead soldier's hands prior to his burial heightens the reader's emotional involvement.

This Paragraph Develops Imagery

It might be easy to become dulled to pain in a war hospital filled with dying men. To prevent this and to personalize the experience, Alcott uses imagery to re-create the events of John's death. The reader can feel that "every breath he draws is like a stab." The image of suffocation tightens our throats as we read about his pain, but we, like Alcott, must learn to "bottle up our tears" as we envision through her simile the nurse as mother and soldier as child. The metaphor of "a gray veil falling that no human hand can lift" softens the death of the soldier while heightening the finality. The concluding metaphor reassures the reader of salvation as she, the writer, allows John into the "dawn of that long day which knows no night."

This Paragraph Develops Tone

As a result of her selection of details, diction, and imagery, Louisa May Alcott creates a scene with a predominant tone of sorrow. Re-creating the death scene of this young soldier, the author chooses those details that emphasize that pain and sorrow, both in herself and in her patient. She chooses to tell of the undelivered letter prior to the soldier's death, which further reinforces the reader's sense of sorrow and pity. Words like "suffering," "wept," "cold," "white," "in agony," help to convey and evoke sadness in the reader. And, the piteous situation is further developed when John's face is described as "lovely and beautiful" after his death. Imagery is also employed to create this tone of sorrow or sadness. Images of suffering, loss, and grief throughout, together with the final metaphor of "a gray veil falling that no human hand can lift," sadly portray the passing of this young Virginian blacksmith into eternity.

DO THIS NOW.

- Write the body of your essay. Time yourself.
- Allow 15–20 minutes to write your body paragraphs.

Here are two actual student essays with comments on each.

Student A

Louisa May Alcott experiences the worst part of war—suffering. Each day brings her   1
in contact with new bloodied men brought in on stretchers, and only a few walk out. She
has to live with their souls on her mind. One soldier, John, is described as a "brave" young
man who fought for "liberty and justice." But, he is suffering. Alcott writes with an
emotional tone about this soldier whom she helps "live" through his final moments. She
obviously retells this story so that her readers can begin to understand the anguish of war.

This chronologically organized story spans two hours, from life to the end of life. It   2
is said that no man should die alone, and Alcott helps this young man to die with the
comfort of one who cares for him. Alcott's diction includes adjectives to describe his
slow drift towards heaven with words like "his limbs grew cold, his face damp, his lips
white . . ." These characteristics added together with the metaphorically imposed "gray
veil" all lead up to his death. John's last words, "tell them that I did my best," symbolize
both his life and his death. From then on, he said nothing and waited to enter his next
life. Though he dies, Alcott hangs on as if trying to keep him from leaving. When
she finally lets him go, four white marks stay on her hand, symbolizing John's lasting
presence.

". . . Many suffer, some swore, some groaned, most endured silently, but none wept."   3
However, John was the exception. He let his emotions go, and his pain was answered
by a caring nurse. Alcott appeals to the reader's emotions with such words as "crying,"
"suffering," "pity," and "awe," that express the extremes of feeling present in the hospital
ward. A man in pain, about to die, should be pitied, especially when his life is about to
be cut short. All his childhood dreams are to go unfulfilled. It is a waste of a "genuine
man." Alcott uses this not only to tell of her experiences in war, but also to clarify for her
reader the devastation of war. Alcott's balanced sentences enhance her story. In paragraph
7, John says, "This is my first battle; do they think it's going to be my last?" Alcott
uses this question to illustrate the shock soldiers feel when faced with death. How can
anyone believe a doctor who tells him he is dying. This shock, on the part of the soldier
illustrates the human horror of war—people die!

Alcott also uses irony to emphasize the sadness of this boy's death. Just an hour after   4
he passes on, another doctor brings in a letter for John. It is just too late. If he had seen it,
maybe it would have put one last sparkle in his eyes before he shut them forever.

The ending of the passage summarizes the entire experience of so many of those who   5
fought in the Civil War. Here was a young man who was very human. He was an average
boy from Virginia who worked as a blacksmith. He had had a regular life and a regular
job until this terrible war. That was when this regular life ceased to exist: John's and pre–
Civil War America.

Having witnessed this young soldier waiting for the "dawn of that long day which   6
knows no night," people should cry and be awe struck at the consequences of war.

Student B

In this excerpt from <u>Hospital Sketches</u> by Louisa May Alcott, she constructs her story to deeply move the reader by re-creating her personal experience as a nurse. Alcott's rhetorical strategies, including diction, imagery and selection of details, help to emphasize the pain and the sorrow which filled the U.S. Army hospital.

A reason why Alcott's excerpt was very successful in helping the reader understand the atmosphere during the Civil War is through her choice of words. The repetition of "hope," reveals that although she and John hoped that he would survive, it was inevitable that he would die, for he had been deeply hurt. Alcott reveals her sympathy and care for this man named John by asking the doctor how long he has to live. She also helps us understand that during the war precious lives were taken away. "The army needed men like John, earnest, brave, and faithful." Alcott even reveals to her readers that having this companionship with John wasn't an easy job. She would have to answer heartbreaking questions, such as "Do they think it's going to be my last?" Telling a person that they won't live for long may be one of the hardest jobs Alcott may have had.

In addition to Alcott's diction, the details which she presents for her readers give the story an even more melancholy effect. She doesn't simply just state how many men were injured or how they were injured. Rather, she writes about her short encounter with the man named John. "John sat with bent head . . . and no outward sign of suffering, till . . . I saw great tears roll down and drop upon the floor." It's like this simple example shows the sadness and grief felt by this young man who was brave and fought for liberty. She reveals the soft side of a soldier. Alcott re-creates her experience by presenting the details of her relationship with John. "I sat down by him, wiped drops from his forehead, stirred the air . . . waited to help him die." She even displays the gradual physical change of the dying human body. "His limbs grew cold, his face damp, his lips white . . ." She also includes a small conversation between John and another injured man who, although a stranger, still had pity and sympathy for him. She also appeals to emotion by adding his mother in the story. She, as a friend, cuts his hair and kisses him for her instead at the grave.

Furthermore, the use of imagery also added to the re-creation of the Civil War scene. She describes John's pain as "every breath he draws is like a stab; for the ball pierced the left lung and broke a rib." With this quotation, it is evident that his pain was great. Alcott also shows the slow deterioration of John. "I saw a gray veil falling that no human hand can lift." This reveals that John's death is inevitable and there was nothing any human could do, but she could play the role of a friend. Alcott also displays the strength of John, how he wished to live, as "heavy breaths still tore their way up for a little longer."

Alcott describes her experience of the Civil War by telling a personal story. She reveals great love and generosity for John. Through this, it helps us understand the true power of human companionship.

Rubrics for Alcott Essay

As we said previously in this chapter, you can view actual AP English Language and Composition rubrics by logging on to the College Board website.

High-Range Essay (9, 8, 7)

- Indicates a complete understanding of the prompt
- Clearly identifies and illustrates the author's intended effect on the reader
- Presents various rhetorical strategies, devices, and elements used by the author to re-create her experience
- Clear, well-organized, and coherent
- Demonstrates a mature writing style
- Thoroughly cites specific references from the text to illustrate and support points being made
- Minor errors/flaws, if any

Note: A 7 essay which is rated in the high range makes the jump from the mid-range because of its more mature style and perception.

Mid-Range Essay (7, 6, 5)

- Refers accurately to the prompt
- Refers accurately to the author's intended effect on the reader
- Presents a less thorough analysis of how Alcott re-creates her experience than the higher-rated essays
- Is less adept at linking strategies and devices to the creation of effect or re-creation of the experience
- Demonstrates writing that is adequate to convey Alcott's assertion
- May not be sensitive to the more subtle strategies employed by Alcott
- A few errors/flaws may be present

Note:
- The 7 paper demonstrates a more consistent command of college-level writing than does the 5 or 6 essay.
- A 5 paper does the minimum required by the prompt. It relies on generalizations and sketchy analysis. It is often sidetracked by plot, and the references may be limited or simplistic.

Low-Range Essay (4, 3, 2, 1)

- Does not respond adequately to the prompt
- Demonstrates insufficient and/or inadequate understanding of the passage and prompt
- Does not clearly identify the author's intended effect on the reader or does not illustrate or supply support for the intended effect
- Underdevelops and/or inaccurately analyzes Alcott's re-creation of her experience
- Demonstrates weak control of the elements of diction, syntax, and organization

Note: A 4 or 3 essay may do no more than paraphrase sections of the passage. A 2 essay may merely summarize the passage. (NO MATTER HOW WELL WRITTEN, A SUMMARY CAN NEVER EARN MORE THAN A 2.)

A 1–2 essay indicates a major lack of understanding and control. It fails to comprehend the prompt and/or the passage. It may also indicate severe writing problems.

Rubrics for Student A Essay

This is a high-range essay for the following reasons:

- Indication of a mature writer [paragraph 2, sentence 3], [paragraph 3, sentences 2 and 3]
- Clear understanding of the author's intended effect on the reader and applies it to a larger context [last paragraph]
- Strong integration of textual support with rhetorical strategies [paragraph 4], [paragraph 5, sentence 1]
- Strong topic adherence and connective tissue
- Interesting and appropriate insights derived from the text [last paragraph]

This high-range essay is well organized, with a strong, mature voice that has a clear point of view together with a well-developed analysis.

Rubrics for Student B Essay

This is a mid-range essay for the following reasons:

- Identifies the intended effect on the reader [paragraph 1, sentence 1], [paragraph 3, sentence 1]
- Adequately develops cited textual references
- Shows understanding of rhetorical devices [paragraph 4]
- Good transitions ("connective tissue")
- Frequently uses awkward syntax [paragraph 2, last 3 sentences], [paragraph 3, last 2 sentences]
- Minor technical errors, such as apostrophes and commas

This mid-range essay is indicative of a writer who understands the text and the prompt. The student is able to choose the obvious rhetorical strategies and devices and relate them to Alcott's purpose with less fully developed analysis in comparison with the high-range papers.

Rapid Review

- Analysis is the study of rhetorical strategies and stylistic elements.
- Your writing reflects your critical thinking.
- Review the types of analysis questions asked on previous exams.
- Always address the prompt.
- Review the rubrics to understand the rating system.
- Remember, the essay on the exam is a first draft.
- Follow a timing strategy for writing the exam essay.
- Carefully analyze the prompt.
- Practice topic adherence.
- Employ close reading and highlighting of the given passage.
- "Work" the material.
- Write your essay and check against models.
- Use echo words.
- Form a study group.
- Read sample essays and rubrics.
- Score your own essays.

CHAPTER 6

Introduction to the Argumentative Essay

IN THIS CHAPTER

Summary: Examination of the argumentative essay and its purpose as it is presented in the AP English Language exam.

Key Ideas
- ✪ Learn to take a position/stand on a situation given in the argumentative prompt.
- ✪ Familiarize yourself with strategies to support your position.
- ✪ Learn the basics of constructing the argumentative essay in response to the AP English Language prompt.

Some Basics

The second type of essay on the Advanced English Language exam is the argumentative essay. Because it is often seen as a "giveaway," many students believe it to be the easiest of the three essays to write. Unfortunately, too many students spend too little time in the actual planning of this essay and, as a result, present an underdeveloped, illogical, or off-topic piece. Although there is a great deal of latitude given for the response to the prompt, the argumentative essay demands careful reading and planning.

What Does the Argumentative Essay Require of Me?

Basically, you need to do three things

- understand the nature of the position taken in the prompt
- develop a position in response to the prompt
- clearly and logically support your claim

What Does It Mean to Develop a Position?

Basically, this is a "So, what do YOU think?" prompt. You are asked to carefully read a passage or statement and to consider your own thoughts and where you stand on the issue. You are NOT being asked to confront the writer or speaker of the given text.

Timing and Planning the Essay

How Should I Approach the Writing of My Argumentative Essay?

Before beginning to actually write the essay, you need to do some quick planning. You could brainstorm a list of ideas, construct a chart, or create an outline. Whatever it is, you MUST find a way to allow yourself to think through the issue and your position.

Once I've Chosen My Position on the Given Issue, How Do I Go About Supporting It?

Remember that you've been taught how to write an argument throughout your school years, and you've even studied it in detail in your AP Comp course this year. Here is a brief overview of the kinds of support/evidence you could include to bolster your argument:

— facts/statistics	— needed definitions	— anecdotes
— details	— recognition of	— contrast and comparison
— quotations	the opposition	— cause and effect
— dialog	— examples	— appeal to authority

Just make certain to choose the strategy or strategies that are most familiar to you and with which you feel most comfortable. Don't try to "con" your reader or pad your essay with irrelevancies.

Does It Matter What Tone I Take in My Argumentative Essay?

The College Board and the AP Comp readers are open to a wide range of approaches. You can choose to be informal and personal, formal and objective, or even humorous and irreverent, and anything in between. Just be certain that your choice is appropriate for your purpose.

Will I Be Penalized for Taking an Unpopular, Unexpected, Irreverent, or Bizarre Position on the Given Issue?

As long as you are addressing the prompt and appropriately supporting your position, there is no danger of your losing points on your essay because you've decided to take a different approach. Your essay is graded for process and mastery and manipulation of language, not for how close you come to the viewpoint of your reader.

How Should I Plan to Spend My Time Writing the Argumentative Essay?

Learning to budget your time is a skill that can be most helpful in writing the successful essay. The following is a sample timeline for you to consider:

- 1–3 minutes reading and working the prompt
- 3 minutes deciding on a position
- 10–12 minutes planning the support of your position
- 20 minutes writing the essay
- 3 minutes proofreading

Working the Prompt

Before beginning to write, you MUST spend some time carefully reading and deconstructing the prompt. (We call this "working the prompt.") Your success depends upon your clearly understanding what is expected of you.

Below is the prompt of the third essay on the Diagnostic/Master exam.

> **In his famous "Vast Wasteland" address to the National Association of Broadcasters in May of 1961, Newton Minow, the Chairman of the Federal Communications Commission, spoke about the power of television to influence the taste, knowledge, and opinions of its viewers around the world. Carefully read the following, paying close attention to how timely it is today, especially in light of the worldwide Internet.**
>
> **Minow ended his speech warning that "The power of instantaneous sight and sound is without precedent in mankind's history. This is an awesome power. It has limitless capabilities for good—and for evil. And it carries with it awesome responsibilities—responsibilities which you and [the government] cannot escape . . ."**
>
> **Using your own knowledge and your own experiences or reading, write a carefully constructed essay that defends, challenges, or qualifies Minow's ideas.**

DO THIS NOW.
Highlight the essential elements of the prompt.
(Time yourself.) How long did it take you? _____
Compare your highlighting of the prompt with ours.

> In his famous "<u>Vast Wasteland</u>" address to the <u>National Association of Broadcasters</u> in May of <u>1961</u>, <u>Newton Minow</u>, the <u>Chairman of the Federal Communications Commission</u>, spoke about the <u>power of television to influence the taste, knowledge, and opinions of its viewers around the world</u>. Carefully read the following, paying close attention to how <u>timely</u> it is today, especially in light of the worldwide <u>Internet</u>.
>
> Minow ended his speech <u>warning</u> that "<u>The power of instantaneous sight and sound is without precedent in mankind's history</u>. This is an <u>awesome power</u>. It has <u>limitless capabilities for good—and for evil</u>. And it carries with it <u>awesome responsibilities</u>—responsibilities which <u>you and [the government] cannot escape</u> . . ."

Using your **<u>own knowledge</u>** and your **<u>own experiences</u>** or **<u>reading</u>**, write a carefully constructed essay that **<u>defends, challenges, or qualifies Minow's ideas</u>**.

For this prompt, anything else you may have highlighted is extraneous.

> The prompt asks the student to defend, challenge, or qualify Minow's ideas. Notice that it does NOT state "all," "some," or a "specific number." Therefore, the student has freedom of choice. (This is similar to the "such as" instructions in other prompts.)

Developing the Opening Paragraph

NOW, BEGIN TO PLAN YOUR ESSAY.

Write your introductory paragraph. Make certain to

- refer specifically to the prompt; and
- clearly state your position on the given issue.

The following are three sample opening paragraphs.

A

I agree with Newton Minow's assertion to the National Association of Broadcasters that "The power of instantaneous sight and sound is . . . an awesome power . . . [with] capabilities for good—and for evil." However, I disagree with his placing the responsibility for this power squarely in the hands of the broadcasters and the government.

B

Imagine—you have limitless capabilities for good and evil—you, not Superman, can control the world with your super powers. And, what are your powers? Do you have x-ray vision, morphability, immortality? NO, you have the most awesome power ever devised—you can instantaneously influence the taste, knowledge, and opinions of mankind around the world. You are Supernet! and you have a super headache because you agree with Newton Minow, who warned the National Association of Broadcasters in 1961 that "You have an awesome responsibility."

C

Nowhere is the awesome power for good and evil of modern technology more clearly seen than in the Internet's pervasiveness and influence. Newton Minow was right on target in 1961 when he warned the National Association of Broadcasters that the power of TV has "limitless capabilities for good—and for evil."

Each of these opening paragraphs does the job required of an introduction to an argumentative essay on the AP English Language and Composition exam.

- Each cites the speaker and the occasion.
- Each clearly states the writer's position on the given issue.

Let's look at what is different about each of the paragraphs.

Sample A qualifies the assertion presented by Minow. The writer agrees with the potential of the power but disagrees about who should take responsibility.

Sample B agrees with Minow's position but treats the assertion in a lighthearted fashion. The reader can expect a humorous and possibly irreverent tone in the essay.

Sample C indicates a writer who has obviously decided to limit the area of the argument to that of the Internet and has chosen to agree with Minow.

Note: Given the subject matter, this prompt does not lend itself easily to a negative position. However, if a creative thinker and writer were to assert such a viewpoint, it would not be penalized.

Which of the above samples is similar to your opening paragraph? Are there any changes you would make in yours?

Developing the Body of the Essay

DO THIS NOW.

— Plan the body of your argumentative essay.

A sample strategy for planning the Minow essay follows. After carefully reading and deconstructing the prompt, we decided to use Minow's own three-part warning to the NAB. We brainstormed for ideas that could be linked to each of the categories. (Remember, ideas about how to organize or approach your essay can sometimes be found in the excerpt itself.)

GOOD	EVIL	RESPONSIBILITY
— education	— promote hate	— laws
— warning of dangers	— distort reality	— censorship
— recognition of heroes	— help terrorists	— self-censorship
— involvement in humankind's achievements	— invasion of privacy	— prior restraint
	— threats to national security	— 1st Amendment
— instant communications with family and friends	— create mass hysteria	— 4th Amendment
		— financial gain
		— copyrights
— medical care	— exploit children	— parental control
— links to the world for the the disabled, elderly, isolated	— fraud	— v-chip
	— conspiracy	— personal checks and balances
	— subvert elections	
— entertainment	— brainwashing	

Once you've completed your initial planning, in our case brainstorming, you must choose those specific items you will be best able to use to support and develop your argument. We limited ours to the following.

GOOD	EVIL	RESPONSIBILITY
— instant communications	— promote hate	— personal checks and balances
— medical treatment	— exploit children	— laws
— entertainment	— create mass hysteria	

This type of chart will provide you as a writer with a structure for your presentation. You are now ready to write the body of your essay based on your carefully considered choices.

Below are three sample body paragraphs which are based on the chart on page 100.

Body Paragraph on "Good"

One of the most rewarding applications of the Internet is its ability to provide instant communication between friends and family. A grandmother-to-be in New York is able to share in the moment by moment experience of her daughter's pregnancy and her grand-daughter Daisy's birth in California through e-mail, scanned photos and quick videos. Likewise, the ability to instantly communicate with others may have saved the life of a doctor stranded at the South Pole. Her contact with medical resources and experts via the Internet enabled her to undergo surgery and treatment for breast cancer. Research and innovations in medical treatment are now available to those around the world via the "Net." Similarly, the ability for instant communication enables millions to enjoy concerts, sports events, theatrical presentations and other cultural activities without ever having to leave home. These wonderful benefits are all because of the fabulous and awesome technological creation—the Internet.

Body Paragraph on "Evil"

The other side of the mass communication coin has the face of evil on it. The Internet offers hate mongers unlimited access to anyone with a connection to the World Wide Web. Groups like the Neo-Nazis can spread their hate messages to susceptible minds via bright, entertaining and engaging websites. What looks like a simple, fun game can easily reinforce the group's hate-filled philosophy to unsuspecting browsers. With the potential for millions of "hits" each week, it does not take a rocket scientist to perceive the danger here. This danger is also present with the minds and bodies of curious and vulnerable young people. Because of its easy access and easy production, "kiddie porn" is both possible and available via the Internet and the films any number of porn sites offer for downloading with the mere click of a keyboard key. Through contacts made through e-mail and/or chat rooms on the Net, children can be easily fooled and led to contact those who would abuse their bodies and minds for a quick profit or cheap thrill. With instantaneous messaging, whether real or imagined, positive or negative, a single person or group can set into motion mass hysteria just by warning of an impending disaster, such as a flood, fire, bomb, poison, and so on. There are obviously many more possibilities floating out there in the ethernet. These are just three of the evil ones.

Body Paragraph on "Responsibility"

Just as there is the potential for both good and evil with regard to mass communication, so too is there the potential for both beneficial and destructive strategies related to responsibilities. The most powerful regulator of our responsibility as individuals is our finger and its power to press a button or double click on a key and to "just say no." With this slight pressure, we are able to exert monumental pressure on those who produce programs, websites, photos, documents, etc., which we find unacceptable. Who better to tell us what to watch, what to do, and what to think? All too often many people prefer to abdicate their personal responsibility and give that power to either the government or the communication industry. We must never forget that dictators target the control and censorship of mass media as the first step in the total control of the minds and hearts of the populace. The laws, which we as citizens of a democracy look to, must never impinge upon our First and Fourth Amendment rights. Each of us has the right of free speech, and each of us has the right to privacy. None of us has the right to harm others or to limit the rights of others; why, then, would we give that right to the communication industry or to the government?

Regarding a concluding paragraph, our advice is to spend your time in planning and writing the body of your essay rather than worrying about a concluding paragraph. With a brief essay, you can be certain that your reader can remember what you've already said, so there is no need to summarize your major points or to repeat the prompt. If you feel you must have a concluding statement/remark, by all means do so. But, make certain it is a FINAL remark that is of interest and is appropriate to your purpose. You may want to use the last sentence of your last body paragraph as your concluding comment. For example, the final sentences in the first and third sample body paragraphs could be used as the conclusion to the essay.

DO THIS NOW.
Spend about 20 minutes writing the body of your essay. Make certain that your essay follows your plan.

Sample Student Essays

The following are two sample student essays.

Student A

When Newton Minow ended his speech in May, 1961, he warned that, "The power of instantaneous sight and sound is without precedent . . . [and] it has limitless capabilities for good—and for evil." I wholeheartedly agree with both Minow's position about modern technology, especially about how it relates to the Internet today and the responsibility facing its users. 1

Scene One—Pre-1980's. Big project. Long haul to the library, gazing despondently until your eyes resemble those of a zombie. Too many books, too little time, in short, just TOO much. Scene Two—mid-1990's. A two-foot walk to the computer, and Voila! All the information you'd ever need is at your fingertips. The Internet has truly revolutionized how people can obtain their information. Now, more than ever, it is easier and quicker to access all types of information from "Exactly what IS that fungus growing on my toe?" to "What are the names of every major river system in the continental United States?" The plethora of information enables people to almost cease the burdensome trip to the library and halt the overwhelming feelings of dread they find as they stare blankly at a stack of books. With the schedule of the typical American today, there's hardly enough time to breathe, nevermind attempting to fit that hour-long trip to the library in the time frame. With the birth of the Internet, people with access to a computer can locate information faster than ever. But, how are we to judge the acceptability of that information? 2

The awesome power of these new technological inventions, such as computers and the Internet, do not always produce, however, grade-A products. People have begun to utilize the Internet to recruit new cult members, to teach people how to build bombs, 3 to teach hate. Basically, anything and everything evil can be posted on the "Net." Scene Three. Mr. Parker, a 75-year-old man from rural Indiana is in severe pain with abdominal cramps. Instead of attempting a two-hour drive to the nearest hospital, he makes it to his computer, logs on to the Internet in hopes of finding out what is wrong with him and in hopes of finding a quick remedy. Following the www's advice, he treats himself for stomach pain. Scene Four. Poor Mr. Parker dies hours later of acute appendicitis.

The Internet has the power to give birth to both good and evil. Today, as our society   4 becomes more and more advanced, we rely more and more on anything that promises to make our busy lives less hectic. The easy way out, it seems, is always the right way in. Call it our American laziness, or call it our penchant to make learning easier, either way you slice it, the Internet has the potential for both positive and negative effects on society. Our responsibility is to find ways to exhibit our ability to distinguish between that which is beneficial and that which is destructive.

Student B

In his now famous address to the National Association of Broadcasters in May,   1 1961, FCC chairman Newton Minow spoke of the unprecedented power that those who control television's programming have over the American public, and how the mass media should be controlled and censored by the government, for it could wield awesome amounts of either good or evil. This assertion, that "television is a vast wasteland" rings true throughout the modern history of American society, especially in light of the global Internet.

There is no doubt that television has greatly altered the very psyche of Americans   2 countless times since Minow's speech. From patriotic events like Neil Armstrong's first step on the moon and the "miracle on the ice" American victory over the Soviet Union in the 1980 Olympic hockey semi-finals, to historical events like Tiananmen Square, the assassination of JFK, and the fall of the Berlin Wall. Television has provided Americans with triumph—the Persian Gulf War—and tragedy—the Columbine massacre. Most importantly, however, it is entertainment for the masses, and is affordable to the point that 95% of Americans watch at least once a week, and this is where it goes awry.

Americans, due to the overwhelming economic prosperity and technological   3 revolution of the last forty years, have become slovenly. We can get almost anywhere in the world within 24 hours via airplane and expect to be waited on while flying there. We drive to work everyday. We have every type of cuisine imaginable less than twenty minutes away, contrasting with several countries which don't have food, period. We have secure incomes, capital growth, and all of the material comforts of the day. We have the Internet, the new mass media which allows for anyone to learn about anything at anytime, anywhere. We are inactive, obese, materialistic, boring people, and television has adapted itself to fit our collective personas. Or possibly, we changed for television.

The nightly news is filled with images of death, suffering, pain, agony, misery, and other horrors that we gobble up because we as middle-class Americans have an infinitesimal chance of ever seeing it. The most popular TV shows are either irreverent comedies like "Seinfeld" and "Friends" with no actual cultural impact, or worse game shows like "Weakest Link" or "Survivor" that reward, in pride and prizes, ruthlessness, emotional warfare, and pointless competition that reinforces those attributes in the 30 million viewers they get every Monday and Wednesday night. The sensationalistic television programming caters to every evil desire we have, so it makes them grow inside us and want more, making us fervent to tune in next week for the next fantastic episode. God forbid they show a rerun.   4

Television has become a wasteland, and it's turning Western culture into one, too. One has to believe Newton Minow knew what he was talking about. In a classic quote from <u>Catch-22</u>, Joseph Heller writes that "There was a general consensus that the platitudes of Americanism were horsesh-t." I wholeheartedly agree.   5

Rating the Essays

High-Range Essays (9, 8)

- Correctly identifies Minow's position regarding the power of television and other forms of mass communication
- Effectively presents a position about Minow's own ideas
- Clear writer's voice
- Successfully defends his or her position
- Presents carefully reasoned arguments making appropriate reference to specific examples from personal experience
- Clear and effective organization
- Effectively manipulates language
- Few, if any, syntactical errors

Mid-Range Essays (7, 6, 5)

- Correctly identifies Minow's position and attitude about television and mass communications
- Understands the demands of the prompt
- Clearly states a position with regard to that of Minow
- Presents a generally adequate argument that makes use of appropriate examples
- Ideas clearly stated
- Less well-developed than the high-range essays
- A few lapses in diction and/or syntax

Low-Range Essays (4, 3, 2, 1)

- Inadequate response to the prompt
- Misunderstands, oversimplifies, or misrepresents Minow's position
- Insufficient or inappropriate examples used to develop the writer's position
- Lack of mature control of the elements of essay writing

For this argumentative essay, almost all of the writers understood that Minow was commenting on the power of television and were able to comment on the timeliness of his assertions. In their essays, student writers attempted to distinguish between good and bad effects of modern technology, especially the Internet, and many illustrated their claims with fine examples of the power of this technology. They recognized the potential for inciting violence, for learning, for conformity, and for influencing political opinions and outcomes. The majority only touched upon power and influence, but the high-range essays recognized the subtlety of the responsibility of television and the Internet.

Most, if not all, student writers agreed with Minow, but few offered any real examination of the need for responsibility with regard to the advances in technology. Some were cautious about First Amendment rights, and a few saw the government as the chief "overseer."

Student A

This is a high-range essay for the following reasons:

- a strong, mature voice willing to be creative as well as analytical;
- clear statement about the writer's position on Minow's assertion;
- overall structure clearly defined through "scenes";
- original illustrations and details to support writer's position;
- tight focus;
- mature vocabulary and sentence structure; and
- brief response to Minow's challenge about responsibility regarding the media.

This high-range essay, although brief, does the work of a mature, clear, and responsive writer. The assertion and support for it are well organized and developed in a very clear writer's voice.

Student B

This is a mid-range essay for the following reasons:

- evidence that the writer understood the question and prompt;
- indication of a writer's voice;
- does not connect all parts of the essay, especially in paragraph 3, with the topic;
- includes interesting and varied details and examples to support the thesis;
- some obviously incorrect assumptions [paragraph 4, sentence 2];
- a few problems with diction and syntax [fragment in paragraph 4, sentence 2]; ["slovenly" in paragraph 3, sentence 1], ["fervent" in paragraph 4, next to last sentence];
- an interesting style and content; and
- does not really address the responsibility issue.

This mid-range essay indicates a writer who is a risk taker and intellectually curious. At times, the writer's enthusiasm seems to get in the way of a clear focus.

Rapid Review

- Create an argument.
  - understand the position or assertion
  - agree, disagree, or qualify
  - take a position, relate to an idea
  - support your point of view

- Work the prompt.
  — read and deconstruct the assignment
  — highlight
- Plan the essay.
- Address the opposition.
- Allow for final remarks.
- Write the essay.
- Read the sample essays and rubrics.
- Score your own essay.

CHAPTER 7

Introduction to the Synthesis Essay

IN THIS CHAPTER

Summary: An introduction to the synthesis essay and its purpose as it is presented on the AP English Language exam.

Key Ideas
- ✪ Learn how the synthesis essay differs from the argumentative and analysis essays.
- ✪ Learn the process of dealing with many texts.
- ✪ Learn the strategies that can be used to incorporate specific texts into your essay.
- ✪ Learn the basics for constructing your response to the synthesis prompt.

Some Basics

What Is the Synthesis Essay on the Exam Like?

Basically, the student is presented with an introduction to and a description of an issue that has varying viewpoints associated with it. Accompanying this is a selection of sources that address the topic. These sources can be written texts that could include nonfiction, fiction, poetry, or even drama, as well as visual texts, such as photos, charts, artwork, cartoons, and so forth.

After carefully reading and annotating the sources, the student is required to respond to the given prompt with an essay that incorporates and synthesizes at least THREE of the sources in support of his position on the subject.

What Is the Purpose of the Synthesis Essay?

The College Board wants to determine how well the student can do the following:

- Read critically
- Understand texts
- Analyze texts
- Develop a position on a given topic
- Support a position on a given topic
- Support a position with appropriate evidence from outside sources
- Incorporate outside sources into the texts of the essay
- Cite sources used in the essay

The synthesis essay is a chance to demonstrate your ability to develop a "researched idea," using not only your personal viewpoint, but also the viewpoints of others. This essay is a reflection of your critical reading, thinking, and writing skills.

What Kinds of Synthesis Essays Can I Expect?

The synthesis essay has two primary approaches.

The first kind of synthesis essay is one you're probably familiar with. This is the expository essay in which you develop your thesis and support it with specific examples from appropriate sources. You could develop this type of synthesis essay using any of the rhetorical strategies, such as:

- Compare and contrast
- Cause and effect
- Analysis

The second kind of synthesis essay presents an argument. Here, you take a position on a particular topic and support this position with appropriate outside sources, while indicating the weaknesses of other viewpoints.

You should be ready to write either of these two types of synthesis essays. Given the nature of the AP Language exam, however, it is more likely that you will be presented with a synthesis essay prompt that requires a response in the form of an argument.

The important thing is to practice composing both types of synthesis essays. Practice. Practice. Being familiar and comfortable with the synthesis process is the crucial factor.

> Don't be put off by the length and/or complexity of the introduction to the subject and the prompt. Remember, you are the one who will choose your position on the topic. And you are the one who chooses which sources to incorporate into your essay.
>
> You can do this—AS LONG AS YOU ADDRESS THE PROMPT AND INCORPORATE AND CITE THE REQUIRED NUMBER OF SOURCES.

How Is the Synthesis Essay Rated?

As with the other essays on the AP Language exam, the synthesis essay is rated on a 9-point scale that is based on the AP Reader's evaluation of this first draft of an essay written in approximately 40 minutes. Here is a sample rubric for the synthesis essay.

A **9** essay has all the qualities of an 8 essay, and the writing style is especially impressive, as is the analysis and integration of the specifics related to the given topic and the given sources.

An **8** essay <u>effectively</u> and <u>cohesively</u> addresses the prompt. It clearly takes a position on the given topic and supports the claim using carefully integrated and appropriate evidence, including at least three of the given sources. The essay will also show the writer's <u>ability to control language</u>.

A **7** essay has all the properties of a 6, only with a <u>more complete</u>, well-developed, and integrated argument or a more mature writing style.

A **6** essay <u>adequately</u> addresses the prompt. The claim is on the given topic and integrates, as well as makes use of, appropriate evidence, including at least three references from the given sources. These elements are less fully integrated and/or developed than scores in the 7, 8, or 9 range. The writer's ideas are expressed with clarity, but the writing may have a few errors in syntax and/or diction.

A **5** essay demonstrates that the writer <u>understands the prompt</u>. The argument/claim/ position about the given topic is generally understandable, but the development and/ or integration of appropriate evidence and at least three of the given sources are limited, strained, or uneven. The writer's ideas are expressed clearly with a few errors in syntax or diction.

A **4** essay is <u>not an adequate response</u> to the prompt. The writer's argument indicates a misunderstanding, an oversimplification, or a misrepresentation of the assigned task. The writer may use evidence that is inappropriate or insufficient to support the argument, or use fewer than three of the given sources. The writing presents the writer's ideas, but it may indicate immaturity of style and control.

A **3** essay is a lower 4 because it is <u>even less effective</u> in addressing the question. It is also less mature in its syntax and organization.

A **2** essay indicates <u>little success in speaking to the prompt</u>. The writer may misread the question, only summarize the given sources, fail to develop the required argument, or simply ignore the prompt and write about another topic. The writing may also lack organization and control of language and syntax. (***Note*: No matter how well written, a summary will never rate more than a 2.**)

A **1** essay is a lower 2 because it is even <u>more simplistic</u>, <u>disorganized</u>, and <u>lacking in control of language</u>.

Timing and Planning the Synthesis Essay

Before Writing

Before you begin to write your essay, you need to perform an important series of tasks. <u>**The first among these tasks is to wisely use the allotted, prewriting 15 minutes of reading time.**</u>

- Read ALL three of the prompts
- Deconstruct the synthesis prompt
- Read and annotate each of the given texts related to the synthesis prompt
- Decide how you will address the synthesis prompt

The second of these tasks is to be aware of the timing of writing your essay. You've been told to open the test booklet and begin to write. Now what? Well, you've already read each of the three prompts and decided what position you're going to take on the synthesis essay. Here's what we recommend as a timeline for writing the synthesis essay:

- 5 to 6 minutes going back to the texts and deciding which you will use in your essay
- 8 to 10 minutes planning the support of your position
- 20 minutes writing the essay
- 3 to 4 minutes checking to make certain you've included at least the minimum number of sources and correctly cited each of them
- 3 minutes proofreading

Working the Prompt

As with the analysis and argument essays, you MUST spend time carefully reading and deconstructing the prompt. This entails your carefully reading and looking for key words, phrases, and other information that make your task clear. DO NOT FORGET TO READ ANY INTRODUCTORY MATERIAL PROVIDED. The introduction will set up the situation and give you any needed background information. Plan to spend about three minutes <u>carefully reading both the introduction and the assignment</u>, and highlighting the important terms and elements of the prompt.

The following is the prompt from the Diagnostic Master exam.

A recent Supreme Court decision has provoked much debate about private property rights. In this decision, the court ruled that the city of New London was within the bounds of the *U.S. Constitution* when it condemned private property for use in a redevelopment plan. This ruling is an example of the classic debate between individual rights versus the greater good.

Carefully read the following sources, including any introductory information. **Then, in an essay that synthesizes at least three of the sources for support, take a position that supports, opposes, or qualifies the claim that the government taking property from one private owner to give to another for the creation of further economic development constitutes a permissible "public use" under the Fifth Amendment.**

Make certain that you take a position and that the essay centers on your argument. Use the sources to support your reasoning; avoid simply summarizing the sources. You may refer to the sources by their letters (Source A, Source B, etc.) or by the identifiers in the parentheses below.

- Source A (*U.S. Constitution*)
- Source B (*60 Minutes*)
- Source C (*Kelo* decision)
- Source D (Koterba, political cartoon)
- Source E (Broder)
- Source F (Britt, political cartoon)
- Source G (CNN and American Survey)

DO THIS NOW.
Time yourself for this activity.
 Highlight the essential elements of the prompt.
 How long did it take you? _____
 Compare your highlighting with ours.

A recent Supreme Court decision has provoked much debate about private property rights. In it, the court ruled that the city of New London was within the bounds of the *U.S. Constitution* when it condemned private property for use in a redevelopment plan. This ruling is an example of the classic debate between individual rights versus the greater good.

Carefully read the following sources, including any introductory information. **Then, in an essay that synthesizes at least three of the sources for support, take a position that supports, opposes, or qualifies the claim that the government taking property from one private owner to give to another for the creation of further economic development constitutes a permissible "public use" under the Fifth Amendment.**

Make certain that you take a position and that the essay centers on your argument. Use the sources to support your reasoning; avoid simply summarizing the sources. You may refer to the sources by their letters (Source A, Source B, etc.) or by the identifiers in the parentheses below.

- Source A (*U.S. Constitution*)
- Source B (*60 Minutes*)
- Source C (*Kelo* decision)
- Source D (Koterba, political cartoon)
- Source E (Broder)
- Source F (Britt, political cartoon)
- Source G (CNN and American Survey)

Notice we have highlighted or underlined the essential parts of both the introduction and the prompt itself. All other words and phrases are nonessential.

> We now know a debate is centering around private property rights and public use for the greater good. We know the U.S. Supreme Court recently handed down a ruling supporting the principle of eminent domain, and we know we must take a position on this debate. And, lastly, we know we must choose at least three of the seven given sources.

Developing the Opening Paragraph

Now that you are aware of what is expected of you, you can begin to plan your essay.

> Before beginning the actual writing, we recommend you jot down a few notes about HOW you are going to present your material. There is no need to construct a formal outline. Simply create a brief listing of the major points you want to include and the order in which you will present them.

DO THIS NOW.
I have decided to use the following sources in my essay:
   Source ___ A ___ B ___ C ___ D ___ E ___ F ___ G

When creating the opening paragraph, most student writers feel more in control if they:

— refer specifically to the prompt and/or introduction
— clearly state their position on the given topic

Now is the time to write your opening paragraph.

DO THIS NOW.

The position I'm going to take on this issue is _____ support _____ oppose _____ qualify

The following are three sample introductory paragraphs.

A

Payday. As usual, the line at the bank drive-thru is a mile long, so Joe Citizen just sits and listens to the radio. This paycheck is especially important to him because it is the final payment on his castle—his home. Mr. Smith has a family waiting back at home for him. Even his dog will be happy to see Joe walk through the door. What Joe Citizen and his family don't know is this: waiting for Joe is a notice from his local government, a letter notifying him that his home and property are being taken, using the right of eminent domain. One has to ask, "Is this fair?" I think not.

B

Every time that my grandparents visit, I have to vacate my bedroom, so they can have a room of their own during their visit. It's always a painful few days because I'm locked out of the room that I've decorated, the room that holds all of my things; it's the room that's "mine." As my mother always says, "It's for the good of the family." But, no matter how much I feel deprived, I always know that I'll have it back in a few days. However, the results would be different if she applied the principle of "eminent domain." I would lose my room permanently, and it would be turned into a real guest room. I would not be a happy family member.

C

Today there is a wide-ranging debate about the individual's right to possess and protect his private property and the right of the government to seize a person's home and land needed for redevelopment that would benefit the entire community. Even though the principle of eminent domain is granted to the government in the *U.S. Constitution*'s Fifth Amendment, it should be used only in the most extreme circumstances.

Each of the previous opening paragraphs could be used to begin the synthesis essay demanded of the eminent domain prompt.

— Each introduces the subject and its context.
— Each clearly indicates the writer's position on the issue.

Let's examine these paragraphs.

Sample A clearly states a position in opposition to eminent domain. This writer tries to place his opinion in the context of a generic man and his family. This brief paragraph begins to indicate the writer's voice. By answering the rhetorical question, the writer emphatically declares a position.

Sample B uses personal experience to present an opposing opinion. By placing the general concept of eminent domain in the context of a very personal experience, the reader hears a real voice that defends private property rights with some exceptions.

Sample C presents an objective statement of the subject and its context. There is no indication of the personal in this introduction, and the reader can expect the objectivity to continue as the writer develops his qualifying essay.

Which of these introductory paragraphs is similar to yours? Are there any changes you would make in your opening? If so, what are they?

Developing the Body of the Essay

DO THIS NOW.

— Plan the body of your synthesis essay.

<u>Take a close look at the planning our writer did for this synthesis essay.</u>

> **Position on issue:** qualifying position on eminent domain
>
> **Sources to use:** (Refer to the sources given in the Diagnostic Master exam)

✔ Source A (*U.S. Constitution*)
  Source B (*60 Minutes*)
✔ Source C (*Kelo* decision)
  Source D (Koterba, political cartoon)
✔ Source E (Broder)
  Source F (Britt, political cartoon)
✔ Source G (CNN and American Survey)

Points to make:

1. The *Kelo* decision + the Fifth Amendment = right of eminent domain. Empathize with private property owners.
2. *60 Minutes* interview to support negative idea of what happens when eminent domain takes private property.
3. Get into the idea of the greater good. Use *60 Minutes* interview with the mayor and the Broder points about the need for urban development to help blighted areas.
4. Use the *Washington Times* survey to support my position of leaning toward those who oppose this type of use of eminent domain.

With these points in mind, our writer is now ready to compose the body of the synthesis essay.

Body Paragraph Based on Point 1 (*Kelo* + Fifth Amendment)

Because of this experience, I can empathize with the home owners affected by the recent 5:4 Supreme Court decision *Kelo v. New London* that cited a section of the Fifth Amendment to the *U.S. Constitution* that states, "nor shall private property be taken for public use, without just compensation" (Source A). The Court ruled that New London, Connecticut, was within its constitutional rights to take private property and give it to another private individual in order to further the economic development of the city (Source C).

- Uses a transition to refer to the opening paragraph
- States empathy with those affected by the *Kelo* decision and summarizes both the case and the Fifth Amendment
- Appropriately cites the sources as directed in the prompt

Body Paragraph Based on Point 2 (*60 Minutes* interview + negative attitude)

Contrary to what the Court sees as "permissible public use" (Source C), I believe that a government taking a person's home or business away and allowing another private individual or company to take it over goes against the idea of our private property rights. A good example of this is the situation in Lakewood, Ohio, where the mayor wants to condemn a retired couple's home in order to make way for a privately owned, high-end condominium and shopping mall. As Jim Saleet said in his interview with *60 Minutes*, "The bottom line is this is morally wrong . . . This is our home . . . We're not blighted. . . . This is a close-knit, beautiful neighborhood" (Source B). The Saleets, who have paid off their mortgage, should be allowed to remain there as long as they want and pass it on to their children. Here, individual rights should prevail.

- Uses the transition device of repeating a phrase from the previous paragraph
- Maintains the personal with *I*
- Backs up personal position with the *60 Minutes* interview of the Saleets
- Appropriately cites the sources as directed in the prompt

Body Paragraph on Point 3 (Qualifying + Broder + *60 Minutes* and mayor)

However, I must also take into consideration the need for cities and states to improve troubled urban areas and clear blighted sections with new construction, tax revenues, and jobs (Source E). If governments are blocked from arranging for needed improvements and income, decline of cities and other areas could result. For example, the mayor of Lakewood, Ohio, Madeleine Cain, claims that the city cannot make it without more tax money coming in. As she sees it, Lakewood needs more money to provide required services. "This is about Lakewood's future. Lakewood cannot survive without a strengthened tax base," Mayor Cain told *60 Minutes* (Source B). Here, it sounds like the greater good should prevail.

- Introduces ambivalence with the transitional word "however"
- Uses both the Broder source and the mayor's words from the *60 Minutes* interview to illustrate and support the qualifying position
- Appropriately cites the sources as directed in the prompt

Body Paragraph Based on Point 3 (Qualifying + Broder)

Legal experts disagree about which of the two positions is the better one. Scott Bullock of the Institute for Justice sees the principle of eminent domain as an important one for government planning and building, but not for private development (Source E). On the other hand, John Echeverria, the executive director of the Georgetown Environmental Law and Policy Institute, sees a danger in legislators going to the extreme in the opposite direction and limiting essential powers of government. "The extremist position is a prescription for economic decline for many metropolitan areas around the country" (Source E).

- Transition created by referring to "the two positions"
- Uses the Broder source to give an overview of both sides of the issue
- Appropriately cites the sources as directed in the prompt and names authorities cited in the source material

> *Note:* This is just one example of the many ways this synthesis essay could be planned and developed. The important thing to remember is YOU MUST PLAN BEFORE YOU WRITE.

DO THIS NOW.
Spend about 20 minutes writing the body of your essay. Make certain that your essay follows your plan and that you cite your sources.

Writing the Conclusion

Now that you've written the intro and body paragraphs, you can't just drop your pen or leave your laptop and walk away. You need to end your essay with a final remark. This concluding idea is the last pertinent thought you want your reader to remember.

ATTENTION. ATTENTION. Avoid final paragraphs that are merely summaries. This is not a lengthy, complicated presentation. Your reader can remember what you've said in the previous paragraphs.

DO THIS NOW.
Spend about five minutes quickly writing the concluding paragraph. Keep in mind what you said in your introduction and what you developed as your major points in the body of your essay.

Now, take a look at our three sample conclusions.

In the case of this synthesis essay, you'll recall that our writer wanted to make four major points. The body paragraphs developed three of those ideas. What to do with the fourth: "Use the *Washington Times* survey to support my position of leaning toward those who oppose this type of eminent domain."

Our writer realizes this could be an important source to solidify the qualifying position, and it brings both sides of the argument together.

The decision is made. Use Source G to develop the concluding paragraph. The following are three sample conclusions that make use of the survey.

A

It seems that there is no right position in all circumstances. According to a *Washington Times* survey, 60% of the American public is against local governments having the power to seize private homes and businesses (Source G). However, there may be times when the greater good has to win the toss.

B

Finally, 60% of the responders to a *Washington Times*/CNN survey opposed the right of eminent domain to local governments. Even though this may seem to be the most compelling position on this issue, there are going to be special circumstances when the greater good trumps private ownership.

C

Ultimately, I have to agree with the large majority of people who responded to recent polls conducted by both the *Washington Times* and CNN. When asked if local governments should be able to take over private homes and businesses, over 60% said "no" (Source G). But, I will have to be open to the possibility that public use and the greater good may, in some cases, be the only viable solution to a complicated problem.

Which of these concluding paragraphs is similar to yours? Are there any changes you would make in your ending? If so, what are they?

Sample Synthesis Essay from the Master Exam

The following is the complete essay that our writer developed for the eminent domain synthesis prompt, which is found in the Master exam.

Every time that my grandparents visit, I have to vacate my bedroom so that they can have a room of their own during their visit. It's always a painful few days because I'm locked out of the room that I've decorated, the room that holds all of my things; it's the room that's "mine." As my mother always says, "It's for the good of the family." But, no matter how much I feel deprived, I always know that I'll have it back in a few days. However, the results would be different if she applied the principle of "eminent domain." I would lose my room permanently, and it would be turned into a real guest room. I would not be a happy family member.

Because of this experience, I can empathize with the home owners affected by the recent 5:4 Supreme Court decision *Kelo v. New London* that cited a section of the Fifth Amendment to the *U.S. Constitution* that states, "nor shall private property be taken for public use, without just compensation" (Source A). The Court ruled that New London, Connecticut, was within its constitutional rights to take private property and give it to another private individual in order to further the economic development of the city (Source C).

Contrary to what the Court sees as "permissible public use" (Source C), I believe that a government taking a person's home or business away and allowing another private individual or company to take it over goes against the idea of our private property rights. A good example of this is the situation in Lakewood, Ohio, where the mayor wants to condemn a retired couple's home in order to make way for a privately owned, high-end condominium and shopping mall. As Jim Saleet said in his interview with *60 Minutes*, "The bottom line is this is morally wrong . . . This is our home . . . We're not blighted. . . . This is a close-knit, beautiful neighborhood" (Source B). The Saleets, who have paid off their mortgage, should be allowed to remain there as long as they want and pass it on to their children. Here, individual rights should prevail.

However, I must also take into consideration the need for cities and states to improve troubled urban areas and clear blighted sections with new construction, tax revenues, and jobs (Source E). If governments are blocked from arranging for needed improvements and income, decline of cities and other areas could result. For example, the mayor of Lakewood, Ohio, Madeleine Cain, claims that the city cannot make it without more tax money coming in. As she sees it, Lakewood needs more money to provide required services. "This is about Lakewood's future. Lakewood cannot survive without a strengthened tax base," Mayor Cain told *60 Minutes* (Source B). Here, it sounds like the greater good should prevail.

Legal experts disagree about which of the two positions is the better one. Scott Bullock of the Institute for Justice sees the principle of eminent domain as an important one for government planning and building, but not for private development (Source E). On the other hand, John Echeverria, the executive director of the Georgetown Environmental Law and Policy Institute, sees a danger in legislators going to the extreme in the opposite direction and limiting essential powers of government. "The extremist position is a prescription for economic decline for many metropolitan areas around the country" (Source E).

Ultimately, I have to agree with the large majority of people who responded to recent polls conducted by both the *Washington Times* and CNN. When asked if local governments should be able to take over private homes and businesses, over 60% said "no" (Source G). But, I will have to be open to the possibility that public use and the greater good may, in some cases, be the only viable solution to a complicated problem.

Rubric for Eminent Domain Synthesis Essay

A **9** essay has all the qualities of an 8 essay, and the <u>writing style</u> is especially <u>impressive</u>, as is the analysis and integration of the specifics related to eminent domain and the given sources.

An **8** essay <u>effectively</u> and <u>cohesively</u> addresses the prompt. It clearly takes a position on eminent domain and supports the argument using carefully integrated and appropriate evidence, including at least three of the given sources. The essay will also show the writer's <u>ability to control language</u>.

A **7** essay has all the properties of a 6 essay, only with a <u>more complete</u>, well-developed, and integrated argument or a more mature writing style.

A **6** essay <u>adequately</u> addresses the prompt. The argument is on eminent domain and integrates, as well as makes use of, appropriate evidence, including at least three references from the given sources. These elements are less fully integrated and/or developed than scores in the 7, 8, or 9 range. The writer's ideas are expressed with clarity, but the writing may have a few errors in syntax and/or diction.

A **5** essay demonstrates that the writer <u>understands the prompt</u>. The argument/claim/position about eminent domain is generally understandable, but the development and/or integration of appropriate evidence and at least three of the given sources are limited or uneven. The writer's ideas are expressed clearly with a few errors in syntax or diction.

A **4** essay is <u>not an adequate response</u> to the prompt. The writer's argument indicates a misunderstanding, an oversimplification, or a misrepresentation of the assigned task. The writer may use evidence that is inappropriate or insufficient to support the argument or may use fewer than three of the given sources. The writing presents the writer's ideas, but may indicate immaturity of style and control.

A **3** essay is a lower 4 because it is <u>even less effective</u> in addressing the question. It is also less mature in its syntax and organization.

A **2** essay indicates <u>little success in speaking to the prompt</u>. The writer may misread the question, only summarize the given sources, fail to develop the required argument, or simply ignore the prompt and write about another topic. The writing may also lack organization and control of language and syntax. (***Note:*** **No matter how well written, a summary will never rate more than a 2.**)

A **1** essay is a lower 2 because it is even <u>more simplistic</u>, <u>disorganized</u>, and <u>lacking in control of language</u>.

Sample Student Essays

Student A

Eminent domain. Two little words that strike fear in the hearts of homeowners all over the country. But what exactly is it anyway? Eminent domain is the power of the government to take privately owned property away for "public use" as long as the original owners are given "fair" compensation for it. (Source A) However, the more the government exercises this power given to it by the Fifth Amendment, the more the public feels the need to curtail it.

I agree with those opposing this governmental sledge hammer. My parents own their own house and have spent much of their lives paying off the mortgage, and now it is finally ours. I would never want to give it away—just compensation or not. The same appears to be true for Jim and Joanne Saleet who live in Lakewood, Ohio, who in a *60 Minutes* interview described their feelings about their mayor, Madeleine Cain, deciding to invoke this right of eminent domain. The mayor's reason for seizing this house that the Saleets "plan to spend the rest of their days [in] and pass on to their grandchildren" is not to build a needed highway or a hospital. NO, it is to build a high-end shopping mall (Source B). This is hardly justifiable—the neighborhood being seized is just your basic middle class suburbia—much like the house you most likely live in. Much like the house 80% of America lives in. 2

Since the Saleets, their neighbors in Scenic Park don't want to leave, the mayor has labeled Scenic Park, ironically enough, as "blighted." This has created a negative picture of the area in the public's mind. Jim Saleet told *60 Minutes*, "You don't know how humiliating this is to have people tell you, 'You live in a blighted area,' and how degrading this is. . . . This is an area that we absolutely love." (Source B) The intent of the new classier condos and mall is to raise Lakewood's property tax revenues, but so far, by calling the area "blighted," all they have done is to lower the reputation of Scenic Park. As Mr. Saleet said, "This is morally wrong, what they're doing here. This is our home." (Source B) 3

Some might say, "Well, this is just one small town example with just one guy's opinion." This is hardly so. In a CNN commissioned survey of 177,987 voters, 66% of those who responded said that local government should never be able to seize homes and businesses. Only 33% said it should be permitted for public use, and only a measly 1% voted to allow eminent domain for private economic development. (Source G) 4

Cities have claimed that invoking the right of eminent domain is being done to further "the greater good." And, yet, as the CNN survey shows, the masses who are supposedly benefiting from it either are not feeling this greater good or just plain don't appreciate it. In either case, something tells me that if most people are not happy about a situation something ought to be done about it. (We are still living in a democracy aren't we?) 5

Some have tried to stop it. But, the Supreme Court ruled on February 22, 2005, in the case of *Kelo v. City of New London* that "the governmental taking of property from one private owner to give to another in furtherance of economic development constitutes a permissible 'public use' under the Fifth Amendment." (Source C) This decision not only went against what the vast majority of the public feels, but it also was made with a very narrow margin of 5:4. This is because the Fifth Amendment doesn't state any specifics regarding what public use is, only that the owner of the property seized must be duly compensated. 6

The Supreme Court's narrow margin of votes demonstrates how heavily disputed this topic is. The public feels that their individual rights are being infringed upon—and I'm on their side. 7

Student B

The debate over government's authority over private property and the seizing of it   1
has been heard ever since the creation of the Constitution. For over two hundred years,
both federal and local governments alike have been taking private property for public use
(with compensation): a power known as eminent domain. While government officials
have used this right to help build public services such as roads and railroad tracks, they
have also used this power under the label of "economic development" to benefit private
corporations that build these projects.

Government should be allowed to take private property only for the creation   2
of public goods and services. This right is stated in the Fifth Amendment of the
Constitution, which deals with the issue of private property rights (Source A). However,
the term "public use" is ambiguous and is open for much interpretation. Eminent
domain should be used to build services like roads and schools. As the nation grows, and
new economic centers develop, there is a need for the creation of new roads. The land
for these roads needs to be taken from somewhere, and often times the only option is to
take land from private owners. A similar situation arises when towns need to build new
schools because of growing population pressures. Scott G. Bullock of the Institute for
Justice concurs when he says, "It [eminent domain] has an important but limited role in
government planning and the building of roads, parks, and public buildings" (Source E).

Although the Supreme Court in *Kelo v. New London* ruled that eminent domain can   3
be used to seize private property to sell to private buyers for economic development that
would benefit a needy area (Source C), the results of this power can cause unnecessary
displacement and pain for the individuals whose homes are part of this "buy out." The
Saleets of Lakewood, Ohio, present one example of this situation. This couple has been
living in their home for 38 years and feels that the government is morally wrong in trying
to evict them from their house in order to create high priced condos and shopping malls.
The area in question is not a run down locale; therefore, it doesn't need renovation. The
mayor of Lakewood claims the city needs money, and that the "area can be used for a
higher and better use" (Source B).

However, it can also be argued that there is always room for improvement when   4
it comes to the use of land, especially because of the ever changing needs and desires
of people and governments. The United States was built on the principle of capitalism
and private enterprise. It is not run with a planned economy as communist nations are.
Therefore, the economy should be allowed to take its own course without government
interference. The invisible hand of the free market guiding the economy has led and will
continue to lead to better outcomes for the entire society.

Additionally, because the government is run by the people and for the benefit of   5
the people, the public's opinion should be taken into consideration. In a recent CNN
poll, only 1% indicated that it affirms the right of eminent domain for private economic
development. While the poll doesn't display everyone's opinion, it is a good indicator of
the attitudes of American citizens (Source G).

Clearly, eminent domain shouldn't be invoked for economic development by private   6
developers. It should be limited to the construction of public services. However, this
debate over property rights, and in a sense, individual rights versus the greater good,
will continue for years to come as the conditions and outlooks of the American people
change.

Rating the Essays

Student A

This is a high-range essay for the following reasons:

- Opening forcefully catches the reader's attention and immediately identifies the subject
- Brings the reader into the conversation with the rhetorical question
- Presents a brief overview of both sides of the debate
- Integrates sources smoothly into the text of the essay
- Uses proper citations
- Utilizes transitions
- Exhibits control of language, for example: parallel structure, punctuation, parenthetical statements, and diction
- Recognizes the opposite position—"Some might say . . ."
- Employs irony to comment on textual material
- Incorporates not only sources, but also provides pertinent comments to develop the argument
- Presents a succinct and straightforward final point
- Presents a true voice

Student B

This is a mid-range essay for the following reasons:

- Clearly takes a position on the issue
- Uses appropriate evidence
- Clearly incorporates sources into the text
- Cites the opposition (paragraph 4)
- Presents a personal opinion (paragraph 4)
- Develops a clear organizational pattern
- Uses good transitions
- Develops a final paragraph that makes a clear statement
- Uses a matter-of-fact voice
- Accomplishes the task demanded by the prompt

Rapid Review

- Read ALL information in the prompt.
- Carefully read and annotate the prompt and the given texts.
- Choose your position on the issue.
- Choose suitable texts from among those given to support your position (choose at least three).
- Plan your essay.
- Write your essay in the allotted time.
- Check your essay to make certain you have cited your sources.
- Proofread.

STEP 4

Review the Knowledge You Need to Score High

CHAPTER **8**   Comprehensive Review—Analysis

CHAPTER **9**   Comprehensive Review—Argument

CHAPTER **10** Comprehensive Review—Synthesis

CHAPTER 8

Comprehensive Review—Analysis

IN THIS CHAPTER

Summary: Examine structure, purpose, and style as evidenced in the modes of discourse.

Key Ideas

✪ Learn the language of analysis and how to use it.

✪ Acquaint yourself with rhetorical strategies.

✪ Learn how selection of detail, subject matter, diction, and syntax contribute to style.

✪ Learn how topic adherence and connective tissue unify your essay.

✪ Understand the difference between active and passive voice.

Some Basics

What Is ANALYSIS?

For the AP English Language exam student, the definition of *analysis* is quite specific. It means that *you* are going to take apart a particular passage and divide it into its basic components for the purpose of examining how the writer develops his or her subject.

Are There Different Types of Analysis?

For the AP English Language exam, the *different types of analysis* include the analysis of structure, purpose, and style.

What Is *DISCOURSE*?

Discourse simply means "conversation." For the writer, this "conversation" takes place between the text and the reader. To communicate with the reader, the writer uses a particular method or combination of methods to make his or her idea(s) clear to the reader.

What Is *RHETORIC*?

Don't let professional jargon throw you. Rhetoric is basically an umbrella term for *all* of the strategies, modes, and devices a writer can employ to allow the reader to easily accept and understand his or her point of view.

What Is a *MODE OF DISCOURSE*?

Here's another piece of the lingo puzzle that you need not fear. Prose can be divided into FOUR primary categories. They are:

1. EXPOSITION: illustrates a point
2. NARRATION: tells a story
3. DESCRIPTION: creates a sensory image
4. ARGUMENTATION: takes a position on an issue and defends it

These are generally referred to as the *modes of discourse.* You should be able to distinguish among them but, do not become bogged down in worrying about these classes. They will be obvious to you. Being familiar with the professional terminology of this course is a way of beginning to develop a common vocabulary needed to discuss writing.

What Are *RHETORICAL STRATEGIES*?

Rhetorical strategies include example, contrast and comparison, definition, cause and effect, process, analysis/division, and classification. The writer may also employ descriptive and narrative strategies. These are the basic approaches a writer uses to tell a story, explain a point, describe a situation, or argue a position. (Modes of discourse, for those in the know.)

What Is the Analysis of *RHETORICAL STRUCTURE*?

Regardless of the length of a passage, the writer will employ one or more strategies to develop the purpose of the piece. Your job is to:

- Carefully read the passage
- Recognize and identify strategies used in the passage
- Determine how these strategies are utilized in the development of the author's purpose

> After this, it is up to you to use your own rhetorical strategies to present the points you want to illustrate in your analysis. Remember, your primary purpose is to analyze the passage. In so doing, you will probably employ one or more of the rhetorical strategies, such as example, cause and effect, or contrast and comparison.

There Is So Much to Know, How Can I Prepare Myself for the Exam?

First, don't panic. You're in an AP English Language course, and you will have a year to become prepared. The work of this course centers on developing those analytical skills required by the AP English Language exam. In this chapter, we are going to provide you with a brief overview of the different rhetorical strategies. For each rhetorical strategy, we will do the following:

- define the term;
- cite examples;
- provide practice with analysis; and
- offer suggestions for writing your own AP essays using that strategy.

Rhetorical Strategies

Example

Definition: <u>Example</u> is a specific event, person, or detail of an idea cited and/or developed to support or illustrate a thesis or topic.

Here is an excerpt from Jane Jacobs's "A Good Neighborhood" that uses examples.

> *Perhaps I can best explain this subtle but all-important balance between people's desire for essential privacy and their wish to have differing degrees of contact with people in terms of the stores where people leave keys for their friends. In our family, we tell friends to pick up the key at the delicatessen across the street. Joe Cornacchia, who keeps the delicatessen, usually has a dozen or so keys at a time for handing out like this. He has a special drawer for them.*
>
> *Around on the other side of our block, people leave their keys at a Spanish grocery. On the other side of Joe's block, people leave them at a candy store. Down a block they leave them at the coffee shop, and a few hundred feet around the corner from that, in a barber shop. Around one corner from two fashionable blocks of town houses and apartments in the Upper East Side, people leave their keys in a butcher shop and a bookshop; around another corner they leave them in a cleaner's and a drug store. In unfashionable East Harlem, keys are left with at least one florist, in bakeries, in luncheonettes, in Spanish and Italian groceries.*

Practice with Analysis

1. Underline the thesis statement.

2. The topic/subject of the passage is _____.

3. The purpose of the passage is to ____ inform ____ persuade ____ entertain.

4. Does the passage contain an extended example? _____

5. The passage contains how many examples? _____

6. Briefly list the examples. _____

7. The organization is ____ chronological ____ spatial ____ least to most important ____ most to least important.

Remarks About the Passage

This informative passage uses a lengthy list of examples to indicate informally the relationship between people and businesses in a neighborhood. There is no single extended example, but rather a series of more than eight examples.

It's a good idea to actually mark up the passage as you answer the analysis questions. It will give you practice and help this process to become second nature to you.

Contrast/Comparison

Definition: <u>Contrast/comparison</u> is a method of presenting similarities and differences between or among at least two persons, places, things, ideas, etc. The contrast/comparison essay may be organized in several ways including:

- Subject by subject—Subject A is discussed in its entirety and is followed by a full discussion of Subject B.
- Point by point—A major point related to Subject A is examined and is immediately followed with a corresponding point in Subject B.
- Combination—In a longer essay, the writer may employ both of the preceding strategies.

Here is an example of a passage that uses contrast/comparison from W. H. Auden's "Work, Labor, and Play."

> *Between labor and play stands work. A man is a worker if he is personally interested in the job which society pays him to do; and that which society views as necessary labor, is from his own point of view voluntary play. Whether a job is to be classified as labor or work depends, not on the job itself, but on the tastes of the individual who undertakes it. The difference does not, for example, coincide with the difference between a manual and a mental job; a gardener or a cobbler may be a worker; a bank clerk, a laborer. Which a man is can be seen from his attitude toward leisure. To a worker, leisure means simply the hours he needs to relax and rest in order to work efficiently. He is therefore more likely to take too little leisure than too much; workers die of coronaries and forget their wives' birthdays. To the laborer, on the other hand, leisure means freedom from compulsion, so that it is natural for him to imagine that the fewer hours he has to spend laboring, the more hours he is free to play, the better.*

Practice with Analysis

1. The topic/subject of the passage is _____.

2. Underline the thesis statement.

3. The purpose of the passage is to ____ inform ____ persuade ____ entertain.

4. The items being compared/contrasted are _____.

5. One example of a comparison in the passage is _____.

6. One example of contrast in the passage is _____.

7. The pattern of development is ____ opposing ____ alternating.

8. The organization is ____ subject to subject ____ point by point ____ combination.

Remarks About the Passage

As with most of your AP contrast/comparison selections, the emphasis is on distinction and contrast. In this passage, the author uses a pattern of alternating points that develops the contrast between work, labor, and leisure.

Cause and Effect

Definition: <u>Cause and effect</u> establishes a relationship: B is the result of A. The cause-and-effect essay can emphasize the cause or the effect, or can treat both equally. It can detail a single cause with many effects, or several causes with a single effect, or any combination.

The organization can present the cause or the effect first. All of this depends upon the intent of the writer. Depending on his or her purpose, the writer can choose to present the most important idea in the beginning, middle, or end. The author can also choose from myriad strategies to develop the cause and effect, such as:

- facts
- statistics
- authorities
- anecdotes
- cases
- real or imagined scenarios

It should be noted that, in some cases, the successful writer of a cause-and-effect essay anticipates and addresses reader objections and/or questions.

Here is an example of a passage using cause and effect from Thomas Hobbes's "Of the Natural Condition of Mankind" (1651).

> *From this equality of ability arises equality of hope in the attaining of our ends. And therefore if any two men desire the same thing, which nevertheless they cannot both enjoy, they become enemies; and in the way to their end (which is principally their own conservation, and sometimes their delectation only), endeavor to destroy or subdue one another. And from hence it comes to pass that where an invader has no more fear than another man's single power, if one plant, sow, build, or possess a convenient seat, others may probably be expected to come prepared with forces united to dispossess and deprive him, not only of the fruit of his labor, but also of his life, or liberty. And the invader again is in like danger of another.*

Practice with Analysis

1. Underline the thesis statement.

2. The topic/subject of the passage is _____.

3. The purpose of the passage is to ____ inform ____ persuade ____ entertain.

4. List the causes. _____

5. List the effects. _____

6. The emphasis is on ____ cause ____ effect ____ causes ____ effects.

7. The passage makes use of ____ statistics ____ facts ____ authorities ____ anecdotes ____ cases ____ real/imaginary scenarios.

Remarks About the Passage

The entire focus of this paragraph is on the singular result of one person's envy for the possessions of another. If both cannot possess it, envy ensues, which leads to dispossession and/or violence.

Classification

Definition: <u>Classification</u> separates items into major categories and details the characteristics of each group and why each member of that group is placed within the category. It is possible to divide the categories into subgroups. The principle of classification should be made clear to the reader. (This is the umbrella term under which everything fits.)

Here is a passage that makes use of classification from Jane Howard's "All Happy Clans Are Alike."

> . . . *If blood and roots don't do the job, then we must look to water and branches, and sort ourselves into new constellations, new families.*
>
> *These new families, to borrow the terminology of an African tribe (the Bangwa of the Cameroons), may consist either of friends of the road, ascribed by chance, or friends of the heart, achieved by choice. Ascribed friends are those we happen to go to school with, work with, or live near. They know where we went last weekend and whether we still have a cold. Just being around gives them a provisional importance in our lives, and us in theirs. Maybe they will still matter to us when we or they move away; quite likely they won't. Six months or two years will probably erase each from the other's thoughts, unless by some chance they and we have become friends of the heart . . . [Those] will steer each other through enough seasons and weathers so that sooner or later it crosses our minds that one of us . . . must one day mourn the other.*

Practice with Analysis

1. The topic/subject of the passage is _____.

2. Underline the thesis statement.

3. The purpose of the passage is to ____ inform ____ persuade ____ entertain.

4. Identify the principle of division/classification. _____

5. List the main subgroups. _____

6. Cite the major characteristic(s) of each subgroup. _____

Remarks About the Passage

This passage briefly details two classes of friends, one by chance and the other by choice. The thesis given at the beginning of the excerpt is stated in general terms that lead the reader to the specific classifications.

Process

Definition: <u>Process</u> is simply "how to" do something or how something's done. Process can have one of two purposes. It can either give instructions or inform the reader about how something is done. It is important to understand that a clear process presentation must be in chronological order. In other words, the writer leads the reader step by step, from beginning to end, through the process. A clear process essay will define necessary terms and will cite any precautions if needed.

Here is a passage that makes use of process from L. Rust Hills's "How to Care for and About Ashtrays."

> *To clean ashtrays the right way, proceed as follows. Take a metal or plastic or wooden (but never a basket) wastebasket in your left hand, and a paper towel in your right. Approach the ashtray that is to be cleaned. Put the wastebasket down on the floor, and with your released left hand pick up the ashtray and dump its contents of cigarette ends, spent matches, and loose ashes (nothing else should be in an ashtray!) into the wastebasket. Then, still holding the ashtray over the basket, rub gently with the paper towel at any of the few stains or spots that may remain. Then put the ashtray carefully back into its place, pick up the wastebasket again, and approach the next ashtray to be cleaned. It should never be necessary to wash an ashtray, if it is kept clean and*

dry. Throughout its whole lifetime in a well-ordered household, an ashtray need never travel more than three feet from where it belongs, and never be out of place at all for more than thirty seconds.

Practice with Analysis

1. Underline the thesis.

2. What is the topic/subject? _____

3. The purpose is to ___ give specific directions ___ be informative.

4. List the major steps given in the selection. _____

5. Is the essay in chronological order? ___ yes ___ no

6. List any words that are defined. _____

7. Were there any other words that should have been defined? _____
_____

8. List any precautions given. _____

9. The process presented is ___ clear ___ unclear ___ complete ___ incomplete.

Remarks About the Passage

The formal tone of such a menial process makes this small paragraph a bit humorous. Its clearly developed ashtray cleaning process is quite complete and needs no added definitions nor precautions.

Definition

Definition: Definition identifies the class to which a specific term belongs and those characteristics which make it different from all the other items in that class. There are several types of definitions: physical, historical, emotional, psychological, and relationship(s) to others.

An essay of definition can be developed using any of the rhetorical strategies, and the writer should decide whether to be serious or humorous.

Here is a passage that uses definition.

BUGDUST

The dinner was fine, the play funny; let's hope my drive home will easily top off a relaxing and rewarding evening. What a surprise! Brightly perched on my car's windshield is a yellow ticket which not so brightly announces that I am being fined $50.00 for an expired parking meter. Grabbing the thing and choking it, I exclaim, "Bugdust!"

Now, let's be honest. This ticket is neither an insect, nor is it dirt. So, am I blind, ignorant or just plain crazy? I hope none of the above. The expletive, "Bugdust," is my personal substitute for the ever-popular, overused and vulgar, four letter curses. My background forces me to avoid these common, rude and inappropriate four letter words. And, heaven only knows that over the years I've had many occasions where I would have loved to use them. For much of my young life, when I found myself in a situation which cried out for some sort of exclamation, I usually reverted to RATS! or CRUMB! Really harsh curses, huh? However, years ago I came upon a substitute by sheer accident.

I was helping out in the kitchen at my sorority house. While chopping onions, I accidentally slipped and cut my thumb quite badly. I really needed a way to express my surprise, pain, and fear. Nothing inside my head would allow me to scream the usual expletives words. (By the way, I sincerely believe that a good deal of money spent on psychotherapy could have been saved had I been able to "just say IT.") In that nanosecond, I wanted, I demanded that my mind come up with something—anything—that I could use. My mind obviously obeyed and began working at a frantic pace. "I hate insects; I hate housework." My mind works in strange ways; it's really warped. (Hmm, that's a word I should also define.) Put two abominable conditions together. Voila! Murf's rule = one new expression = BUGDUST. What a mind!

The people around me during the birth of this little word-gem said, "What the *@#?! does that mean?" I had to stop for a second. They were right. What did it mean? It was not the incinerated remains of a roach colony. It was not the unkempt environs of a roach motel. It was a way for me to say that I was monumentally angry. It was also a way for me to say I was hurting. It was original and ME.

Years have passed. And, so today . . .

It's 15°; it's snowing and icy; I'm cold. Let's shop. I join the rest of the universe at the supermarket. Heaven only knows one needs rice crispy treats in the house when it snows. What I don't need is the keys locked in my car. BUGDUST!

I'm doing 7 mph behind a 1965 Volkswagen Beetle being driven by its original owner. I miss the green light. I'm late for my dental appointment. BUGDUST!

And, into cyberspace . . . My computer just crashed. BUGDUST!

Practice with Analysis

1. Underline the thesis.

2. The topic/subject is _____.

3. The purpose is to ____ inform ____ persuade ____ entertain.

4. The attitude of the writer is ____ serious ____ humorous.

5. To what class does the word being defined belong? _____

6. List the major rhetorical strategies used. _____

7. The definition is ____ historical ____ physical ____ emotional ____ psychological ____ relationship(s) to others.

8. Do you, as a reader, have an understanding of the definition presented? _____

9. Briefly state your understanding of the term. _____

Remarks About the Passage

The topic of the essay is the definition of the expletive *bugdust*. The thesis is the fifth sentence of the second paragraph. The primary purpose is to inform using humor. The rhetorical strategies used throughout the essay are example [paragraph 1] and anecdote [paragraphs 3 and 4]. The definition of *bugdust* is primarily emotional [last two sentences in paragraph 3 and the last two sentences in paragraph 4].

Now it's your turn. Write a paragraph that defines a favorite word that is special or unique to you or your friends or family. Choose an attitude and go for it. When finished, ask yourself the same analytical questions you asked for the sample essay.

Narration

Definition: <u>Narration</u> is nothing more than storytelling. There is a beginning, a middle, and an end. Moreover, there's a point to it—a reason for recounting the story that becomes clear to the reader. There should be a focus to the story as well. For example, your point might be that lying gets you into trouble. To illustrate this, you might focus on an anecdote about the repercussions of a specific lie you told your parents. Narration requires a specific point of view, such as:

- 1st person
- 3rd person omniscient
- 3rd person objective
- Stream of consciousness

A narrative generally revolves around a primary tension and employs character, plot, and setting. The point the author is trying to make corresponds to the literary term *theme*. The development of a narrative may be extended and fully developed or brief to support or illustrate the subject of an essay.

The following excerpt from "Death of a Soldier" by Louisa May Alcott is an example of a narrative.

> *John was dying. Even while he spoke, over his face I saw a gray veil falling that no human hand can lift. I sat down by him, wiped drops from his forehead, stirred the air about him with a slow wave of a fan, and waited to help him die. For hours he suffered dumbly, without a moment's murmuring: his limbs grew cold, his face damp, his lips white, and again and again he tore the covering off his breast, as if the lightest weight added to his agony.*
>
> *One by one, the other men woke, and round the hospital ward appeared a circle of pale faces and watchful eyes, full of awe and pity; for, though a stranger, John was beloved by all. "Old boy, how are you?" faltered one. "Can I say or do anything for you anywheres?" whispered another.*
>
> *"Take my things home, and tell them that I did my best."*

Practice with Analysis

1. The topic/subject is _____.

2. The purpose is to ____ inform ____ persuade ____ entertain.

3. The focus is _____.

4. The point of view is ____ first person ____ third person objective ____ third person omniscient ____ stream of consciousness.

5. The setting is _____.

6. The main character(s) is/are _____.

7. The gist of the plot is _____.

8. List the sequence of the major events (beginning, middle, end)

_____

_____

Remarks About the Passage

This brief excerpt is enough of a story to allow you to identify the basic narrative elements. Employing the first person point of view, Alcott provides a beginning, middle, and ending to this episode that occurs in a hospital ward. Focusing on the boy's death, the author illustrates the quality of John's character.

Description

Definition: <u>Description</u> is writing that appeals to the senses. It can be objective, which is scientific or clinical, or it can be impressionistic, which tries to involve the reader's emotions or feelings. Description can also be direct or indirect, and the organization can be as follows:

- Chronological
- Spatial
- Emphasizing the most important detail
- Emphasizing the most noticeable detail

To create his or her description, the writer can employ any or all of the following literary devices:

- Analogy
- Concrete, specific words
- Appeal to the senses
- Personification
- Hyperbole
- Contrast and comparison
- Onomatopoeia
- Other figurative language

The following excerpt from Charles Dickens's *Bleak House* uses description.

> *Fog everywhere. Fog up the river, where it flows among green aits and meadows; fog down the river, where it rolls defiled among tiers of shipping and waterside pollutions of a great (and dirty) city. Fog on the Essex marshes, fog on the heights, fog creeping into the cabooses of [coal barges]. Fog lying out on the yards, and hovering in the rigging of great ships; fog drooping on the gunwales of barges and small boats. Fog in the eyes and throats of ancient Greenwich pensioners, wheezing by the firesides of their wards; fog in the stem and bowl of the afternoon pipe of the wrathful skipper, down in his close cabin; fog cruelly pinching the toes and fingers of his shivering little 'prentice boy on deck. Chance people on the bridges peeping over the parapets into a nether sky of fog, with fog all round them, as if they were up in a balloon, and hanging in the misty clouds.*

Practice with Analysis

1. Underline the thesis.

2. The topic/subject of the passage is _____.

3. The description is ____ objective ____ impressionistic.

4. The passage contains examples of

   - ____ analogy, ex. _____
   - ____ concrete words, ex. _____

- ____ imagery, ex. _____
- ____ contrast/comparison, ex. _____
- ____ personification, ex. _____
- ____ onomatopoeia, ex. _____
- ____ other figurative language, ex. _____

5. The intended effect is to ____ inform ____ persuade ____ entertain.

Remarks About the Passage

In its appeal to the senses, this loaded passage about fog contains about every descriptive device possible to re-create the almost palpable scene for the reader.

About Style

What Is Style?

Ask yourself a question—What is the difference between the comedy of Bill Cosby and Eddie Murphy? We would all agree that they are both funny, but we would also say that each man has his own style. What makes Cosby's comedy different from Murphy's? Consider the following:

- Subject matter
- Language (diction)
- Pacing
- Selection of detail
- Presentation—body language
- Attitude toward his material
- Attitude toward his audience

   This is what we call style. You do this all the time. You know Jennifer Lopez has a different style than does Barbra Streisand.

   If we were to give you two literary passages, you could probably tell which was written by Hemingway and which was written by Dickens. How would you know? Simple; you would use the same principles you considered with the two comedians:

- Subject matter
- Selection of detail
- Point of view
- Diction
- Figurative language/imagery
- Attitude
- Tone
- Pacing/syntax
- Organization

   See how easy it is? The AP English Language and Composition exam expects you to be able to recognize and to explain how these elements function in a given passage.

How Do I Talk About Style?

You need to understand and to refer to some basic writing terms and devices. These include subject matter, selection of detail, organization, point of view, diction, syntax, language, attitude, and tone.

What follows is a brief review of each of these *elements of style*. In this review, we define each device, cite examples, and provide practice for you. (In addition, we have incorporated suggested readings and writing for you.)

Subject Matter and Selection of Detail

Since these two are dependent on each other, let's look at them together. Unlike the poor, beleaguered AP Comp student who is assigned a topic, each author makes a conscious decision about what he or she will write. (In most instances, so do you.) It is not hit or miss. The author wants to make a point about his or her subject and makes numerous conscious decisions about which details to include and which to exclude. Here's an example. Two students are asked to write about hamburgers. One is a vegetarian, and one is a hamburger fanatic. You've already mentally categorized the details each would choose to include in making his or her points about hamburgers. Got it? <u>Selection of detail is part of style.</u>

Note: Many authors become associated with a particular type of subject matter: for example, Mario Puzo with organized crime (*The Godfather*), Steven King with horror and suspense (*The Shining*), Upton Sinclair with muckraking (*The Jungle*). This, then, becomes part of their recognized style.

Think about a couple of your favorite writers, rock groups, singers, comedians, and so on and list their primary subjects and selection of details.

Organization

The way in which a writer presents his or her ideas to the reader is termed *organization*. You do this every day. For example, look at your locker. How are your books, jacket, gym clothes, lunch, and other things arranged in it? If someone else were to open it, what conclusion would that person draw about you? This is your personal organization. The same can apply to a writer and his or her work. Let's review a few favorite patterns of organization.

Writers can organize their thoughts in many different ways, including:

- Chronological
- Spatial
- Specific to general
- General to specific
- Least to most important
- Most to least important
- Flashback or fast-forward
- Contrast/comparison
- Cause/effect

As with your locker, an outside viewer—known here as the reader—responds to the writer's organizational patterns. Keep these approaches in mind when analyzing style. (You might want to make marginal notes on some of your readings as practice.)

Point of View

Point of view is the method the author utilizes to tell the story. It is the vantage point from which the narrative is told. You've had practice with this in both reading and writing.

- *First person:* The narrator is the story's protagonist. (I went to the store.)
Here is an example from Charles Dickens's *The Personal History of David Copperfield*.

  Whether I shall turn out to be the hero of my own life, or whether that station will be held by anybody else, these pages must show. To begin my life with the beginning of my life, I record that I was born (as I have been informed and believe) on a Friday, at twelve o'clock at night. It was remarked that the clock began to strike, and I began to cry, simultaneously.

- *Third person objective:* The narrator is an onlooker reporting the story. (She went to the store.)
  Here is an example from Sinclair Lewis's *Elmer Gantry*.

  Elmer Gantry was drunk. He was eloquently drunk, lovingly and pugnaciously drunk. He leaned against the bar of the Old Home Sample Room, the most gilded and urbane saloon in Cato, Missouri, and requested the bartender to join him in "The Good Old Summer time," the waltz of the day.

- *Third person omniscient:* The narrator reports the story and provides information that the character(s) is unaware of. (She went to the store unaware that in three minutes she would meet her unknown mother selling apples on the corner.)
  Here is an example from Evan S. Connell's *Mrs. Bridge*.

  Her first name was India—she was never able to get used to it. It seemed to her that her parents must have been thinking of someone else when they named her. Or were they hoping for another sort of daughter? As a child she was often on the point of inquiring, but time passed, and she never did.

- *Stream of consciousness:* This is a narrative technique that places the reader in the mind and thought process of the narrator, no matter how random and spontaneous that may be (e.g., James Joyce's *Ulysses*).
  Here is an example from William Faulkner's *As I Lay Dying*.

  I dont know what I am. I dont know if I am or not. Jewel knows who he is, because he does not know that he does not know whether he is or not. He cannot empty himself because he is not what he is and he is what he is not. Beyond the unlamped wall I can hear the rain shaping the wagon that is ours . . . And then I must be, or I could not empty myself for sleep in a strange room. And so if I am not emptied yet, I am is.

- *Chorus:* Ancient Greek plays employed a chorus as a narrative device. The chorus, as needed, could be a character, an assembly, the playwright's voice, the audience, or an omniscient forecaster.
- *Stage manager:* This technique utilizes a character who comments omnisciently (e.g., *Our Town*, *The Glass Menagerie*).
- *Interior monologue:* This technique reflects the inner thoughts of the character.
  Here is an example from Christopher Isherwood's *Goodbye to Berlin*.

  I am a camera with its shutter open, quite passive, recording, not thinking. Recording the man shaving at the window opposite and the woman in the kimono washing her hair. Some day, all this will have to be developed, carefully printed, fixed.

Diction

Diction, also termed *word choice*, refers to the conscious selection of words to further the author's purpose. Once again, place yourself in the writer's position. How would you describe your date last weekend to your parents? Your peers? Yourself? We're guessing you used different words (and selection of details) for each audience. And, may we say, "good choice."

That personal note out of the way, a writer searches for the most appropriate, evocative, or precise word or phrase to convey his or her intent. The author is sensitive to denotation, connotation, and symbolic aspects of language choices.

For example, let's look at **"The evening invaded the street."** Here James Joyce chooses a strong verb to express his thought. What do you associate with this word? Does it affect you? What if he had said, "The evening caressed the street?" Diction makes a difference. (By the way, the first example is from "Eveline," which is a story about a character's personal war with herself.)

Diction is placing the right word in the right place. It is a deliberate technique to further the author's purpose or intent. Diction builds throughout a piece so that ideas, tone, or attitude are continually reinforced. You should be able to identify and link examples of specific diction to the ideas, purpose, tone, or intent of the passage.

Let's Try Another

Here is the bare-bones sentence outline of a paragraph.

> *She heard the story and accepted its significance. She wept in her sister's arms. She went to her room alone.*

Here is how Kate Chopin actually wrote her paragraph in "The Story of an Hour":

> *She did not hear the story as many women have heard the same, with a paralyzed inability to accept its significance. She wept at once, with sudden, wild abandonment in her sister's arms. When the storm had spent itself she went away to her room alone. She would have no one follow her.*

Now, you highlight those changes in words/phrases which transform the whole tone of the passage.

In this brief paragraph that describes Louise's reaction to the news of her husband's death, we can easily see diction at work. The first and last lines use a negative word to establish her separation from other women. The adjective *paralyzed* is also contrasted with Louise's *sudden, wild abandonment*. The *storm* of grief is *spent*—as are her emotional responses. She is going *away* to be *alone* with herself.

See how the diction enriches the paragraph. Here, the reader begins to get a feeling for Louise's unique character.

> When writing your essay write, "Diction IS . . . " or "An example of Salinger's diction IS. . . ." Avoid saying, "Salinger *uses* diction." It is a little point, but it is one that indicates a mature writer is at work.

Figurative Language and Imagery

Imagery is the written creation of sensory experience achieved through the use of figurative language. Figurative language includes the following:

- Analogy
- Sensory description
- Poetic devices, which include:
  — metaphor
  — simile
  — hyperbole
  — onomatopoeia

— personification
— oxymoron
— metonymy
— synecdoche
— alliteration
— assonance
— consonance

As an example, here is a passage excerpted from Herman Melville's "Nantucket."

> *And thus have these naked Nantucketers, these sea hermits, issuing from their ant-hill in the sea, overrun and conquered the watery world like so many Alexanders; parceling out among them the Atlantic, Pacific, and Indian oceans, as the three pirate powers did Poland. Let America add Mexico to Texas, and pile Cuba upon Canada; let the English overswarm all India, and hang out their blazing banner from the sun; two thirds of this terraqueous globe are the Nantucketer's. For the sea is his; he owns it, as Emperors own empires; other seamen having but a right of way through it. Merchant ships are but extension bridges; armed ones but floating forts; even pirates and privateers, though following the sea as highwaymen the road, they but plunder other ships, other fragments of the land like themselves, without seeking to draw their living from the bottomless deep itself. The Nantucketer, he alone resides and riots on the sea; he alone, in Bible language, goes down to it in ships; to and fro ploughing it as his own special plantation.* There *is his home; there* lies his business, *which a Noah's flood would not interrupt, though it overwhelmed all the millions in China. He lives on the sea, as prairie dogs in the prairie; he hides among the waves, he climbs them as mountain goats climb the Alps. For years he knows not the land; so that when he comes to it at last, it smells like another world, more strangely than the moon would to an Earthsman. With the landless gull, that at sunset folds her wings and is rocked to sleep between billows; so at nightfall, the Nantucketer, out of sight of land, furls his sail, and lays him to his rest, while under his very pillow rush herds of walruses and whales.*

Can you recognize the different examples of figurative language used in this paragraph? List several now.

Syntax

Risking your closing the book, we are going to use the dreaded "G" word—*grammar*. Grammar refers to the function of words and their uses and relationship in a sentence. <u>Syntax is the grammatical structure of sentences</u>. Without syntax, there is no clear communication. It is the responsibility of the author to manipulate language so that his or her purpose and intent are clear to the reader.

Note: When we refer to syntax in the context of rhetorical analysis, we are not speaking of grammatical correctness, but rather of the deliberate sentence structure the author chooses to make his or her desired point.

We assume that you are already familiar with the basics of sentence structure and are able to recognize and clearly construct:

- phrases;
- clauses;
- basic sentence types: declarative, interrogative, imperative, exclamatory;
- simple sentences;
- compound sentences;

- complex sentences; and
- compound–complex sentences.

We also assume that you have a good working knowledge of:

- punctuation,
- spelling, and
- paragraphing.

If you are in doubt about any of these, refer to the English handbook section of your composition textbooks. We also recommend *The Elements of Style* by Strunk and White. And, don't forget, your teacher is your major resource who can provide you with information and practice. Be honest with yourself. If you need help, get it early in the term.

Carefully read the following passage for *more practice with syntax.*

> *It struck eight. Bella waited. Nobody came.*
>
> *She sat down on a gilt chair at the head of the stairs, looked steadily before her with her blank, blue eyes. In the hall, in the cloakroom, in the supper-room, the hired footmen looked at one another with knowing winks. "What does the old girl expect? No one'll have finished dinner before ten."*
>
> — *(Mr. Loveday's Little Outing; "Bella Gave a Party," Evelyn Waugh, 1936)*

Did you notice the following syntactical elements and their effects in this selection?

- Short declarative sentences
  — Repetitiveness is like the ticking of a clock
  — Immediately introduces tension
- Simple declarative sentence beginning with subject/verbs
  — Parallel structure with phrases beginning with *in*
  — Pacing: clock ticking away time, uncaring
- Periodic sentence draws attention to the setting rather than the footmen
- Ends with a rhetorical question: reader drawn into the tension

You can see from just a brief analysis of the sentence structure of this passage that syntax plays an important role in the creation of character, setting, and tension.

> We recommend that you choose brief passages from works which you study in your AP Comp class and practice this process on them throughout the year.

Here is a sentence structure activity you can use to review creating sentences using coordination and subordination.

Consider the following set of sentences.

I write.
I have a writing problem.
The problem is wordiness.
This tendency leads me somewhere.
It leads me to my writing awkward sentences.
These sentences confuse my readers.
I must edit my writing.
I must be very careful.

Rewrite this set of simple sentences THREE different ways, with each new sentence containing ALL of the information given. Each new sentence is to emphasize a different simple sentence (main clause) given in the original set. Bracket the clause you are emphasizing in each new sentence.

> You might wish to work on this type of activity throughout the year with your class or with an AP Comp study group that you have formed.

Tone and Attitude

We are guessing that these terms have confused you, as indeed, they have confused our own students in the past. <u>Both terms refer to the author's perception and presentation of the material and the audience</u>.

Tone, which often reinforces the mood of a piece, is easy to understand. Think of Edgar Allen Poe and the prevailing mood and tone of a short story such as "The Telltale Heart." There is no doubt that the single effect of this story is macabre horror, which clearly establishes the tone.

<u>An author's attitude is not just the creation of a mood. It represents the stance or relationship the author has toward his or her subject</u>. This type of analysis may require that you "read between the lines," which is the close reading of diction and syntax.

There are some basics for you to consider when determining tone and attitude.

The author can indicate several attitudes toward the reader:

• Talking down to the reader as an advisor
• Talking down to the reader as a satirist
• Talking eye-to-eye with the reader as an equal
• Talking up to the reader as a supplicant or subordinate

The attitude may also be formal or informal.

• Formal tends to use diction and syntax that are academic, serious, and authoritative.
• Informal is more conversational and engages the reader on an equal basis.

In "The Telltale Heart," it is fairly obvious that the diction and syntax help to create a macabre tone. At the same time, Poe's highly academic and mature diction and syntax create a formal attitude as he relates his tale to his reader as an equal.

Jonathan Swift in "A Modest Proposal" presents a satiric attitude as he speaks down to (instructs) his audience. Likewise, Charles Lamb in "A Dissertation on Roast Pig" engages his reader with an informal attitude in his satire.

If you want to see a subservient or subordinate attitude, see Chief Seattle's speech in our Practice Exam #1, essay question #1. Here, you will see how he employs diction and syntax to create a mocking humility that would serve his greater purpose.

<u>The following is a list of adjectives often used to describe tone and attitude in a literary work. Feel free to add your own appropriate words.</u>

bitter	objective	idyllic
sardonic	naïve	compassionate
sarcastic	joyous	reverent
ironic	spiritual	lugubrious
mocking	wistful	elegiac
scornful	nostalgic	gothic
satiric	humorous	macabre

vituperative	mock-serious	reflective
scathing	pedantic	maudlin
confidential	didactic	sentimental
factual	inspiring	patriotic
informal	remorseful	jingoistic
facetious	disdainful	detached
critical	laudatory	angry
resigned	mystified	sad
astonished		

> Be aware that tone and attitude are frequently described using a *pair* of words in the multiple-choice section of the AP English Language and Composition exam. For example: *bitter and disdainful.* Both adjectives must apply for the choice to be correct.

What follows is a set of activities that can provide practice in recognizing and analyzing tone and attitude. We suggest you try them as you progress through your AP Comp course. Consider the following passages:

Passage A

I am looking at a sunset. I am on the rim of the Grand Canyon. I have been on vacation for the past two weeks which I have been planning for over a year. I have always wanted to visit this geographic location. There are many people also looking at the same sight that I see. This is the first time I have witnessed this place and this event. There are many varied colors while this sunset is taking place. The sun disappears behind the Canyon walls, and darkness comes quickly after that.

Passage B

It was Monday morning. The sun was out, and I walked into the meeting. I was expecting to find some new people there. They were. I was introduced to them. The room was warm. Coffee was served. The meeting began, and the subject was our budget for the next year. There was discussion. I did not agree with many of the people there. A vote was taken after a period of time. The new budget was passed.

Passage C

I am looking at the new Wondercar. I am trying to decide whether or not to purchase or lease this car. It offers ABS, four-wheel drive, a V-8 engine, and the following extras: CD player, AC, power windows, door locks, etc., tinted glass, heated leather seats, a cellular phone, and luggage and ski racks. I would like the color forest green. The purchase price is $48,500. The monthly leasing payment after a $6,000 down payment would be $589.00 for three years.

Using your knowledge of tone, rewrite each of the above passages so that a specific tone is evident to your reader. Identify that tone/attitude. Once you have written the new passage, highlight those changes in diction and syntax which help you to create the tone and attitude you wanted.

Here is another activity that will allow you to practice your skills in analyzing tone and attitude:

Locate reviews of films, music, plays, cars, sports events, or teams—anything you can find that has been reviewed or criticized. These reviews can come from newspapers and/or periodicals you locate in an actual publication, or they can be from a *real* newspaper or periodical with articles posted on the Web. We suggest that you cut them out or print them out from the Internet.

Under each review:

- Cite the source and the date of the review
- State the *tone* the reviewer has
- Underline those words and/or phrases (*diction*) used in the review that support and/or develop this *tone*

As an extra practice, you might try this. Follow the directions above. Only this time, you will be collecting the reviews for only *one* film, sports event, and so forth. Let's see. You could try the *New York Times*, *USA Today*, the *Wall Street Journal*, *Time*, *Newsweek*, *People*, or *Entertainment Weekly*. Of course, you may know of others. Terrific; feel free to use them.

Again, try this with your class or study group. The more the merrier.

The following may serve as a final look at our review of style. We have been taking a rather concentrated look at some of the components of what the experts call "literary" style. As you know, two of the major components of style are: (1) the types of sentences an author chooses to use (*syntax*); and (2) word choice (*diction*). Below is a sample paragraph that provides some further practice with these two areas. *This is the first, bare-bones draft.*

> *Last night was chilly. I went into New York City. I went to see a reading of a play. It was a new play. It was a staged reading. It was read at the Roundabout Theater. The Roundabout Theater is on Broadway. It is on the corner of 45th Street. The play was written by Ruth Wolf. She writes about historical people. This play is about Mary Shelley. She was the wife of Percy Bysshe Shelley. Percy B. Shelley was a poet. He is a very famous Romantic poet. Mary Shelley wrote books. She wrote <u>Frankenstein</u>. Many people know this novel. Many people really like the story. There were more than 200 people there. The play was long. It had two acts. It takes place in France and Italy. It also takes place in heaven and hell. There are three main characters. One character is Mary Shelley. One character is Percy B. Shelley. One character plays the archangel and the devil. There is a lot of talking. There is little action. I liked the talking. I wished there was more action. It is called a comedy. Many of the scenes were not comical. The play could not make up its mind. I do not think it will be produced.*

1. Now, using your knowledge of syntax and diction, rewrite this paragraph using coordination, subordination, phrases, and so forth.
2. Once you have written a revised paragraph, work with someone and REWRITE it in a **new and different** way.

Here's an example of one way to revise the passage.

> *Last night, I went into chilly New York City to see a staged reading of a new play at the Roundabout Theater on the corner of 45th and Broadway. Ruth Wolf, who is known for her productions about historical figures, has written a play about Mary Shelley, the wife of the Romantic poet Percy Bysshe Shelley. Many people know Mary Shelley as the author of the popular novel <u>Frankenstein</u>. The play takes place in France, Italy, heaven, and hell with main characters Mary herself, Percy B. Shelley, and an archangel who doubles as the devil. The drama contains much dialog and very*

little action, which I sorely missed. Billed as a comedy, this play seemed to be unable to make up its mind between being a comedy or a serious tragedy. Because of this problem, I don't believe this play has a real chance of being produced.

The "Connective Tissue" Issue

Throughout this book, we use the term *connective tissue*. For us, this "tissue issue" has four components. The most obvious refers to transitions between paragraphs or sections of a piece. The other three are not as readily recognizable as is transition, but you need to know that they play a major role in the coherence of a written work. The mature reader and writer will learn to recognize and employ these elements:

- Transition—indicates a logical connection between ideas
- Subject consistency—the subjects of the main clauses in a sequence of sentences are consistent (inconsistency is often the result of passive voice)
  Example: no: The <u>photography</u> was by Ansel Adams. <u>I</u> have always been a fan of this great photographer. The <u>temptation</u> to buy the photo due to the price was quite strong.
  yes: <u>I</u> have always been a fan of the great photographer Ansel Adams. Because of the price of one of his photographs, <u>I</u> was tempted to buy it.

- Tense consistency—the use of the same tense throughout the selection
  Example: no: When I have driven to work, I always used the same route.
  yes: I always use the same route when I drive to work.

- Voice consistency—use of the active voice and avoidance of the passive voice when possible
  Example: no: The bear was seen when Tim opened the door.
  yes: Tim opened the door and saw the bear.

Note: Another method of creating cohesion and topic adherence is the use of "echo words" or synonymous words or phrases throughout the selection.

Those authors you recognize as good writers are skilled at building connective tissue. You should be able to recognize it and to employ it in your own work.

<u>The following is a guide to transitional words and phrases.</u>

Most often used and most "natural" transitions in sentences or brief sequences of sentences:

- and
- but
- or
- nor
- for
- yet

Some other commonly used transitions between paragraphs or sections of longer works:

- Numerical: first, second, third, primarily, secondly, and so forth
- Sequential: then, finally, next
- Additional: furthermore, moreover, again, also, similarly
- Illustrative: for example, for instance, to illustrate
- Contrast, comparison, alternative: on the other hand, nevertheless, conversely, instead, however, still
- Cause and effect: therefore, consequently, as a result, accordingly
- Affirmation: of course, obviously, indeed

Here is an activity that will provide practice with transitions. Using one of your essays, highlight all of the transitions and complete the following:

The following are the *transition words/phrases* that I have used to connect each paragraph to the one before it.

#1: _____

#2: _____

#3: _____

#4: _____

#5: _____

#6: _____

#7: _____

#8: _____

#9: _____

#10: _____

If you find that you are missing a needed transition between paragraphs, indicate that on the appropriate line that corresponds to that paragraph. Then, write the needed transitional word or phrase.

> *Note:* This practice activity should be one which you do as often as possible. You may wish to do this type of editing with your class or study group. No matter how you do it, just DO IT.

Voice: Pen, Paper, Action!

Writing is a living process. Good writing moves the reader clearly from point to point. Voice and pacing play a major role in this process. Subjects are responsible for their actions. In the context of rhetorical analysis, the *first type of voice* is that "picture" of yourself as a writer that you consciously try to create for your reader. Just how do you want your reader to "see" and "hear" you: as confident, mature, knowledgeable, witty, reverent, friendly, caring, audacious . . .? What? This first type of voice is the result of all of the elements that make up **style**.

And, one of those components is the *second type of voice*. This type of voice refers to *active* or *passive voice*, which simply is the relationship between the subject and its verb. Almost every instructor or writer who teaches says one thing—"Use ACTIVE voice."

Just What Is ACTIVE VOICE?

To answer this question, look at the following sentences:

> ***The ball was thrown by Jessica.***

1. What is the subject? _____

2. What is the verb tense? _____

3. Is the verb simple or compound? _____

4. What is the prepositional phrase? _____

5. How many words are in the sentence? _____

Jessica threw the ball.

1. What is the subject? _____

2. What is the verb tense? _____

3. Is the verb simple or compound? _____

4. Is there a prepositional phrase? _____

5. How many words are in the sentence? _____

Which of the two sentences has the subject of the sentence doing the action? ____
Which one has the subject being acted upon? ____

> When the writing lets the reader know that the subject is *doing the acting*, you have ACTIVE VOICE. <u>When the subject is acted upon or is the goal of the action, and, therefore, NOT responsible, you have PASSIVE VOICE</u>.

With this information, now identify which of the two sentences above is active and which one is passive. Without doubt, we know you chose the second as active and the first as passive. Good for you.

Here's another example:

The treaty was signed last night.

Who signed the treaty? Whom do we blame if the treaty fails? We don't know, do we? Passive voice avoids responsibility. It is a primary tool of those who want to obfuscate or of those who lack confidence and decisiveness. Why not give the true picture and write:

Last night, the President of the United States and the President of Mexico signed a mutual defense treaty.

Here's a practice activity for you.

> *The huge red building was entered at the sound of the bell. Instructions were yelled at us by a mean-looking **old lady**. A crowd of six-year-olds was followed down a long hallway, up some steps, and down another corridor by me clutching my lunchbox. Mrs. Nearing's room was looked for. Our destination was reached when we were loudly greeted by a tall, black-haired woman. A tag was pressed to my chest after my name was asked and a tag was printed by her. Several big six-year-olds could be seen inside the room by me. The door was closed with a loud bang. The glass near the top of the door was kept from shattering by a network of wires. The wires were observed to be prison-like. So, back in school was I.*

You should have noticed that every sentence is written in the passive voice. Awkward and tedious, isn't it? Now, it's your turn. Rewrite this passage by simply changing all of the passive constructions into active voice.

Compare Your Revision with Ours

At the sound of the bell, I entered the huge, red building with hundreds of other kids. Just inside the entrance, a mean-looking old lady yelled instructions at us. I clutched my lunchbox and followed a crowd of other six-year-olds down a long hallway, up some steps, and down another corridor as we looked for Mrs. Nearing's room. I knew we had reached our destination when a tall, black-haired woman loudly greeted us. She asked me my name, then she printed it on a sticky tag and pressed it to my chest. Once inside the room, I could see several other kids my age, some of them BIG. Finally, Mrs. Nearing closed the door with a loud bang. A network of wires kept the glass near the top of the door from shattering. These wires looked like the bars of a prison to me. I was back in school.

Have you noticed that many sentences written in passive voice contain a prepositional phrase beginning with *by*? That *by*-phrase immediately following the verb (usually compound) can be a clue that you have passive voice at work in the sentence. GET RID OF IT, if you can.

Note: There are times when you deliberately want to use passive voice, but it should be a very conscious choice on your part. Here are four questions to ask yourself.

- Do you want to avoid stating who/what is responsible for an action?
- Is there a specific goal or effect that you wish to emphasize?
- Do you want to create a "special effect"?
- Do you want to sound "academic" and avoid using the dreaded "first person" responsibility?
- If you can answer a loud "yes" to any or all of these questions, then you may decide to employ passive voice.

Let's hear your voice—loud and clear! Take responsibility for what you think, say, and write. This is your voice. It is the real you. Give it life. Don't suffocate it.

Pacing

Pacing is the "movement" of a literary piece from one point to another. The primary component of pacing is syntax: sentence length, sentence type, and punctuation. There are several ways to add variety and pacing to your writing by:

- using a mixture of sentence types, known as sentence variety;
- using the rhetorical question;
- using the imperative sentence;
- using the exclamatory sentence; and
- varying the beginnings of sentences.

For example, if you were to compose a brief paragraph about writing an AP English Language and Composition essay, you could write:

I like to write essays for AP Comp class. I like to think through an idea, and I like to try out different approaches to discussing an idea. My AP teacher gives us lots of time to prepare our essays. He gives us a topic. Then, he has us do an outline and then a first draft. We have our first draft read by a member of our peer group. I do my revision after this. I also read my essay aloud to someone. Then, I'm ready to hand it in to my instructor for grading.

Note that all the sentences begin with subject and verb. All the sentences, except for the second one, are simple. The second is no more than a compound sentence made up of two very simple main clauses. Do you feel the tediousness and immaturity of this paragraph? There is *nothing* grammatically wrong with any of the sentences. However, would you be happy with this paragraph if you had written it? Something is missing, and that something has to do with *pacing*.

Rewrite this paragraph so that there is a variety of sentences and sentence beginnings. How does your revision compare with ours?

> *Because I like to think through ideas and try different approaches to presenting an idea, I really enjoy my AP Comp class. Another reason for my enjoying writing essays is my AP teacher's approach to composition. For him and, therefore, for us, writing is not a quick, hit-or-miss assignment. After we choose a topic, Mr. Damon allows plenty of time for preparation, which includes outlining, writing the first draft, and reading by our peer groups. It is only after completing these steps that I revise and write the final draft I will submit for grading. It's a good plan.*

A Few Words About Coherence

Coherence is accepting your responsibility as a writer to "deliver the goods." Your reader has expectations you are obliged to meet.

- Basically, the reader looks for some kind of announcement as to what is to follow (the thesis, assertion, claim).
- Near the end of the introduction, the reader expects to find some hints about the major points that you will discuss in your piece of writing.
- The body of the presentation will develop the discussion of each major point.
- The reader will expect to be led logically from one major point to another via "connective tissue."
- The reader expects some sort of final comment or remark, not a summary. Among the many possibilities, this final "point" could be:
  — an interpretation of the significance of the points of your discussion;
  — a prediction;
  — an anecdote;
  — a question; or
  — a quote.

Make certain that your ending/conclusion is related to your discussion. Don't introduce new or irrelevant ideas or comments. Also, make sure that the final comment is consistent in tone and attitude with the rest of the paper.

Just as the reader has particular expectations of you as a writer, YOU have expectations when you read the writing of others and when you complete a rhetorical analysis of another's written work. Ask the very same questions that are asked of you.

An Essay Editing and Revision Template

We are going to provide you with a template for editing and revision that we recommend you use throughout the year for your own essays. The more you use this template for your own writing, the more comfortable you will be when it comes to analyzing the writing of others. It will become almost second nature to you.

Before you begin to write the revised draft of your essay, respond to each of the following *carefully*. If possible, ask for input from your peers. Read aloud to each other. *Listen* to what you have written.

"For me, having an audience who gives me feedback is really important and helps me to see what needs to be revised."
—Jessica K.,
    AP student

The title of my essay is _____.

I will organize my essay using (a rhetorical strategy) _____.

The thesis of my essay is in the _____ paragraph.

My intended tone/attitude is _____.

I have used the following rhetorical devices/elements to create this tone:

_____ in paragraph _____   _____ in paragraph _____

_____ in paragraph _____   _____ in paragraph _____

_____ in paragraph _____   _____ in paragraph _____

_____ in paragraph _____   _____ in paragraph _____

_____ in paragraph _____   _____ in paragraph _____

_____ in paragraph _____   _____ in paragraph _____

_____ in paragraph _____   _____ in paragraph _____

_____ in paragraph _____   _____ in paragraph _____

The following are the *transition words/phrases* I have used to connect each paragraph to the one before it.

#1: _____

#2: _____

#3: _____

#4: _____

#5: _____

#6: _____

#7: _____

#8: _____

#9: _____

#10: _____

I use the _____ tense as the predominant tense in my essay.
I have checked the verbs in each of my paragraphs. They are *all* in the predominant tense *except*:

    #1: _____ (tense) _____ Reason for using this tense is _____. (You must do this with each paragraph and with each verb.)

I have _____ sentences in my essay. _____ of them begin with the subject. _____ of them begin with a participle phrase. _____ of them begin with a relative clause. _____ of them begin with an adverbial clause. _____ of them begin with a prepositional phrase. _____ of them begin with an infinitive. _____ of them begin with a gerund.

I have _____ simple sentences in my essay; _____ compound sentences; _____ complex sentences; _____ compound-complex sentences.

I think I need to add more sentence variety to my presentation. _____ yes _____ no

I have made certain that there is a variety of sentence structures in my essay. _____ yes _____ no

My conclusion _____ *is* _____ *is not* a summary of what I have already said in my essay. If it is not a summary, identify the type of ending you have created. _____ _____

I have discussed this inventory of my first draft with _____. These are the suggested areas for improving my essay:

The *major* things I have to work on when I revise my essay are:

Rapid Review

- Analysis is the deconstruction of a passage into its components in order to examine how a writer develops a subject.
- The AP English Language exam requires the analysis of structure, purpose, style.
- Discourse is conversation between the text and the reader.
- Rhetoric is a term for all of the strategies, modes, and devices a writer employs.
- There are four major modes of discourse:
  — exposition
  — narration
  — description
  — argumentation
- Rhetorical strategies are used to develop the modes of discourse:
  — example
  — comparison and contrast
  — definition
  — cause and effect
  — process
  — analysis
  — classification
- Practice each of the rhetorical strategies.
- Style is the unique writing pattern of a writer.
- Style comprises:
  — subject matter
  — selection of detail
  — organization
  — point of view
  — diction
  — syntax

      — language
      — attitude
      — tone
- Practice with stylistic devices.
- Review words that describe tone.
- Review "connective tissue":
      — transition
      — subject consistency
      — tense consistency
      — voice consistency
- Practice using active and passive voice.
- Practice recognizing pacing in professional writing and in your own essays by sentence variety:
      — construction
      — openings
      — types
- Utilize rubrics to gauge your essays.

CHAPTER 9

Comprehensive Review—Argument

IN THIS CHAPTER

Summary: Experience why everything is an argument. Examine the process for presenting a position that others will understand and accept.

Key Ideas
- ✪ Learn the format for the basic argumentative essay.
- ✪ Learn the difference between deduction and induction.
- ✪ Become familiar with logical fallacies.
- ✪ Practice reading and evaluating an argument.

Some Basics

What Is ARGUMENT?

In its broadest sense, all writing is argument. It is the presentation and defense or support of a specific thesis, assertion, or claim. This thesis can be a strongly held belief, a critical view of an issue, a presentation of an insight, a search for the truth, or even a description of that mountain view that moved you to tears that you hope others will share. To convince the reader to accept the position, the writer provides support using objective facts or logical evidence, and sometimes, even emotional appeals.

You can find argument almost anywhere: from ads in your favorite magazine or on television to academic journals, from "*Peanuts*" to political cartoons, from letters to the editor of *Sports Illustrated* to editorials in the *New York Times*, and from a plea to your parents to a President's speech to the nation. Possibly the only writing that is not an argument is a piece that offers no support for a claim.

What Is the Difference Between Argument and Persuasion?

The intended results of each of these strategies is where the difference lies. ALL persuasion is a type of argument. The goal of an argument is to have you accept the writer's thesis. However, with persuasion, after you've accepted the position of the writer, the goal is to have you get moving and *do something.* For example:

ARGUMENT: Walking is necessary for good health.

PERSUASION: I want you to walk every day for good health.

What Does the AP Expect Me to Be Able to Do with an Argumentative Essay?

Most frequently, the AP exam will present you with a prompt that could be:

- A brief excerpt
- A quotation
- A statement
- An anecdote

You will then be directed to <u>defend</u> (agree with), <u>challenge</u> (disagree with), or <u>qualify</u> (agree with some and disagree with other parts of the text) the:

- Author's position
- Statement's main idea
- Narrative's main point

Other types of argumentative prompts will ask you to:

- Write an essay indicating which idea among a given set is more valid
- Explore the validity of an assertion

No matter which type of argumentation prompt is given, the AP expects you to be able to:

- Take a position on the issue or situation
- Support your position using your own experience, reading, and/or observations

How Do You Argue a Point or Position?

Basically, support for your position on an issue should be rational and logical, not emotional. It should be objective rather than biased (one-sided). This support can be developed using any of the rhetorical strategies and devices we've reviewed for you in Chapter 8.

The classical formula for an argument is:

1. Present the issue/situation/problem.
2. State your (writer's) assertion/claim/thesis.
3. Support your claim.
4. Acknowledge and respond to real or possible opposing views.
5. Make your final comment or summary of the evidence.

The order of the presentation can be varied, and any of the rhetorical strategies can be employed. You must make certain that your support/evidence is appropriate and effective.

The Argument

Your argument can be:

- **Ethical**—an appeal to the reader's good sense, goodwill, and desire to "do the right thing"
- **Emotional**—an appeal to the reader's fear, patriotism, and so forth
- **Logical**—an appeal to inductive and deductive reasoning
  - *Induction*: forming a *generalization* from a set of specific examples. (Example: Margo has 17 stuffed teddy bears, 3 stuffed cows, 11 monkeys, 4 camels, and 6 stuffed elephants. Margo loves to collect stuffed animals.)
  - *Deduction*: reaching a probable *conclusion* based on given premises. A *premise* is a proposition that is proven or taken for granted. (Example: All high school seniors at this high school must write a research paper. Sean is a senior at this high school. Therefore, Sean must write a research paper.)

Be aware that conclusions can be drawn from implicit premises. These can include:

- Universal truths
- Possibilities that the reader will readily accept
- Familiar sayings
- Facts that everyone, including the reader, knows

Deduction uses the syllogism. A **syllogism** is the format of a formal argument that consists of a

Major premise:	*All A are C.*	*"All lions are cats."*
Minor premise:	*B is A.*	*"Leonard is a lion."*
Conclusion:	*Therefore, B is C.*	*"Leonard is a cat."*

You could also say, "Because Leonard is a lion, he is a cat." In this instance, you have suppressed one of the premises. However, you are confident that most people would agree that all lions are cats. Therefore, you would feel confident in leaving out that premise. But, you must be very careful, because you could end up with what we call a **logical fallacy**.

Logical fallacies are mistakes in reasoning and fall into several categories.

- *Non sequitur argument:* This Latin phrase means "does not follow." This is an argument with a conclusion that does not follow from the premise. (Example: Diane graduated from Vassar. She'll make a great lawyer.)
- *Begging the question:* Here is a mistake in which the writer assumes in his or her assertion/ premise/thesis something that really remains to be proved. (Example: Taking geometry is a waste of time. High school students should not be required to take this course.)
- *Circular reasoning:* This mistake in logic restates the premise rather than giving a reason for holding that premise. (Example: I like to eat out because I enjoy different foods and restaurants.)
- *Straw-man argument:* Here is a technique we've all seen and heard used by politicians seeking election. The speaker/writer attributes false or exaggerated characteristics or behaviors to the opponent and attacks him on those falsehoods or exaggerations. (Example: You say you support allowing people under eighteen to drive alone. I'll never be able to understand why weak-willed drivers like you are willing to risk your life and the lives of all other drivers with these crazy teenagers on the road.)

- *Ad hominem argument:* This literally means to "argue against the man." This technique attacks the person rather than dealing with the issue under discussion. (Example: We all know Sam has several speeding tickets on his record. How can we trust him to vote for us on the issue of a trade agreement with Europe?)
- *Hasty generalization:* A person who makes a hasty generalization draws a conclusion about an entire group based on evidence that is too scant or insufficient. (Example: The veterinarian discovered a viral infection in five beagles. All beagles must be infected with it.)
- *Overgeneralization:* This is what we call stereotyping in most cases. Here, the writer/speaker draws a conclusion about a large number of people, ideas, things, etc. based on very limited evidence. (Example: All members of group A are not to be trusted.) Words such as *all, never, always,* and *every* are usually indicative of overgeneralization. It's best to use and to look for qualifiers (*some, seem, often, perhaps, frequently,* etc.) that indicate that the writer has an awareness of the complexities of the topic or group under discussion.
- *Post hoc argument:* This fallacy cites an unrelated event that occurred earlier as the cause of a current situation. (Example: I saw a black cat run across the street in front of my car five minutes before I was hit by a foul ball at the ball park. Therefore, the black cat is the cause of my bruised arm.)
- *Either/or argument:* With this fallacy, the writer asserts that there are only two possibilities, when, in reality, there are more. (Example: Tomorrow is April 15; therefore, I must mail in my tax return, or I will be arrested.)

There are several other categories of logical fallacies, but these are the most frequently encountered.

> During the year, carefully read editorials or ads in the print media. Check to see if you can locate any logical fallacies. It might be beneficial to do this with your class or study group.

The following activities provide you with some practice with induction, deduction, and analogy.

Induction: If induction is the process that moves from a given series of specifics to a generalization, these are the possible problems:

- The generalization covers many unobserved persons, objects, etc.
- If the conclusion begins with ALL, any exception would invalidate the generalization.
- Cited facts are incorrect.
- Assumed connections are incorrect.
- Assumption is a conclusion NOT supported by the evidence.

Practice:

A. Write a conclusion for the following:
   1. Television network USBC's drama series won this year's Emmy for Best Dramatic Series.
   2. USBC won the Emmy for Best Comedy Series.
   3. USBC won the Emmy for Best Talk Show.

   4. *Therefore,* _____.

Are there any possible weaknesses in your conclusion?

B. Carefully read the following and briefly explain the possible error in the conclusion.
  1. The 43rd U.S. President is a Yale graduate.
  2. The 42nd U.S. President was a Yale Law School graduate.
  3. The 41st U.S. President was a Yale graduate.
  4. The last seven presidents were college graduates.
  5. *Therefore,* the President of the U.S. must have a college degree.

Deduction: If deduction is the process of moving from a general rule to a specific example (A = B; C = B; Therefore, C = A.), these are the possible problems:

- Not *all* of the given A falls into the given B category. There are exceptions.
- The given category B is incorrect.
- The second statement is *not* true or is incorrect. Therefore, the conclusion is invalid.
- The truth of the third statement is in question.

Practice:

A. Carefully read the following. Assume that statements 1 and 2 are true. Briefly state the possible error of the conclusion.
  1. Some Japanese cars are made in the United States.
  2. Toyota is a Japanese car.
  3. *Therefore*, all Toyotas are made in the United States.

B. Carefully read the following. Assume that statements 1 and 2 are true. Briefly state the possible error of the conclusion.
  1. No eagles are flamingos.
  2. All flamingos are birds.
  3. Therefore, no eagles are birds.

Analogy: If analogy is an argument based on similarities, these are the possible problems.

- Accepting the totality of the analogy by never questioning that there are differences between/among the items being compared that could invalidate the argument or conclusion.
- Exaggerating the similarities.

Practice:

A. Briefly identify the analogy in the following:

Both the doctor and the teacher must have special knowledge. People select their own doctors; therefore, people should be allowed to pick their own teachers.

B. Briefly explain the mistake in the following:

Both 2-year-olds and 10-year-olds have two legs, two eyes, two ears, and two arms. Ten-year-olds can read and write. Therefore, 2-year-olds should be able to read and write.

Reading the Argument

KEY IDEA

In the multiple-choice section of the AP English Language exam, you are asked to read several selections, many of which are argumentative. Remember two very important points. No matter how brief or how lengthy the text is:

1. There is a rhetorical context with a
   - writer
   - occasion or situation
   - audience

Any good argument will effectively utilize and address each of these elements.

2. Don't make the mistake of evaluating an argument based simply on who wrote it. Don't confuse the messenger with the message.

   With this in mind, your task is to read the given text critically and to:

   - Determine who the speaker is, what the situation is, and who the audience is.
   - Identify the position of the speaker.
   - Check off the points made in support of the assertion.

   You can easily accomplish these three tasks by highlighting, underlining, checking, making marginal notes, or even outlining (if you have time). Once you have completed your initial reading, you need to ask yourself several questions. In the case of the actual AP English Language and Composition exam, your test makers will ask you the questions based on these points.

1. Are there any judgments in the presentation?
   — Evidence is needed to support judgments.

2. Recognize that fact is <u>not</u> the same as interpretation.
   — Fact: You know it with certainty and can verify it.
   — Interpretation: An explanation of the meaning and/or importance of a specific item.

   You must be able to distinguish between the two.

3. Distinguish between literal and ironic statements. Recognizing the difference between these two terms can save you from misreading the text.
   — Ironic: Saying the opposite from what you really mean, as in satire.
   — Clues to be aware of: diction, subject, selection of detail.
   — Literal: What you read is what is the reality.

4. Do not evaluate an argument based on its form. Look at the content. It's easy to be misled by "fabulous" writing.

Below is a checklist that functions as a rubric for the evaluation of any rhetorical argument.

— **A clearly developed thesis is evident.**
— **Facts are distinguished from opinions.**
— **Opinions are supported and qualified.**
— **The speaker develops a logical argument and avoids fallacies in reasoning.**
— **Support for facts is tested, reliable, and authoritative.**
— **The speaker does not confuse appeals to logic and emotion.**
— **Opposing views are represented in a fair and undistorted way.**
— **The argument reflects a sense of audience.**
— **The argument reflects an identifiable voice and point of view.**
— **The piece reflects the image of a speaker with identifiable qualities (honesty, sincerity, authority, intelligence, etc.).**

As practice, read the following editorial, which appeared in a recent teachers' newsletter.

Misters King and Prince could not have picked a more ironic day to have their anti-teacher tirade printed in Today's News *than on Tuesday, January 13. Here were Matt King, executive director of the conservative magazine* The Right Position, *and Ray Prince, the chief economist for the conservative Small Business Conference, showing their poisonous fangs in their hissy-fit against the state's teachers' union and the state's education department.*

Here were two cobras from the antiteacher snake pit posturing about the need to end tenure and to create charter schools. These, said the two vipers, are among the steps "needed to revitalize education in our area and across the state." Later in their column, they continued with "declining student performance in recent years" is indicative of poor teaching quality.

May I direct King and Prince to pages A5 and A28 of this very same Today's News *edition. In this article were the names of 74 (4 of them from New High School) Intel competition semifinalists out of a total of 144 in our state. With about 50% of the state's semifinalists, this and our neighboring county had MORE winning contestants and MORE participants than any other region in the country. This is MORE than half the national total of 300 . . . [and] "more than six times as many as the second-ranked state, which had 21 semifinalists and the third-ranked state, which had 19."*

Hmmm . . . now, let me think. Which speaks more loudly about teacher quality and student motivation: the negative nagging of King and Prince or the positive professionalism and performance represented by the Intel story? I daresay—no contest. And, this type of professional proficiency and dedication is part and parcel of the standards and goals of ALL our state teachers.

They would have to count the extraordinary number of national, state, and local awards our professionals and their pupils have earned. They would have to count the number of scholarships, volunteer hours, and AP courses our students have amassed. They would have to listen to a litany of academic awards, associations, and degrees with which our teachers are connected. They would have to read the hundreds of thank-you letters former students have written to their teachers.

They would have to acknowledge that their scaly agenda needs to be shed.

Rather than casting a "shadow over education" in this state, our teachers shine a bright light on the snake pits created by ignorance and negativity.

Let's Use the Argument Checklist on This Editorial

1. The <u>thesis</u> is that Mr. King and Mr. Prince are incorrect about their position to end tenure and create charter schools. These two are wrong when they say "our area needs to revitalize education."
2. <u>Facts are distinguished from opinion</u>. Facts include the number of Intel scholarships in paragraph 3; the comparison of the writer's area with other school districts in paragraph 3, and the number of awards, etc. associated with the writer's school. Opinion is obvious in the analogy established between Mr. King and Mr. Prince and snakes.
3. Some <u>opinions are supported and others are not</u>. In some cases, numbers are cited, and in other cases, generalizations are used.
4. The editorial <u>avoids fallacies in most instances</u>. However, the emotional appeal and arguing from analogy is present.

5. The <u>editorial is developed using induction</u>. A possible fallacy here revolves around whether or not what is true about one school district may be true about all other school areas or for all teachers and students.

6. The <u>facts used come from current newspapers</u>. The writer cites statistics and gives the source. The comparison between New High School and other schools and school districts is based on statistics and facts.

7. The author <u>uses both logic and emotion</u>. The facts and statistics are given in separate paragraphs. Emotional and analogical aspects of the argument are in opinionated sections of the editorial.

8. The <u>opposing views</u> of King and Prince are presented to illustrate the position of the columnists factually.

9. The <u>audience</u> is obviously teachers and those involved in education.

10. The <u>point of view</u> of the writer is clearly negative toward King and Prince and positive toward the condition of education in the writer's school district and state.

11. The editorial reflects a writer who is sincere, angry, confident, and willing to find support for the assertion.

Note: Each of these statements about the given editorial could also be turned into multiple-choice questions. Keep in mind that the writers of the AP English Language and Composition exam are aware of all of the preceding information and will base their questions on the assumption that you are also familiar with it and can recognize the elements of argument when you read them.

Writing the Argument

While the multiple-choice section of the exam will present you with specific questions about specific texts, the argumentative essay in the second section of the test requires that you compose *your own argument* based on a given excerpt, quotation, statement, or anecdote.

You will have to plan and write your argument knowing that the AP reader will be evaluating your presentation based on the major points we have just reviewed.

How Should I Go About Writing My Argument?

We invite you to compose an argumentative essay based on the following prompt. We will take you through the prewriting process.

> *In a recent* USA Today *op-ed piece, titled "Poor Suffer from Lack of Internet Access," Julianne Malveaux stated, "While the Internet has hardly caused the gap between the [lower and higher rungs on the economic ladder], it is one of the many things that have made the gap greater."*
>
> —(Julianne Malveaux, *USA Today*, June 22, 2001)

In an effective, well-organized essay, defend, challenge, or qualify Ms. Malveaux's assertion.

The Planning/Prewriting Process

What follows is an example of the prewriting process that addresses the given prompt.

1. Reread the prompt and highlight important terms, ideas, etc.
2. *Take a position*. Defend "it is one of the many things that have made the gap greater."

3. *My topic is:* Internet is one cause of the widening gap between the haves and the have-nots.

4. *My thesis statement is:* I agree with Julianne Malveaux when she states that access to the Internet has widened the gap between the haves and the have-nots.

5. *I will develop my argument using:*
   —personal anecdote
   — specific examples of the gap (at least three)
   — statistics and facts that I can remember from the news, and other sources

6. The *specifics I will use to support my assertion are*:
   (Make certain examples are introduced, discussed, and linked to my thesis.)

7. I will use the *inductive* technique to develop my argument.

8. I will *end my argument* with the image of a single child with her nose against a window peering into a room filled with children using computers. The child outside is not alone. Behind her are many, many others, and they all look as if they are growing more and more anxious and angry at being left outside.

This planning took about 10 to 12 minutes to develop. Based on this planning, writing the essay is easy. As a class assignment or as personal practice, you would:

- Write your first draft
- Have the initial argument checklist completed by one of your peers
- Complete your second draft
- Complete the revision activity either by yourself or with a member of your peer reading group

If you have practiced this process throughout the year or semester, when the AP English Language exam rolls around, you will find this kind of writing second nature to you.

Rapid Review

- Argument can be ethical, emotional, or logical.
- Inductive reasoning forms generalizations.
- Deductive reasoning reaches conclusions based on given premises.
- A premise is a proven proposition or one that is taken for granted.
- A syllogism is the format of a formal argument:
  — All A is C.
  — B is A.
  — Therefore, B is C.
- Logical fallacies are intended or unintended errors in reasoning.
- Rhetorical fallacies are used to manipulate the audience.
- Read editorials and ads to try to locate any fallacies that may be present.
- Do practice exercises with induction and deduction and analogy.
- All argument has a rhetorical context: the writer, the occasion, and the audience.
- When reading arguments, locate judgments and find supporting evidence.
- Be certain to recognize and to separate fact from interpretation.
- Evaluate the argument according to the given rubrics.
- When writing an argument, make certain to:
  — address the prompt
  — take a position
  — state your thesis
  — develop your position with evidence

CHAPTER 10

Comprehensive Review—Synthesis

IN THIS CHAPTER

Summary: Examine the synthesis purpose and process.

Key Ideas
✪ Practice with reading and evaluating different types of texts from various mediums, including graphics.
✪ Work with summary, paraphrase, and inference.
✪ Learn different approaches to incorporating sources into the text of your essay.

Some Basics

What Is the Synthesis Essay?

Synthesis is the process in which you, as the writer, develop a thesis and, in the course of developing this thesis,

- you investigate a variety of sources, both print and visual;
- you choose which of these sources to include in your presentation;
- you respond to these sources and discuss how they relate to your position on the topic.

Note: A well-respected and experienced Advanced Placement English instructor, Jodi Rice, uses the following example to clarify the idea of *synthesis*: You're having a dinner party, and you consult two recipes you've been given and use bits of each to create your own, new dish. You let your dinner guests know that you invented the dish, but that you used and combined recipes from your grandmother and from the newspaper. You don't take credit for those two recipes, but you <u>do</u> take credit for what you did with them.

In the case of the AP Language exam, you only have time to write a first draft, and it must be clear, organized, logical, and thoughtful. In developing each of your major points, make certain to:

- Relate it to the thesis/claim
- Use specific examples (personal and otherwise)
- Use selected sources to support the major point
- Incorporate sources into the development of your point by using
  — Attribution and introduction of cited sources
  — Transitions
  — Mix of direct quotations, summary, and paraphrases

A Few Comments Before Beginning

Your AP Language class, as well as other courses across the curriculum, has taught you how to conduct, evaluate, and present research. You most likely have completed at least one research paper that required you to develop a thesis on a particular subject; to find, read, and annotate outside sources related to the topic; to determine which of the sources to use in support of your thesis; to incorporate these sources into your research paper; and to appropriately cite your sources.

If you've written this type of paper before, whether brief or lengthy, you're well on your way to being able to compose a successful synthesis essay.

The synthesis essay also requires you to be familiar with both <u>analysis</u> and <u>argument</u>. Because of this, we strongly urge you to review Chapters 5, 6, 8, and 9. Those skills needed to develop a successful essay of analysis or argument are requisites for composing a <u>synthesis</u> essay.

This chapter briefly reviews strategies and provides you with practice activities specifically related to writing the synthesis essay as it would most probably appear on the AP English Language exam.

Let's begin.

Note: We will use the synthesis prompt and sample essay from the Diagnostic Master exam (Chapter 3) as the basis for the following review segments.

Strategies

Strategy 1: Critical Reading of Texts

A word about the texts: The several texts you will be given for the synthesis prompt will be related to the topic, and you can be assured that each text has been evaluated and judged to be appropriate, of acceptable quality, and representing several points of view.

Critical reading of texts specifically for the synthesis essay demands that you determine the following:

- Purpose/thesis
- Intended audience
- Type of source (primary, secondary)
- Main points
- Historical context
- Authority of the author
- How the material is presented
- Type of evidence presented
- Source of the evidence
- Any bias or agenda
- How the text relates to the topic
- Support or opposition toward the thesis

Practice with Critical Reading

Our example: Here is a text provided in the Diagnostic Master exam's synthesis essay.

Source E
Broder, John M., "States Curbing Right to Seize Private Homes." *New York Times*, February 21, 2006.
The following passage is excerpted from an article published in the *New York Times*.

> *"Our <u>opposition</u> to eminent domain is <u>not across the board</u>," he* [<u>Scott G. Bullock</u> of the Institute for Justice] *said. "It has an <u>important but limited role in government planning</u> and the building of roads, parks, and public buildings. What <u>we oppose</u> is eminent domain <u>abuse for private development</u>, and we are encouraging legislators to curtail it."*
>
> *<u>More neutral observers expressed concern that state officials</u>, in their zeal to protect homeowners and small businesses, <u>would handcuff local governments</u> that are trying to revitalize dying cities and fill in blighted areas with projects that produce tax revenues and jobs.*
>
> *"It's fair to say that many states are on the verge of seriously overreacting to the Kelo decision," said <u>John D. Echeverria</u>, executive director of the Georgetown Environmental Law and Policy Institute and an authority on land-use policy. "<u>The danger is that some legislators</u> are going to <u>attempt to destroy</u> what is a significant and sometimes painful but essential <u>government power</u>. The extremist position is a <u>prescription for economic decline</u> for many metropolitan areas around the county."*

Our writer's critical reading of the passage provides the following information:

1. <u>Thesis</u>: ". . . What we oppose is eminent domain abuse for private development, and we are encouraging legislators to curtail it."
2. <u>Intended audience</u>: generally educated readers
3. <u>Main points</u>:
   A. qualified opposition to eminent domain
   B. opposed to eminent domain for private development
   C. acknowledges that there are those who see their position as handcuffing local officials
   D. Echeverria says, "The danger . . . " He fears legislation could destroy essential government power.

4. <u>Historical context:</u> 2006 in response to *Kelo* decision
5. <u>How material is presented:</u> Thesis + expert's direct quotation + acknowledgment of opposition + expert's direct quotation
6. <u>Type of evidence presented:</u> direct quotations of experts in the field
7. <u>Source of evidence:</u> expert opinions
8. <u>Any bias or agenda:</u> both sides of issue are presented
9. <u>How text relates to the topic:</u> specific statements for and against eminent domain
10. <u>Support or not for thesis:</u> one quotation supports a qualifying position: "I can empathize with the home owners affected by the recent 5:4 Supreme Court decision." The other quotation could be used to recognize those who would oppose it.

Note: This is a process that does not necessarily require that every point be written out. You could easily make mental notes of many of these items and jot down only those that you think you could use in your essay. You may prefer to annotate directly on the text itself.

Practice

Now, you complete a critical reading of another text from the Master exam on eminent domain.

Source C

Kelo v. New London. U.S. Supreme Court 125 S. Ct. 2655.
The following is a brief overview of a decision by the U.S. Supreme Court in 2005.

> Suzette Kelo, et al. v. <u>City of New London</u>, et al., <u>*125 S. Ct. 2655 (2005)*</u>, *more commonly* Kelo v. New London, *is a land-use law case argued before the <u>United States Supreme Court</u> on <u>February 22, 2005</u>. The case arose from a city's use of <u>eminent domain</u> to condemn privately owned real property so that it could be used as part of a comprehensive redevelopment plan.*
>
> *The owners sued the city in Connecticut courts, arguing that the city had misused its eminent domain power. The power of eminent domain is limited by the <u>Fifth</u> and <u>Fourteenth Amendments to the United States Constitution</u>. The Fifth Amendment, which restricts the actions of the federal government, says, in part, that "private property [shall not] be taken for public use, without just compensation"; under Section 1 of the Fourteenth Amendment, this limitation is also imposed on the actions of <u>U.S. state</u> and local governments. Kelo and the other appellants argued that economic development, the stated purpose of the Development Corporation, did not qualify as public use.*
>
> *The Supreme Court's Ruling: This 5:4 decision holds that the governmental taking of property from one private owner to give to another in furtherance of economic development constitutes a permissible "public use" under the Fifth Amendment.*

1. Purpose/thesis: _____

_____

2. Intended audience: _____

3. Main points: _____

_____

4. Historical context: _____

5. How material is presented: _____

6. Type of evidence presented: _____

_____

7. Source of evidence: _____

8. Any bias or agenda: _____

9. How text relates to topic: _____

_____

10. Support or opposition for my thesis: _____

What Types of Visual Texts Can I Expect on the AP Language Exam?

You can expect to encounter a variety of visual sources on the AP Language exam. They may include:

- Political cartoons
- Charts and graphs
- Posters
- Advertising
- Paintings
- Photographs

As with the steps involved in the critical reading of written material, visuals also require critical analysis. The following are steps you should consider when faced with a visual text:

- Identify the subject of the visual.
- Identify the major components, such as characters, visual details, and symbols.
- Identify verbal clues, such as titles, taglines, date, author, and dialogue.
- Notice position and size of details.
- Does the visual take a positive or negative position toward the issue?
- Identify the primary purpose of the visual.
- Determine how each detail illustrates and/or supports the primary purpose.
- Does the author indicate alternative viewpoints?

What Follows Is a Sample Critical Reading of a <u>Political Cartoon</u> Taken from the Master Exam

One type of text that could be used for the synthesis essay prompt on the AP English Language exam is the political cartoon. No, AP Language has not turned into a history or journalism course. But, it does recognize the variety of texts that can be created to advance or illustrate a particular thesis. The political cartoon does in a single- or multiple-frame presentation what would take hundreds of words in an essay, editorial, and so forth. It is a visual presentation of a specific point of view on an issue.

> *Note:* Even though the synthesis essay prompt may include political cartoons, or charts, or surveys, you are not required to use any of them. Your choice of texts depends on your purpose.

When dealing with a political cartoon, here are the specific steps to consider that are adapted from the critical reading of a visual.

- Identify the subject of the cartoon.
- Identify the major components, such as characters, visual details, and symbols.
- Identify verbal clues, such as titles, taglines, date, cartoonist, and dialogue.
- Notice position and size of details within the frame.
- Does the cartoon take a positive or negative position toward the issue?
- Identify the primary purpose of the cartoon.
- Determine how each detail illustrates and/or supports the primary purpose.
- Does the cartoonist indicate alternative viewpoints?

Notice that a political cartoon assumes the reader is aware of current events surrounding the specific issue. So, we recommend you begin to read a newspaper or news magazine regularly and/or watch a daily news program on TV. Even listening to a five-minute news summary on the radio as you drive to and from errands or school can give you a bit of background on what's happening in the world around you.

Example: Source D, political cartoon
The following political cartoon appeared in an Omaha, Nebraska, newspaper.

Jeff Koterba, *Omaha World Herald*, NE

1. <u>Subject of the cartoon:</u> eminent domain.

2. <u>Major components:</u> one chicken, one cow in a barnyard.

3. <u>Verbal clues:</u> Print size and form indicates the chicken is very excited, even panicked, while the cow is calm and unimpressed.

4. <u>Position and size of details:</u> The chicken and cow are drawn mostly to scale and perspectives with the chicken taking center stage.

5. <u>Position of the cartoonist:</u> Sees fears surrounding eminent domain as overexaggerated.

6. <u>Primary purpose of the cartoon:</u> Ridicule those who believe that all is lost if eminent domain remains in effect.

7. <u>How details illustrate the primary purpose:</u> Size and form of print indicates the chicken's state of mind. The sigh of the calmly chewing cow indicates its recognition of the chicken's silly warning. The chicken's last warning that says the cow is a threatening monster is just wrong and over the top.

8. <u>Indication of alternative viewpoints:</u> Yes, both sides are indicated.

As pointed out previously, each of these steps is important in understanding a political cartoon, but it is not necessary that you write out each of them every time you come across one in the newspaper, and so forth. Most of the analysis is done quickly in your mind, but when you are practicing techniques and strategies, it is most beneficial to write out, just as our writer did, each of the previous eight steps.

Practice critically reading political cartoons that you find in newspapers and news magazines. You might even try a few included in your history textbook.

Strategy 2: Selecting Sources

Once you've carefully read the prompt, critically read each of the given texts, and decided on your claim, you must choose which of the sources you will use in your essay. This choice is dependent on your answers to the following:

- What is your purpose?
- Is the text background information or pertinent information?
- Does the source give new information or information that other sources cover?
- Is this information that will add depth to the essay?
- Does this text reflect the viewpoints of any of the other texts?
- Does this text contradict the viewpoints of any of the other texts?
- Does the source support or oppose your claim?

Our writer has to make some important decisions about the seven texts provided in the Master synthesis essay prompt. As the writer answers each of the previous questions, he or she will decide which texts to use in the essay.

<u>My purpose:</u> to qualify the support and opposition to eminent domain
<u>Background information:</u> *Constitution* (Source A) *Kelo* decision (Source C)
<u>Pertinent information:</u> *60 Minutes* (Source B) Broder (Source E) Survey (Source G)

A helpful technique to answer the next several questions is to construct a quick chart that incorporates all of the sources at once. The following is a sample of such a chart.

SOURCE	TYPE OF INFO	ADDS DEPTH	REFLECTS VIEWS OF OTHER TEXTS	SUPPORT OF CLAIM
A	Primary and covered by Sources C and E	Yes	No	Yes and no
B	Covered by Sources C–G	Yes	Yes	Yes
C	Covered by Sources A, D, E	Yes	Yes, Sources D, G	Yes and no
D	Covered by Sources A, C	Not really	Yes, Sources A, C	Yes and no
E	Covered by Sources B, F, G	Yes	Yes, Sources B, F, G	Yes and no
F	Covered by Sources B, E, G	Not really	Yes, Sources B, E, G	Yes and no
G	Covered by Sources B–F	Yes	Yes, Sources B–F	Yes

There certainly is a great deal of information to gather and consider. The good news is that the more practice you have with this process, the more quickly you will be able to complete the task. Writing the answers to the previous questions for each of the given texts is a good practice technique for you. But, when it comes to a timed writing situation, you will be annotating the given texts as you read them and jotting down brief notes that reflect the type of thinking our writer performed previously. You will NOT have time to write answers to each question for each text. But, you WILL be thinking about them as you read and as you plan.

Practice responding to these questions using editorials, letters to the editor, and editorial cartoons that revolve around current events issues in which you have an interest. Don't ignore your school and local newspapers, and columnists in news magazines and newspapers. **Become an informed reader and citizen!**

After carefully considering each of the given texts, our reader has decided to eliminate both political cartoons because neither seems to add much depth. The other five sources can be used to develop a position.

Strategy 3: Choosing Which Parts of the Selected Texts to Use

Pay no attention to those texts you have eliminated. For those sources you have chosen to include in your essay, do the following:

* Review the notes/highlights on each of your chosen passages.
* Ignore those items you have not annotated.
* Determine if each excerpt contributes to the development of your thesis.
  — Identify the major point each will support.
  — Does it strengthen your position or not (if not, ignore it)?
  — How much of the excerpt will you use?
  — Why have it in your essay?
  — What comments can you make about it?

For example: You might construct a chart such as the following:

SOURCE:	A	B	C	E	G
	–Use all of excerpt	–City ¶ 1	–ID Kelo case ¶ 1	–Bullock "." 1st line in title	–Survey ID
	–Use in Intro	–Background ¶ 1	–Summary in ¶3	–Echeverria"." Line 1, ¶3	–Major result lines 1 & 2
		–1st "." ¶ 2			
		–Mayor's position"." ¶7			
		–Blighted ¶8			

Our writer now has a clear idea of what part(s) of each text to use. The next task is to plan the essay. The following are some planning notes:

INTRO: *Background*
                Basic prompt info
                My room when grandmother visits
                My position—qualify

POINT 1:   Kelo *decision* + *Saleets (oppose current ruling)*
Saleets' mayor (supports ruling)
My comments
POINT 2:   *Broder* = *Bullock & Echeverria (both qualify and for ruling)*
Survey

With this brief outline in mind, our writer knows where to place each of the chosen excerpts. If this were a class situation that allotted time for prewriting plans, more details would be possible when constructing the outline.

Note: Our writer chose to jot down a brief outline, but could have chosen to plan the essay in a number of different ways, such as:

- Mapping
- Charting

As we stated earlier in this chapter, for the AP English Language exam, you only have time to write a first draft, and it must be clear, organized, logical, and thoughtful. In developing each of your major points, make certain to:

- Relate it to the thesis/claim
- Use specific examples (personal and otherwise)
- Use selected sources to support the major point
- Incorporate sources into the development of your point
  — Attribution and introduction of cited sources
  — Transitions
  — Mix of direct quotations, summary, and paraphrases

A Note About Summary, Paraphrase, and Inference

No doubt you have been constructing summaries, paraphrases, and inferences as you learned the techniques of close reading and research. As a quick review, here are the definitions of these processes and an example of each. If you have any further questions, we strongly recommend you ask your instructor for clarification and further examples and/or practice.

Summary

If you want to summarize a text, you read closely and locate those key words and/or phrases that enable you to reduce the piece into its essential point(s).

Example: The previous *New York Times* article by Broder

Number of words in given text: 175

Number of key words underlined: 47

Summary based on the key words and phrases: *For many, the debate about eminent domain centers around opposing local governments using it to seize private property for private development or supporting eminent domain because cities face economic disaster without this necessary power.* (34 words)

Comments: The writer has whittled the original down by more than 73 percent to its essential point.

<u>Practice</u> this strategy on newspaper or magazine articles that you read regularly.

Note: Many online databases provide abstracts of longer articles when you perform a search. You might want to seek these out and read them to see how they are constructed to emphasize only the main points of the articles (Jodi Rice).

Paraphrase

To paraphrase a given text or part of a text, you transpose the original material into your own words. This will probably be close to the number of words in the original. In most cases, you need to cite the original.

Example: The first paragraph in the previous Source C

<u>Paraphrase:</u> Kelo v. New London *is an eminent domain case that was presented to the U.S. Supreme Court in February of 2005. The argument centered around New London using the power of eminent domain to seize private property so that it could be sold and used in the redevelopment of a section of this city (Source C).*

Comments: The original contains 67 words and two sentences, and the 54-word paraphrase is also two sentences long. Our writer has eliminated specific court numbers and the day of the month and combined several phrases into briefer and more direct ones. **Because this background on the *Kelo* case is NOT common knowledge and because our writer is NOT a recognized expert in this field, a citation is necessary.**

<u>Practice</u> this technique on sections of your own course textbooks and on newspaper or magazine articles you read regularly. You might also try to paraphrase the Master exam synthesis prompt itself, both the introduction and the assignment.

Inference

An inference is the process of drawing a conclusion based on specific material. By carefully considering the important information provided in the text, the reader reaches a conclusion or makes a judgment.

Example: Source B given in the synthesis essay prompt

<u>Inference:</u> *Considering the amount of time given to the Saleets as compared to the mayor of their town, one could conclude that* 60 Minutes *is more inclined to side with the homeowners over the local government in this eminent domain confrontation.*

Comments: Seven out of the ten paragraphs in this interview are positively related to the Saleets or their problem. The rhetorical question and answer given by the voiceover in paragraph five is indicative of the position of *60 Minutes,* and the diction used to describe both sides of the issue is more favorable toward the position of the Saleets.

<u>Practice</u> making inferences based on editorials or letters to the editor that you find in your local newspapers. Go a step further. Take a close look at ads you find in the magazines you read regularly and draw some conclusions about their purpose, their intended audience, and the specific way the ads are presented. <u>Remember, you must be able to support each of your inferences from specifics found in the text itself.</u>

Strategy 4: Incorporating Sources into the Text of Your Essay

Let's be realistic. The synthesis essay is not just a list of direct quotations from sources related to the topic. Once you have chosen your passages, you need to place them appropriately and interestingly within the actual text of your essay in the order that you've planned to best support your thesis/claim.

Just how do you do this? You could select from among the following techniques:

Direct quotation—full citation provided at beginning of the sentence

> *John Broder, in his February 21, 2006,* New York Times *article titled "States Curbing Right to Seize Private Homes," quotes Scott G. Bullock of the Institute for Justice: "Our opposition to eminent domain is not across the board . . . What we oppose is eminent domain abuse for private development, and we are encouraging legislators to curtail it."*

Direct quotation—citation placed outside the text

> *In a* 60 Minutes *interview presented on July 4, 2004, Jim Saleet, a homeowner being adversely affected by the current eminent domain policy, stated, "The bottom line is this is morally wrong . . . This is our home . . . We're not blighted. . . . This is a close-knit, beautiful neighborhood" (Source E).*

Paraphrase of and direct quotation from the third paragraph—citation placed outside of the text

> *John D. Echeverria, an authority on land-use policy, sees a danger arising from legislatures doing away with many of the powers of eminent domain. For the Director of the Georgetown Environmental Law and Policy Institute, if this policy change takes place across the country, there is a real danger that many urban areas will experience "economic decline" (Source E).*

Combination of direct quotation and paraphrase—citation provided outside of text; note the use of the ellipsis

> *In 2005, a 5–4 Supreme Court decision in the* Kelo v. New London *case ruled that ". . . the government taking of property from one private owner to give to another in furtherance of economic development constitutes a permissible 'public use' under the Fifth Amendment" (Source C).*

Notice that each of the examples integrates the source material into the text. The information is not just plopped down on the page. Take a close look at how our writer integrates the second example into the following paragraph in his essay.

> *Contrary to what the Court sees as "permissible public use" (Source C), I believe that a government taking a person's home or business away and allowing another private individual or company to take it over goes against the idea of our private property rights. A good example of this is the situation in Lakewood, Ohio, where the mayor wants to condemn a retired couple's home in order to make way for a privately owned, high-end condominium and shopping mall. As Jim Saleet said in his interview with* 60 Minutes *presented on July 4, 2004, "The bottom line is this is morally wrong . . . This is our home . . . We're not blighted. . . . This is a close-knit, beautiful neighborhood." The Saleets, who have paid off their mortgage, should be allowed to remain there as long as they want and pass it on to their children. Here, individual rights should prevail.*

Comments: Our writer uses the sources to establish negative feelings toward the current policy. The writer then refers to the *Kelo* decision in a summary and proceeds to introduce the context of the Saleet reference with the transition phrase, "A good example of this is . . . " Cohesiveness is achieved by referring to Source C, which was previously cited in the essay. The actual quotation is incorporated into the text with an introductory dependent clause. Two related sentences follow that reemphasize the writer's own position.

Practice: As you read, become aware of HOW professional writers incorporate sources into their writing. Use these as models to practice incorporating outside sources into your own sentences and/or essays.

> *Note:* You might want to take a close look at reviews of movies and books. In many cases, you will find they include direct quotations from the dialog of the film or passages from the book.

Strategy 5: Writing the Conclusion

Our writer has used each of the excerpts in the body of the essay, EXCEPT for the survey information. Although this number is quite important, it does not fit into the development of the body paragraphs. Therefore, the writer decides to incorporate this survey result into the conclusion. It will contribute to a strong final statement. Following are three different ways to use the survey.

Direct quotation—citation after sentence

> *68% of survey respondents said that they "favored legislative limits on the government's ability to take private property away from owners . . . " (Source G).*

Direct quotation—citation within sentence

> *According to a survey conducted by CNN on July 23, 2005, 66% of those responding said "never" to the question, "Should local governments be able to seize homes and businesses?"*

Paraphrase—citation outside sentence

> *In recent polls conducted by both the* Washington Times *and CNN, over 60% said no when asked if local governments should be able to take over private homes and businesses (Source G).*

Carefully consider how this sentence is incorporated into the concluding paragraph.

> *Ultimately, I have to agree with the large majority of people who responded to recent polls conducted by both the* Washington Times *and CNN. When asked if local governments should be able to take over private homes and businesses, over 60% said "no" (Source G). But, I will have to be open to the possibility that public use and the greater good may, in some cases, be the only viable solution to a complicated problem.*

Comments: The source material is sandwiched between two effective sentences. The first presents our writer's position and leads the reader to the cited excerpt employed to make the point. The last sentence begins with the word "But," which indicates that the writer is qualifying the cited sources in this paragraph and throughout the essay.

Final Comment

Remember, you MUST establish a position, and each source you choose to use MUST support and develop your position.

Rapid Review

- Establish a position on the issue.
- Critically read all given texts and any introductory material provided.
- Annotate your sources using the critical reading guidelines.
- Select appropriate sources to support your position and purpose.
- Choose appropriate excerpts from each of the selected sources that can help develop the thesis.
- Summarize, paraphrase, and draw inferences from selected material.
- Make certain you properly cite each source you incorporate into the essay.
- Construct a conclusion that clearly states a strong, final point.
- Proofread.

STEP **5**

Build Your Test-Taking Confidence

Practice Exam 1
Practice Exam 2

PRACTICE EXAM 1

ANSWER SHEET FOR MULTIPLE-CHOICE QUESTIONS

1. _____

2. _____

3. _____

4. _____

5. _____

6. _____

7. _____

8. _____

9. _____

10. _____

11. _____

12. _____

13. _____

14. _____

15. _____

16. _____

17. _____

18. _____

19. _____

20. _____

21. _____

22. _____

23. _____

24. _____

25. _____

26. _____

27. _____

28. _____

29. _____

30. _____

31. _____

32. _____

33. _____

34. _____

35. _____

36. _____

37. _____

38. _____

39. _____

40. _____

41. _____

42. _____

43. _____

44. _____

45. _____

46. _____

47. _____

48. _____

49. _____

50. _____

51. _____

52. _____

53. _____

54. _____

I _____ did _____ did not complete this part of the test in the allotted 1 hour.

I had _____ correct answers. I had _____ incorrect answers. I left _____ blank.

I have carefully reviewed the explanations of the answers, and I think I need to work on the following types of questions:

PRACTICE EXAM I
ADVANCED PLACEMENT ENGLISH LANGUAGE

Section I

Total Time—1 hour

Carefully read the following passages and answer the questions that follow.

Questions 1–10 are based on the following passage excerpted from Charles Dickens's *Pictures from Italy*.

Magnificently stern and sombre are the streets of beautiful Florence; and the strong old piles of building make such heaps of shadow, on the ground and in the river, that there is another and different city of rich forms and fancies, always lying at our feet. Prodigious palaces, constructed for defence, with small distrustful windows heavily barred, and walls of great thickness formed of huge masses of rough stone, frown, in   5 their old sulky state, on every street. In the midst of the city—in the Piazza of the Grand Duke, adorned with beautiful statues and the Fountain of Neptune—rises the Palazzo Vecchio, with its enormous overhanging battlements, and the Great Tower that watches over the whole town. In its court-yard—worthy of the Castle of Otranto in its ponderous gloom—is a massive staircase that the heaviest wagon and the stoutest   10 team of horses might be driven up. Within it, is a Great Saloon, faded and tarnished in its stately decorations, and mouldering by grains, but recording yet, in pictures on its walls, the triumphs of the Medici and the wars of the old Florentine people. The prison is hard by, in an adjacent court-yard of the building—a foul and dismal place, where some men are shut up close, in small cells like ovens; and where others look through   15 bars and beg; where some are playing draughts, and some are talking to their friends, who smoke, the while, to purify the air and some are buying wine and fruit of women-vendors; and all are squalid, dirty, and vile to look at. "They are merry enough, Signor," says the Jailer. "They are all blood-stained here," he adds, indicating, with his hand, three-fourths of the whole building. Before the hour is out, an old man, eighty years   20 of age, quarrelling over a bargain with a young girl of seventeen, stabs her dead, in the market-place full of bright flowers; and is brought in prisoner, to swell the number.

Among the four old bridges that span the river, the Ponte Vecchio—that bridge which is covered with the shops of Jewellers and Goldsmiths—is a most enchanting feature in the scene. The space of one house, in the center, being left open, the view   25 beyond is shown as in a frame; and that precious glimpse of sky, and water, and rich buildings, shining so quietly among the huddled roofs and gables on the bridge, is exquisite. Above it, the Gallery of the Grand Duke crosses the river. It was built to connect the two Great Palaces by a secret passage; and it takes its jealous course among streets and houses, with true despotism: going where it lists, and spurning every obstacle   30 away, before it.

1. The purpose of the passage is to
   A. condemn the squalor of Florence
   B. entice visitors to Florence
   C. praise the Grand Duke
   D. present the dichotomy existing in Florence
   E. reveal the author's worldliness

2. The primary rhetorical strategy used by the author is
   A. narration
   B. description
   C. analysis
   D. process
   E. argument

3. In developing his purpose, the author uses all of the following rhetorical devices except:
   A. spatial organization
   B. metaphor and simile
   C. comparison and contrast
   D. imagery
   E. chronological order

4. Which of the following lines contains an example of paradox?
   A. line 17
   B. lines 18–19
   C. lines 4–5
   D. lines 26–27
   E. line 29

5. The most probable function of the selected detail which focuses on the murder of the young girl by the old man (20–22) is
   A. to emphasize the brutality of the citizens
   B. to establish a tone of pathos
   C. to criticize the city's government
   D. to warn visitors about the dangers of the city
   E. to emphasize the contrasts evident in the city

6. The abrupt shift caused by a lack of transition between paragraphs 1 and 2 serves to do all of the following except:
   A. reemphasize the unexpected nature of murder
   B. reinforce the idea that there is no connection between the two paragraphs
   C. reinforce the element of contrast
   D. reinforce the author's style
   E. immediately whisk the reader to a place of safety away from the murder scene

7. What can be inferred from the following details taken from the passage
   — "small distrustful windows" (4)
   — "walls of great thickness" (5)
   — "enormous overhanging battlements" (8)
   — "secret passage" (29)
   A. Florence was not architecturally sound.
   B. Florence was designed to protect its artwork.
   C. Florence had experienced both warfare and intrigue.
   D. Florence was unsuited for habitation.
   E. Florence was preparing for war.

8. Lines 11–22 contain examples of which of the following rhetorical device?
   A. antithetical images
   B. anecdotal evidence
   C. parallel structure
   D. denotation
   E. inversion

9. If one were building a house of horrors, which of the following would be best suitable as a model or inspiration?
   A. Piazza of the Grand Duke (6–7)
   B. Fountain of Neptune (7)
   C. Palazzo Vecchio (8)
   D. Ponte Vecchio (23)
   E. Gallery of the Grand Duke (28)

10. Which of the following terms has most probably undergone a shift in meaning from Dickens's time to its current usage?
    A. "stately" (12)
    B. "squalid" (18)
    C. "enchanting" (24)
    D. "jealous" (29)
    E. "obstacle" (30)

Questions 11–20 are based on the following passage from Margaret Atwood's "Origins of Stories."

Our first stories come to us through the air. We hear voices.   1

Children in oral societies grow up within a web of stories; but so do all children.   2
We listen before we can read. Some of our listening is more like listening in, to the
calamitous or seductive voices of the adult world, on the radio or the television or in our
daily lives. Often it's an overhearing of things we aren't supposed to hear, eavesdropping
on scandalous gossip or family secrets. From all these scraps of voices, from the
whispers and shouts that surround us, even from ominous silences, the unfilled gaps in
meaning, we patch together for ourselves an order of events, a plot or plots; these, then,
are the things that happen, these are the people they happen to, this is the forbidden
knowledge.

We have all been little pitchers with big ears, shooed out of the kitchen when the   3
unspoken is being spoken, and we have probably all been tale-bearers, blurters at the
dinner table, unwitting violators of adult rules of censorship. Perhaps this is what writers
are: those who never kicked the habit. We remained tale-bearers. We learned to keep
our eyes open, but not to keep our mouths shut.

If we're lucky, we may also be given stories meant for our ears, stories intended for   4
us. These may be children's Bible stories, tidied up and simplified and with the vicious
bits left out. They may be fairy tales, similarly sugared, although if we are very lucky
it will be left in. In any case, these tales will have deliberate, molded shapes, unlike
stories we have patched together for ourselves. They will contain mountains, deserts,
talking donkeys, dragons; and, unlike the kitchen stories, they will have definite
endings. We are likely to accept these stories being on the same level of reality as the
kitchen stories. It's only when we are older that we are taught to regard one kind of
story as real and the other kind as mere invention. This is about the same time we're
taught to believe that dentists are useful, and writers are not.

Traditionally, both the kitchen gossips and the readers-out-loud have been mothers   5
or grandmothers, native languages have been mother tongues, and the kinds of stories
that are told to children have been called nursery tales or old wives' tales. It struck me
as no great coincidence when I learned recently that, when a great number of prominent
writers were asked to write about the family member who had the greatest influence
on their literary careers, almost all of them, male as well as female, had picked their
mothers. Perhaps this reflects the extent to which North American children have been
deprived of the grandfathers, those other great repositories of story; perhaps it will come
to change if men come to share in early child care, and we will have old husbands' tales.
But as things are, language, including the language of our earliest-learned stories, is a
verbal matrix, not a verbal patrix . . .

11. One reason Atwood gives for the presence of
stories in children's lives is
A. scandalous gossip
B. family secrets
C. supernatural influences
D. listening
E. radio and television

12. The close association between the reader and
the author is immediately established by
A. a first person, plural point of view
B. placing the reader into a family situation
C. using accessible diction and syntax
D. being emotional
E. appealing to the child in the reader

13. The last sentence of paragraph 2, "From all these scraps . . ." to "forbidden knowledge," contains all of the following except:
    A. parallel structure
    B. a periodic sentence
    C. prepositional phrases
    D. a compound-complex sentence
    E. an ellipsis

14. The phrase "forbidden knowledge" in the last sentence of the second paragraph can best be categorized as
    A. a paradox
    B. a biblical allusion
    C. hyperbole
    D. antithesis
    E. understatement

15. According to the author, the writer is like a child because
    A. "We are likely to accept these stories being of the same level of reality as the kitchen stories" [paragraph 4]
    B. ". . . we are taught to regard one kind of story as real . . ." [paragraph 4, next to last line]
    C. "We remained tale-bearers" [paragraph 3]
    D. "We will have old husbands' tales" [paragraph 5]
    E. ". . . the kinds of stories that are told to children have been called nursery tales . . ." [paragraph 5]

16. A careful reading of the last two paragraphs of the excerpt can lead the reader to infer that
    A. society does not value the storyteller
    B. women should be the storytellers
    C. storytelling should be left to children
    D. men can never be storytellers
    E. the author is a mother herself

17. The predominant tone of the passage is best stated as
    A. scathingly bitter
    B. sweetly effusive
    C. reverently detailed
    D. wistfully observant
    E. aggressively judgmental

18. The author makes use of which of the following rhetorical strategies?
    A. narration and description
    B. exposition and persuasion
    C. process and analysis
    D. anecdote and argument
    E. cause and effect

19. A shift in the focus of the passage occurs with which of the following?
    A. "If we're lucky" [paragraph 4]
    B. "Perhaps this is what writers are . . ." [paragraph 3]
    C. "Traditionally, . . ." [paragraph 5]
    D. "Perhaps this reflects the extent to which North American children have been deprived of the grandfathers . . ." [paragraph 5]
    E. "But as things are, language, including the language of the earliest-learned stories . . ." [paragraph 5]

20. The primary purpose of the passage is to
    A. plead for men to tell more stories
    B. criticize censorship
    C. idealize children
    D. analyze storytelling
    E. look at the sources of storytelling

Questions 21-32 are based on the passage taken from an article by E. J. Graff titled "What Makes a Family?" that appears in *What is Marriage For?* published by Beacon Press, Boston, in 1999.

Most historians warn readers that to grasp "family" history, you must first abandon   1
the idea that you already know what "family" means. "Family" seems to be a word
invented by Humpty Dumpty, who told Alice that "a word means what I say it means,
what I say it should mean, neither more nor less; the question is, which is to be master,
that is all." Historians always remind us of the word's etymology. Our "family" is   5
related to its root in the Roman "*familia*" just about as closely as a Chevy Suburban is
related to an elephant and a camel-drawn caravan. Sure, both of them move, but who's
inside and what are they doing there?

Inside the Roman *familia* was everyone in the household: legitimate children,
adopted adults, secretaries, and other dependents, slaves of various ages. "The Romans   10
rarely used it to mean family in the sense of kin," writes Roman family historian
Suzanne Dixon.[1] What counted, rather, was ownership. The words for children, slaves,
and servants were so often interchanged that historians can't always tell how many of
which lived under one roof. And for good reason. The patriarch's rule was complete:
he could educate, beat, sell, give, indenture, marry off, endow, or kill any one of them,   15
almost at will.[2]

He could, of course, care for his *familia* as well. Romans lived with their slaves and
servants so closely that it "in some ways resembled kinship, even if the slaves were
always in the position of poor relations," explains Dixon.[3] [She] also cites one hard-
fought custody battle between a freed slave and her former owners over who would keep   20
the ex-slave's daughter, Patronia Iusta, a custody battle as vicious as that over Baby M.[4]

Romans didn't consider birth the only way to acquire offspring. Just as they felt free
to expose (in other words, kill) any child they didn't need, they also felt free to adopt—
adults, that is. Adoption's goal was not to nurture a child, but to install an heir to carry
on the house, a goal better served by adults—and so nearly all adoptions were of grown   25
men (yes, men). Adoptees were usually nephews or grandsons or cousins, sometimes
adopted through a will. As one historian explains, "A citizen of Rome did not 'have' a
child . . . The Romans made no fetish of natural kinship.[5] Choice, not biology, made a
familia."

. . . the Roman's idea that "family" meant everyone under one roof, biologically   30
related or not, lasted until the eighteenth century's end.[6]

Historians and anthropologists frankly throw up their hands and admit that they
can't define "family" in a way that works universally. "Before the eighteenth century,
no European language had a term for the mother-father-children group,"[7] one pair
of historians writes, mainly because that grouping—although widespread—wasn't   35
important enough to need its own word. A 1287 Bologna statute defined "family" to
include a father, mother, brothers, sisters, daughters-in-law (sons brought home their
wives), but Italy was an exception. For Northern and Western Europe, the extended
family is a myth. New-marrieds almost always launched their own households—if their
parents signed over the farm, the contract often included a clause insisting that the   40
old folks must be built their own separate dwelling—socialized as much or more with
neighbors and work partners, as well as with kin. Rather, the European family, like
the Roman, included people we'd consider legal strangers: they were grouped together
in that word "family," not by blood, but by whether they lived under one roof. "Most
households included non-kin inmates, sojourners, boarders, or lodgers occupying rooms   45
vacated by children or kin, as well as indentured apprentices and resident servants,

employed either for domestic work about the house or as an additional resident labour force for the field or shop," writes historian Lawrence Stone of the British between 1500 and 1800. "This composite group was confusingly known as a 'family.'"[8] A baker might have a family of a dozen or fifteen, including four journeymen, two apprentices, two maidservants, and three or four bio-children, all of whom worked, lived, and ate under his roof, at his table, and by his rules. A baronet might have a family of thirty-seven, including seven daughters and twenty-eight servants. Or was that ten daughters and twenty-five servants? Historians grind their teeth as they try to figure out from church, census, and tax records which "menservants" and "maids" were children, stepchildren, or nephews, and which were hired labor. Children, apprentices, servants—all were under the master's rule.

    In other words, until very recently, not love, not biology, but labor made a family.

___

[1] *"The Romans rarely used it to mean family"*: Dixon, 2. [All notes are the author's, except 4, 13, 14, 23–26, 33, and 35.]

[2] The Roman patriarch's legal authority to kill his family members was used mostly for newborns; there were social limits on his right to kill his family's adults, although the symbolic threat could be usefully wielded. Dixon, 36, and Susan Treggiari, personal communication.

[3] *"in some ways resembled kinship"*: Dixon, 114.

[4] *Baby M*: The child in a nationally publicized legal case in which a surrogate mother fought the biological father for legal custody.

[5] "A citizen of Rome did not 'have' a child": Veyne, "The Roman Empire," in Ariès and Duby, vol. 1, 9.

[6] For fuller discussions of the frustrating plasticity of "the family" (and, therefore, the impossibility of defining it and studying it as a single phenomenon), see, for instance, Dixon, Ch. 1; Gies and Gies, introduction; Burguière and Lebrun, "The One Hundred and One Families of Europe," in Burguière et al., vol. 2, 1–39; Cherlin, 85–87; Stone, FSM, 37–66; Laslett, Oosterveen, and Smith, introduction; and de La Roncière, "Tuscan Notables on the Eve of the Renaissance," in Ariès and Duby, vol. 2, 157–170.

[7] *"Before the eighteenth century no European language"*: Gies and Gies, 4.

[8] *"Most households included non-kin"*: Stone, FSM, 28. For illuminating glimpses of demographic and family historians straining to determine which "servants" were or were not biological children, see, for instance, Laslett, Oosterveen, and Smith, and Rotberg and Rabb.

21. The thesis of the entire passage can be found in line(s)
A. 1–2
B. 9–10
C. 22
D. 27–29
E. 33–36

22. The purpose of the first paragraph is to
A. criticize historians
B. define *family*
C. prove the author's scholarly intent
D. ease the reader into a scholarly topic
E. establish the time frame of the passage

23. Footnote 4 is an example of a(n)
A. primary source
B. secondary source
C. assumption of the reader's background
D. author's aside
E. link to other sources

24. The opening sentence of the passage is an example of a(n)
A. cautionary tale
B. analogy
C. paradox
D. ad hoc argument
E. interrogative

25. The primary rhetorical technique employed by the author to develop this passage is
A. cause and effect
B. narration
C. description
D. process
E. definition

26. The tone of the passage can most accurately be described as
A. sarcastic and vituperative
B. conversational and scholarly
C. formal and pedantic
D. erudite and exhortative
E. humorous and detached

27. According to the passage, today's modern family most resembles that found in
    A. Rome in the time of the emperors
    B. Bologna in the thirteenth century
    C. Pre-eighteenth-century western Europe
    D. Great Britain between the sixteenth and nineteenth centuries
    E. Pre-modern northern Europe

28. Lines 32–33 ("historians . . . universally") can be read as a reinforcement of a concept expressed in lines
    A. 2–5
    B. 9–10
    C. 22–24
    D. 27–29
    E. 41–44

29. Footnote 6 does all of the following, <u>except</u>:
    A. provide primary sources for further calculations and estimates
    B. reinforce the concept of the amorphous nature of the term *family*
    C. demonstrate the breadth of the author's research
    D. point to references that the reader can access for further study
    E. disclaim any lapses or inadequacies in the author's discussion of the subject

30. The author's anticipation of readers' questions is demonstrated by her use of
    A. diction
    B. rhetorical questions
    C. direct quotations
    D. parentheticals
    E. ellipsis

31. An ambiguous piece of information is found in which of the following footnotes?
    A. 2
    B. 5
    C. 6
    D. 7
    E. 8

32. Which of the following was not critical in the evolution of the historical definition of family?
    A. common living quarters
    B. proprietary rights
    C. inheritance
    D. economic needs
    E. sanguinity

Questions 33–43 are based on the following passage from Ralph Waldo Emerson's Oration before the Phi Beta Kappa society, at Cambridge University, August 31, 1837, entitled "The American Scholar."

It is remarkable, the character of the pleasure we derive from the best books. They impress us with the conviction that one nature wrote and the same reads. We read the verses of one of the great English poets, of Chaucer, of Marvell, of Dryden, with the most modern joy,—with a pleasure, I mean, which is in great part caused by the abstraction of all *time* from their verses. There is some awe mixed with the joy of our   5 surprise, when this poet, who lived in some past world, two or three hundred years ago, says that which lies close to my own soul, that which I also had well-nigh thought and said. But for the evidence thence afforded to the philosophical doctrine of the identity of all minds, we should suppose some pre-established harmony, some foresight of souls that were to be, and some preparation of stores for their future wants, like the fact   10 observed in insects, who lay up food before death for the young grub they should never see.

It would not be hurried by any love of system, by an exaggeration of instincts, to underrate the Book. We boil grass and the broth of shoes, so the human mind can be fed by any knowledge. And great and heroic men have existed who had almost no other   15 information than by the printed page. I only would say that it needs a strong head to bear that diet. One must be an inventor to read well. As the proverb says, "He that would bring home the wealth of the Indies, must carry out the wealth of the Indies." There is then creative reading as well as creative writing. When the mind is braced by labor and invention, the page of whatever book we read becomes luminous with   20 manifold allusion. Every sentence is doubly significant, and the sense of our author is as broad as the world. We then see, what is always true, that as the seer's hour of vision is short and rare among heavy days and months, so is its record, perchance, the least part of his volume. The discerning will read, in his Plato or Shakespeare, only the least part,—only the authentic utterances of the oracle;—all the rest he rejects, were it never   25 so many times Plato's and Shakespeare's.

Of course, there is a portion of reading quite indispensable to a wise man. History and exact science he must learn by laborious reading. Colleges, in like manner, have their indispensable office,—to teach elements. But they can only highly serve us when they aim not to drill, but to create; when they gather from far every ray of various   30 genius to their hospitable halls, and by the concentrated fires, set the hearts of their youth on flame. Thought and knowledge are natures in which apparatus and pretension avail nothing. Gowns and pecuniary foundations, though of towns of gold, can never countervail the least sentence or syllable of wit. Forget this, and our American colleges will recede in their public importance, whilst they grow richer every year.   35

33. In context, the word "oracle" in line 25 can best be interpreted to mean the
A. visionary writer
B. inventive writer
C. popular writer of a time
D. intuitive writer
E. writer as critic

34. In line 17, the word "diet" refers to
A. "Broth of shoes" [paragraph 2, sentence 2]
B. "Boiled grass" [paragraph 2, sentence 2]
C. "Any knowledge" [paragraph 2, sentence 2]
D. "Any love" [paragraph 2, sentence 1]
E. "Printed page" [paragraph 2, sentence 3]

35. The speaker characterizes the great writers as being able to
A. surprise the reader
B. present universal truths
C. create harmony in their writing
D. be philosophical
E. write about nature

36. The speaker's attitude toward great writers in the fourth sentence of paragraph 1 (lines 5–8) might best be described as
A. skeptical
B. confused
C. accusative
D. validated
E. patronizing

37. The speaker's tone in the passage can best be described as
A. pretentious
B. analytical
C. satirical
D. ambiguous
E. servile

38. All of the following lines use figurative language except:
A. "It is remarkable, the character of the pleasure we derive from the best books. They impress us with the conviction that one nature wrote and the same reads."
B. ". . . and some preparation of stores for their future wants, like the fact observed in insects . . ."
C. "We boil grass and the broth of shoes, so the human mind can be fed by any knowledge."
D. "I would only say that it needs a strong head to bear that diet. One must be an inventor to read well."
E. "Gowns and pecuniary foundations, though of towns of gold, can never countervail the least sentence or syllable of wit."

39. After reading the passage, the reader can infer that the author desires to
A. praise the work of current writers
B. change the curriculum of the college
C. change college administration
D. warn against relying on academic appearances
E. criticize the cost of college

40. The pronoun "this" in the last sentence of the passage refers to
A. "But they can only highly serve us when they aim not to drill, but to create . . ."
B. "History and exact science he must learn by laborious reading."
C. "Thought and knowledge are natures in which apparatus and pretension avail nothing."
D. "Forget this, and our American colleges will recede in their public importance . . ."
E. "When the mind is braced by labor and invention, the page of whatever book we read becomes luminous with manifold allusion."

41. According to the speaker, the characteristics of the discerning reader include all of the following except:
A. brings himself to the work
B. makes connections with the past
C. discards irrelevancies
D. approaches difficult readings willingly
E. aspires to be a writer

42. Paragraphs 1 and 2 develop their ideas by means of
  I. metaphor and simile
 II. allusion
III. paradox
A. I
B. II
C. III
D. I and II
E. I, II, and III

43. The purpose of the third paragraph is to
A. defend the role of reading
B. praise history and science
C. delineate the qualities of an ideal college
D. inspire student scholars
E. honor college instructors

Questions 44–54 are based on the following excerpt from Joseph Conrad's *The Secret Sharer*.

On my right hand there were lines of fishing stakes resembling a mysterious system of half-submerged bamboo fences, incomprehensible in its division of the domain of tropical fishes, and crazy of aspect as if abandoned forever by some nomad tribe of fishermen now gone to the other end of the ocean; for there was no sign of human habitation as far as the eye could reach. To the left a group of barren islets, suggesting ruins of stone walls, 5 towers, and blockhouses, had its foundations set in a blue sea that itself looked solid, so still and stable did it lie below my feet; even the track of light from the westering sun shone smoothly, without that animated glitter which tells of an imperceptible ripple. And when I turned my head to take a parting glance at the tug which had just left us anchored outside the bar, I saw the straight line of the flat shore joined to the stable sea, 10 edge to edge, with a perfect and unmarked closeness, in one leveled floor half brown, half blue under the enormous dome of the sky. Corresponding in their insignificance to the islets of the sea, two small clumps of trees, one on each side of the only fault in the impeccable joint, marked the mouth of the river Meinam we had just left on the first preparatory stage of our homeward journey; and, far back on the inland level, a larger and 15 loftier mass, the grove surrounding the great Paknam pagoda, was the only thing on which the eye could rest from the vain task of exploring the monotonous sweep of the horizon. Here and there gleams as of a few scattered pieces of silver marked the windings of the great river; and on the nearest of them, just within the bar, the tug steaming right into the land became lost to my sight, hull and funnel and masts, as though the 20 impassive earth had swallowed her up without an effort, without a tremor. My eye followed the light cloud of her smoke, now here, now there, above the plain according to the devious curves of the stream, but always fainter and farther away, till I lost it at last behind the miter-shaped hill of the great pagoda. And then I was left alone with my ship, anchored at the head of the Gulf of Siam. 25

44. Within the passage, the long, sinuous sentences emphasize the
A. narrator's sense of anticipation
B. objectivity of nature
C. insecurity of the narrator
D. passive nature of the journey
E. fearful tone of the passage

45. In the next to last sentence of the passage (lines 21–24), "devious curves" most likely is used to reinforce
A. the unpredictability of the water
B. the hidden nature of the stream
C. the concept of the complexity of what lies beneath the surface of the story
D. the mystery of nature
E. all of the above

46. The passage as a whole can best described as
A. an interior monologue
B. a melodramatic episode
C. an evocation of place
D. a historical narrative
E. an allegory

47. The first sentence of the passage helps to establish tone by means of
A. structure that reflects the strangeness of the experience described
B. parallel structure that contrasts with the chaos of the situation
C. alliteration to heighten the imagery
D. irony to create a sense of satire
E. hyperbole that exaggerates the danger of the situation

48. Which of the following ideas can be supported based on the third sentence (lines 9–12) beginning with "And when I . . ."?
    A. The speaker enjoys watching boats sailing on the horizon.
    B. The speaker wants to revel in the beauty and grace of nature.
    C. The speaker responds to the symmetry and balance of nature.
    D. The speaker realizes how vulnerable man is in the universe.
    E. The speaker is fearful of the earth and sea.

49. All of the following contribute to the feeling of solitude except:
    A. ". . . the impassive earth had swallowed her up without an effort . . ."
    B. "a group of barren islets"
    C. "the grove surrounding the great Paknam pagoda"
    D. "the monotonous sweep of the horizon"
    E. "ruins of stone walls, towers, and blockhouses"

50. The passage is organized primarily by means of
    A. spatial description
    B. definition
    C. chronological order
    D. order of importance
    E. parallelism

51. In the third to last sentence of the passage (lines 18–21) beginning with "Here and there . . . ," the figure of speech used to describe "the windings of the great river" is
    A. personification
    B. simile
    C. apostrophe
    D. antithesis
    E. symbol

52. The writer emphasizes his solitude by using all of the following rhetorical techniques except:
    A. heavy descriptive emphasis placed on setting
    B. overt statement of the absence of other people
    C. tracking the departure of the tugboat
    D. diction that emphasizes desertion and neglect
    E. contrasting the present situation with previous times

53. A characteristic of the author's style is
    A. succession of allusions
    B. the use of emotional language
    C. terse sentence structure
    D. vividness of contrasting images
    E. shifts in points of view

54. The tone of the passage can best be described as
    A. cynical
    B. reflective
    C. sarcastic
    D. elegiac
    E. apathetic

END OF SECTION I

Section II

Total Time—2 hours

Question 1

(Suggested time 40 minutes. This question counts as one-third of the total score for Section II.)

Carefully read Chief Seattle's oration to Governor Isaac I. Stevens, who had just returned from Washington, D.C., with orders to buy Indian lands and create reservations. In a well-written essay, identify Chief Seattle's purpose and analyze the rhetorical strategies he uses to convey his purpose. Consider such items as figurative language, organization, diction, and tone.

. . . Yonder sky that has wept tears of compassion upon my people for centuries untold, and which to us appears changeless and eternal, may change. Today is fair. Tomorrow it may be overcast with clouds. My words are like the stars that never change. Whatever Seattle says the great chief at Washington can rely upon with as much certainty as he can upon the return of the sun. The White Chief says that Big Chief at Washington sends us greetings of friendship and goodwill. This is kind of him for we know he has little need of our friendship in return. His people are many. They are like the grass that covers vast prairies. My people are few. They resemble the scattering trees of a storm-swept plain. The great, and I presume—good White Chief sends us word that he wishes to buy our lands but is willing to allow us enough to live comfortably. This indeed appears just, even generous, for the Red Man no longer has rights that he need respect, and the offer may be wise, as we are no longer in need of an extensive country.   1

There was a time when our people covered the land as the waves of a wind-ruffled sea cover its shell-paved floor, but that time long since passed away with the greatness of tribes that are now but a mournful memory. I will not dwell on, nor mourn over, our untimely decay, nor reproach my paleface brothers with hastening it as we too may have been somewhat to blame.   2

Youth is impulsive. When our young men grow angry at some real or imaginary wrong, and disfigure their faces with black paint, it denotes that their hearts are black, and our old men and old women are unable to restrain them. Thus it was when the white men first began to push our forefathers further westward. But let us hope that the hostilities between us may never return. We would have everything to lose and nothing to gain.   3

Our good father at Washington—for I presume he is now our father as well as yours—our great and good father, I say, sends us word that if we do as he desires he will protect us. But can that ever be? Your God is not our God! Your God loves your people and hates mine. He folds his strong protecting arms lovingly about the pale face—but he has forsaken his red children—if they really are his. Our God, the Great Spirit, seems also to have forsaken us. Our people are ebbing away like a rapidly receding tide that will never return. How then can we be brothers? We are two distinct races with separate origins and separate destinies.   4

To us the ashes of our ancestors are sacred and their resting place is hallowed ground. You wander far from the graves of your ancestors and seemingly without regret. Your dead cease to love you and the land of your nativity as soon as they pass the portals of the tomb and wander away beyond the stars. Our dead never forget the beautiful world   5 that gave them being . . . and often return to visit, guide, console, and comfort the lonely hearted living.

It matters little where we pass the remnant of our days. They will not be many. The Indians' night promises to be dark. Not a single star of hope hovers above his horizon. Tribe follows tribe, and nation follows nation like the waves of the sea. It is the order of nature, and regret is useless. Your time of decay may be distant, but it will surely come, for even the white man whose God walked and talked with him as friend with friend, cannot be exempt from the common destiny. We may be brothers after all. We will see. 6

And when the Last Red Man shall have perished, these shores will swarm with the invisible dead of my tribe, and when your children's children think themselves alone, they will not be alone. At night when you think your cities are deserted, they will throng with the returning hosts that once filled them and still love this beautiful land. The White Man will never be alone. 7

Let him be just and deal kindly with my people, for the dead are not powerless. 8

Question 2

Suggested Writing Time: 40 minutes

A new word has entered the American vocabulary: *affluenza*. A 1997 PBS documentary titled *Affluenza* introduced this new term and defined it: " n. 1. The bloated, sluggish, and unfulfilled feeling that results from efforts to keep up with the Joneses. 2. An epidemic of stress, overwork, waste, and indebtedness caused by dogged pursuit of the American Dream. 3. An unsustainable addiction to economic growth."

Since then, scholars, journalists, political leaders, artists, and even comedians have made America's ever-increasing consumption the subject of dire warnings, academic studies, social commentary, campaign promises, and late-night TV jokes.

Carefully read the following sources (including any introductory information). **Then, in an essay that synthesizes at least three of the sources, take a position that supports, opposes, or qualifies the claim that Americans are never satisfied. They are constantly wanting new things and are never content with what they have. There is a superabundance of "stuff," and Americans have lost their sense of meaning. As Sheryl Crow's 2002 lyrics state,** *"it's not having what you want. It's wanting what you've got."*

Make certain that you take a position and that the essay centers on your argument. Use the sources to support your reasoning; avoid simply summarizing the sources. You may refer to the sources by their letters (Source A, Source B, etc.) or by the identifiers in the parentheses below.

Source A (Aristotle's *Ethics*)
Source B (*The Declaration of Independence*)
Source C (John Stuart Mill's *Utilitarianism*)
Source D (Cartoon by Jim Sizemore)
Source E (Jessie H. O'Neill's *The Golden Ghetto: The Psychology of Affluence*)
Source F (Lewis Lapham's *Money and Class in America*)
Source G ("Wealth" by Andrew Carnegie)

Source A
Aristotle's *Nicomachean Ethics*

> *Certainly the future is obscure to us, while happiness, we claim, is an end and something in every way final. . . . If so, we shall call happy those among living men in whom these conditions are, and are to be fulfilled.*

Happiness is desirable in itself and never for the sake of something else. But honor, pleasure, reason, and every virtue we choose indeed for themselves, but we choose them also for the sake of happiness, judging that by means of them we shall be happy. Happiness, on the other hand, no one chooses for the sake of these, nor, in general, for anything other than itself. Happiness, then, is something final and self-sufficient.

He is happy who lives in accordance with complete virtue and is sufficiently equipped with external goods, not for some chance period but throughout a complete life.

To judge from the lives that men lead, most men seem to identify the good, or happiness, with pleasure: which is the reason why they love the life of enjoyment. The mass of mankind are evidently quite slavish in their tastes, preferring a life suitable to beasts.

With regard to what happiness is (men) differ, and the many do not give the same account as the wise. For the former think it is some plain and obvious thing, like pleasure, wealth, or honor. They differ, however, from one another—and often even the same man identifies it with different things, with health when he is ill, with wealth when he is poor.

Source B

The Declaration of Independence
From the opening paragraph of The Declaration of Independence.

We hold these Truths to be self-evident, that all Men are created equal, that they are endowed by their Creator with certain unalienable Rights: that among these are Life, Liberty, and the Pursuit of Happiness. That to secure these Rights, Governments are instituted among Men, deriving their just Powers from the Consent of the Governed . . .

Source C

Utilitarianism, written by John Stuart Mill, an eighteenth-century British philosopher, in 1863. Available at http://www.utilitarianism.com/mill2.htm.
The following is an excerpt from Chapter 2 entitled "What Utilitarianism Is."

. . . The creed which accepts as the foundation of morals, Utility, or the Greatest Happiness Principle, holds that actions are right in proportion as they tend to promote happiness, wrong as they tend to produce the reverse of happiness. By happiness is intended pleasure, and the absence of pain; by unhappiness, pain, and the privation of pleasure. . . .

. . . no intelligent human being would consent to be a fool, no instructed person would be an ignoramus, no person of feeling and conscience would be selfish and base, even though they should be persuaded that the fool, the dunce, or the rascal is better satisfied with his lot than they are with theirs. They would not resign what they possess more than he for the most complete satisfaction of all desires which they have in common with him. If they ever fancy they would, it is only in cases of unhappiness so extreme, that to escape from it they would exchange their lot for almost any other, however undesirable in their own eyes. A being of higher faculties [humans] requires more to make him happy, is capable probably of more acute suffering, and certainly accessible to it at more points, than one of the inferior type [animals]: but in spite of these liabilities, he can never really wish to sink into what he feels to be a lower grade

of existence. . . . Whoever supposes that this preference takes place at a sacrifice of happiness—that the superior being, in anything like equal circumstances, is not happier than the inferior—confounds two very different ideas, of happiness and content. It is indisputable that the being whose capacities of enjoyment are low, has the greatest chance of having them fully satisfied; and a highly endowed being will always feel that any happiness which he can look for, as the world is constituted, is imperfect. But he can learn to bear its imperfections, but only because he feels not at all the good which those imperfections qualify. It is better to be a human being dissatisfied than a pig satisfied; better to be Socrates dissatisfied than the fool satisfied. And if the fool, or the pig, are of different opinion, it is because they only know their own side of the question. The other party to the comparison knows both sides.

Source D

Cartoon by Jim Sizemore

Available at http://www.cartoonstock.com/blowup.asp?imageref=jsi0087&artist=Sizemore,+Jim&topic=consumerism.

This cartoon appeared in a recent issue of *The New Yorker.*

"Something is missing."

Source E

O'Neill, Jesse H. *The Golden Ghetto: The Psychology of Affluence,* The Affluenza Project: Milwaukee, Wisconsin, 1997.

The following is adapted from passages in Jesse H. O'Neill's book and from the mission statement of The Affluenza Project founded by O'Neill. Available at http://www.affluenza.com.

The malaise that currently grips our country comes not from the fact that we don't have enough wealth, but from a terrifying knowledge that has begun to enter our consciousness that we have based our entire lives, our entire culture and way of being on the belief that "just a little bit more" will finally buy happiness.

Although many people in our culture are beginning to question the assumptions of the American Dream, we still live in a time of compulsive and wasteful consumerism. Statistics to consider:

- *Per capita consumption in the United States has increased 45 percent in the past twenty years.*
- *During the same period, quality of life as measured by the index of social health has decreased by roughly the same percentage.*
- *The average working woman plays with her children forty minutes a week—and shops six hours.*
- *Ninety-three percent of teenage girls list shopping as their favorite pastime.*

Source F

Lapham, Lewis. *Money and Class in America: Notes and Observations on Our Civil Religion*, Grove Press: New York, 1988.

The following is a passage from Mr. Lapham's text.

I think it fair to say that the current ardor of the American faith in money easily surpasses the degrees of intensity achieved by other societies in other times and places. Money means so many things to us—spiritual as well as temporal—that we are at a loss to know how to hold its majesty at bay. . . .

Henry Adams in his autobiography remarks that although the Americans weren't much good as materialists they had been "so deflected by the pursuit of money" that they could turn "in no other direction." The natural distrust of the contemplative temperament arises less from the innate Philistinism than from a suspicion of anything that cannot be counted, stuffed, framed or mounted over the fireplace in the den. Men remain free to rise or fall in the world, and if they fail it must be because they willed it so. The visible signs of wealth testify to an inward state of grace, and without at least some of these talismans posted in one's house or on one's person an American loses all hope of demonstrating to himself the theorem of his happiness. Seeing is believing, and if an American success is to count for anything in the world it must be clothed in the raiment of property. As often as not it isn't the money itself that means anything; it is the use of money as the currency of the soul.

Against the faith in money, other men in other times and places have raised up countervailing faiths in family, honor, religion, intellect and social class. The merchant princes of medieval Europe would have looked upon the American devotion as sterile stupidity; the ancient Greek would have regarded it as a form of insanity. Even now, in the last decades of a century commonly defined as American, a good many societies both in Europe and Asia manage to balance the desire for wealth against the other claims of the human spirit. An Englishman of modest means can remain more or less content with the distinction of an aristocratic name or the consolation of a flourishing garden; the Germans show to obscure university professors the deference accorded by Americans only to celebrity; the Soviets honor the holding of political power; in France a rich man is a rich man, to whom everybody grants the substantial powers that his riches command but to whom nobody grants the respect due to a member of the National Academy. But in the United States a rich man is perceived as being necessarily both good and wise, which is an absurdity that would be seen as such not only by a Frenchman but also by a Russian. Not that the Americans are greedier than the French, or less intellectual than the Germans, or more venal than the Russians, but to what other tribunal can an anxious and supposedly egalitarian people submit their definitions of the good, the true and the beautiful if not to the judgment of the bottom line?

Source G

"Wealth" written by Andrew Carnegie[1] published in *North American Review*, CCCXCI, June 1889. Available at http://facweb.furman.edu/~benson/docs/carnegie.htm.
The following is excerpted from the article by Andrew Carnegie.

> *The problem of our age is the proper administration of wealth, so that the ties of brotherhood may still bind together the rich and poor in harmonious relationship. The conditions of human life have not only been changed, but revolutionized, within the past few hundred years. In former days there was little difference between the dwelling, dress, food, and environment of the chief and those of his retainers. The Indians are today where civilized man then was. When visiting the Sioux, I was led to the wigwam of the chief. It was just like the others in external appearance, and even within the difference was trifling between it and those of the poorest of his braves. The contrast between the palace of the millionaire and the cottage of the laborer with us today measures the change which has come with civilization.*
>
> *This change, however, is not to be deplored, but welcomed as highly beneficial. It is well, nay, essential for the progress of the race, that the houses of some should be homes for all that is highest and best in literature and the arts, and for all the refinements of civilization, rather than that none should be so. Much better this great irregularity than universal squalor. Without wealth there can be no Maecenas.[2] The "good old times" were not good old times. Neither master nor servant was as well situated then as today. A relapse to old conditions would be disastrous to both—not the least so to him who serves—and would sweep away civilization with it. But whether the change be for good or ill, it is upon us, beyond our power to alter, and therefore to be accepted and made the best of. It is waste of time to criticize the inevitable.*
>
> [1] *Late nineteenth-century American capitalist and philanthropist*
> [2] *Patron of the arts in ancient Rome*

Question 3

In his essay "The Wilderness Idea," Wallace Stegner states the following.

> *Without any remaining wilderness we are committed wholly, without chance for even momentary reflection and rest, to a headlong drive into our technological termite-life, the Brave New World of a completely man-controlled environment.*

Write a well-constructed essay that defends, challenges, or qualifies Stegner's statement using your own knowledge, experience, observation, or reading.

END OF SECTION II

ANSWER KEY

1. D	19. C	37. B
2. B	20. E	38. A
3. E	21. A	39. D
4. A	22. D	40. C
5. E	23. C	41. E
6. B	24. C	42. D
7. C	25. E	43. C
8. A	26. B	44. D
9. C	27. B	45. E
10. D	28. A	46. C
11. D	29. A	47. A
12. A	30. D	48. C
13. E	31. A	49. C
14. B	32. E	50. A
15. C	33. A	51. B
16. A	34. E	52. E
17. D	35. B	53. D
18. B	36. D	54. B

Explanations of Answers to the Multiple-Choice Section

The Dickens Passage

1. **D.** The very first sentence indicates the author's purpose. Here, the reader is told directly that Florence is both fanciful and somber, rich and stern.

2. **B.** This selection is based on a quite specific description of Florence and an area within the city. To correctly answer this question, the student needs to be familiar with the different types of rhetorical strategies.

3. **E.** The reader is brought from the general street scene to a specific prison and then to a specific scene outside the prison. Metaphors, similes, and imagery are found throughout the selection, such as "small cells like ovens," "distrustful windows." Contrast and comparison are provided with such phrases as "faded and tarnished Great Saloon" placed next to the "walls which record the triumphs of the Medici." The passage does *NOT* follow a specific timeline.

4. **A.** The test taker needs to know the definition of paradox and must be able to recognize it in a given text. Here, smoke is being used to purify the air even though it is in itself a pollutant.

5. **E.** Dickens is not warning people away from Florence, nor is he criticizing its government. What the text and its selection of details do is to reinforce the idea of Florence being a city of contrast (youth and age, life and death, bright flowers and squalid prisons).

6. **B.** There is no support from a close reading of the text that will allow you to defend choice B, which sees no connection between the two scenes described. Obviously both reveal aspects of Florence. Both are descriptive, with the second paragraph containing the selective contrast with the first paragraph.

7. **C.** Distrustful and secret are indicative of "intrigue," and building thick walls and huge battlements points to the need for protection from aggression. No other choice provides these same inferences.

8. **A.** A close look at each of the selected lines reveals opposites being placed side by side. This is the nature of antithesis.

9. **C.** The Palazzo Vecchio is described using such terms as "ponderous gloom," "faded" and "tarnished" and "mouldering." These are evocative of a place that is creepy and frightening. None of the other choices projects these qualities.

10. **D.** In Dickens's time, "jealous" was used to indicate the state of being watchful or closely guarded. If you look at the context of the line, you can see that "jealous" has nothing to do with our current use of the word.

The Atwood Passage

11. **D.** Although you might be inclined to accept A, B, or E as possible correct choices, you should be aware that these are specific things the child hears. Each of these would cancel the other out, because they would be equally valid. Choice C is nowhere to be found in the selection. Therefore, the appropriate choice is D, listening.

12. **A.** The very first word of the selection is "Our." This immediately links the writer and the reader. Both are vested with this choice of pronoun.

13. **E.** If you look carefully, you find examples of all of the choices except E. An ellipsis is punctuation comprising three periods. You find none in this sentence. Its function is to notify the reader that a piece of the text has been omitted.

14. **B.** The question makes reference to wanting or seeking something not permitted, such as Adam and Eve being warned not to eat of the forbidden fruit from the tree of knowledge. The other choices are simply not appropriate to the relationship between *forbidden* and *knowledge*.

15. **C.** This is a rather easy question. The entire third paragraph supports this idea.

16. **A.** The answer is clearly supported in the last sentence of paragraph 4. That which is immediately practical and helpful in a very tangible way is the more valuable.

17. **D.** Words, phrases used, and specific details given in this passage support the adjective "wistful" (paragraphs 3 and 4). She is observant throughout the passage as she provides details of the child acquiring her stories. The writer's wistfulness is reiterated in the last paragraph as she states her yearning for men to share in the language of storytelling.

18. **B.** The only choice that presents two strategies actually present in the text is B. The entire passage employs exposition to support the author's purpose. Even the final paragraph, which attempts to persuade, uses exposition to strengthen the appeal to have men welcomed into the language of storytelling. (If you are not crystal clear about the terminology used in the choices, this may be one of those questions you choose to skip, because it can be time consuming trying to determine the correct choice.)

19. **C.** The abruptness of "Traditionally," provides no real connection with the previous paragraph or the previous sentence. It is an obvious break that grabs the reader's attention and leads him or her to Atwood's point.

20. **E.** Throughout the passage, Atwood is taking a close look at the beginnings of storytelling. Although she does attempt to persuade us of the need to encourage men to tell their stories, this is not the primary purpose of the piece. It is important to also notice that the title is a clue to this answer.

The Family Passage

21. **A.** The entire passage is concerned with the concept of family in general, not just the Roman and pre-modern era family. The choices other than A all concern these.

22. **D.** Through humor, exaggeration, common allusions, and rhetorical questions, the author invites the reader to join her family as a prelude to a scholarly examination of the roots of the word *family*.

23. **C.** The footnote identifies a case that some readers may not be familiar with. No sources are cited or referenced. The footnote is strictly informative.

24. **C.** This is a vocabulary question that demands you know and can identify each of the terms. Knowing the definition of each can only lead you to choose C.

25. **E.** Each piece of information provided in the passage is given in terms of defining what a *family* is.

26. **B.** The first paragraph establishes the conversational tone with its lighthearted references. But, the author's use of footnotes, direct quotations from experts, and historical references all indicate a scholarly presentation.

27. **B.** If one closely reads the passage, the only location cited that has a family unit consisting of a mother, father, and children is Bologna in the thirteenth century.

28. **A.** The word *family* does NOT have a universal definition. Each culture and time period defined it according to its own circumstances.

29. **A.** This footnote contains NO specifics that were gathered via observation and experience. There is no data from census, and so forth.

30. **D.** Even though the reader can locate instances of choices C and E in both paragraphs, they are not responding to a probable reader-generated question. The parentheticals come immediately after a word or phrase that could raise questions from a reader.

31. **A.** The comment separated only by commas leaves the reader unclear as to whom the *personal communication* refers: Dixon, Treggiari, or the author.

32. **E.** Lines 24–25, 27–29, 43–44, and 56–57 support choices A, B, C, and D.

The Emerson Passage

33. **A.** If you go back to the next to last sentence of paragraph 2, you will see the phrase "the seer's hour of vision." Your knowledge of synonyms will lead you to choose A.

34. **E.** Using the process of substitution, it is not difficult to eliminate all choices other than "the printed page."

35. **B.** For Emerson, the universal crosses barriers between time and place. This idea is supported in the third sentence of paragraph 1.

36. **D.** Using the process of elimination while looking carefully at the given lines, you will discover that the only answer that correctly relates to Emerson's attitude is D. All the others are negative.

37. **B.** Vocabulary is a key factor in this question. In this passage, Emerson is "taking apart" the qualities of a great writer, book, and college. This is what an analytical essay does.

38. **A.** In the first two sentences of paragraph 1, Emerson is setting up the parameters of his argument. There is no figurative language here.

39. **D.** Carefully reading the last paragraph, especially the last three sentences, can only lead you to choose D. None of the other choices is logical within the context of the passage.

40. **C.** Antecedents come *before* the given pronoun, and as close as possible to that pronoun. With this in mind, the fifth sentence of paragraph 3 is the only choice that correctly and logically fits the criteria.

41. **E.** If you pay close attention to the second paragraph, you will find all the choices, except E.

42. **D.** Emerson alludes to "great English poets" in the first paragraph, and to a proverb and other writers in the second paragraph. Similes and metaphors can be found throughout both paragraphs, but no paradox is evident.

43. **C.** Because this is an analytical passage, including the final paragraph, C is the only acceptable choice.

The Conrad Passage

44. **D.** The very nature of sentences that are long and flowing serves to create a corresponding mood of passivity, ease, and timelessness. This lack of tension in the structure is not indicated in any of the other choices.

45. **E.** Each of the choices deals with what is yet unknown to the narrator and the reader. The phrase "devious curves" foreshadows the complexity of the novella itself.

46. **C.** This exemplifies that choosing the correct answer can be dependent on the student's knowing definitions of terms and ability to recognize them in context. No other choice is acceptable in characterizing this passage.

47. **A.** This compound-complex sentence sets the task for the reader with its convoluted structure and imagery. This reflects the very essence the narrator is presenting to the reader of the strangeness of the experience.

48. **C.** The diction, which includes "joined," "edge to edge," and "half brown, half blue," supports the idea of balance and corresponding symmetry.

49. **C.** Choices A, B, D, and E all reinforce the feeling of abandonment and aloneness. Choice C does not contribute to this impression of isolation; it is rather just a descriptive detail.

50. **A.** By its very definition, spatial description will provide the reader an opportunity to sense the setting by means of directions, scale, dimension, and color.

51. **B.** Just find the word *as,* and you will easily locate the simile comparing the light to scattered pieces of silver.

52. **E.** A careful reading of the passage uncovers each of the given choices except E. Nowhere in the excerpt does the narrator indicate a contrast between the current situation and a previous one.

53. **D.** The passage contains no allusions, has no real emotional diction, and maintains a constant first person point of view. And, most obviously, it does not rely on short, direct sentences. Therefore, the only choice is D.

54. **B.** The entire passage involves the reader in the narrator's thoughtful and reflective observations about his or her surroundings.

Sample Student Essays

Rubrics for Seattle Passage

High-Range Essay

- Clearly identifies Seattle's purpose and attitude
- Successfully and effectively analyzes the rhetorical strategies used to accomplish the author's purpose
- Effectively cites specifics from the text to illustrate rhetorical devices and their meanings and effects on the oration
- Indicates a facility with organization
- Effectively manipulates language
- Few, if any, syntactical errors

Mid-Range Essay

- Correctly identifies Seattle's purpose and attitude
- Understands the demands of the prompt
- Cites specific examples of rhetorical devices found in the text and effects on the oration
- Ideas clearly stated
- Less well-developed than the high-range essays
- A few lapses in diction or syntax

Low-Range Essay

- Inadequate response to the prompt
- Misunderstands, oversimplifies, or misrepresents Seattle's purpose and attitude
- Insufficient or inappropriate use of examples to develop the demands of the prompt
- Lack of mature control of elements of essay writing

Students apparently found the question quite accessible. Most recognized the figurative language used in the passage and were able to incorporate examples into their essays. They were able to recognize the purpose and emotional appeal of Seattle's oration. The more perceptive writers recognized the subtleties of Seattle's manipulation of the situation—his implied sarcasm and his subtle threatening predictions.

Chief Seattle Passage—Student Sample A

In his oration to Governor Isaac I. Stevens, Chief Seattle attempts to convince the whites that they should deal fairly with the Native Americans despite their inferior status. Through the use of rhetorical strategies and devices like figurative language, organization, diction, and tone, he appeals both to the pride and the reason of the Governor, reminding him that, though weak, the Natives are not powerless.

Chief Seattle begins his oration in a friendly manner, appealing to the Governor and the white's pride while recognizing their superior status. He refers to the Governor as "the great" and "the good White Chief" throughout the piece, hoping the governor will look favorably on his subordinance despite the mocking that is hidden in his words. Seattle takes responsibility for the plight of the Natives, another strategy that undoubtedly makes him more respectable and admirable to the Governor, although he does not necessarily believe his people are truly at fault. In yet another attempt to get or remain on the Governor's "good side," Seattle says that the young Indian warriors' "hearts are black," blaming them and not the whites for the warfare and distrust that characterizes the Native American–American relationship. To increase his own credibility, Seattle uses the simile "my words are like the stars that never change," once more emphasizing his steadfastness and ability to work with the Americans. By presenting himself as inferior, apologetic, responsible and respectful, Seattle attempts to win Stevens' favor.

In addition to promoting his own respectability, Seattle emphasizes differences between his people and the Americans. Appreciating the Americans' "generosity" and "friendship and goodwill," Seattle points out the differences between the two peoples in a respectful manner. He calls the whites his "paleface brothers," but is certain to point out that they believe in different supreme beings, have different customs, are "two distinct races with separate origins and separate destinies." With rhetorical questions like "How then can we be brothers?" Seattle suggests that the two peoples cannot intermingle through no fault of their own. Instead of blaming the Americans, he implies that they are just and kind and that the peoples' lack of friendship is just the way it's supposed to be.

Despite his calm, almost compromising attitude throughout his oration, Chief Seattle does, at certain points, warn Governor Stevens of the power of his people. Short of belligerent, these comments are often made in a manner that implies rather than openly affirms Native American strength and lack of fear. With the emotional statement "Indians' night promises to be dark," Seattle almost suggests that his people have nothing to lose if the relationship with the Americans goes sour. They have already lost so much that they will fight to the end. Seattle warns that "these shores will swarm with the invisible dead of my tribe . . . the White Man will never be alone." Thus, he reminds Stevens that, even though his people are but "the scattering trees of a storm-swept plain," they are strong—a force to be reckoned with. In a respectful manner, he manages to threaten Stevens and clearly deliver his message that the tribe will not so easily be destroyed.

In addition to warning the Governor, acting respectfully and emphasizing the inherent differences between the two peoples, Chief Seattle gives a sense of the unfair treatment his tribe has suffered. In his oration so deeply saturated with figurative language, balanced sentences, carefully chosen diction, and hidden implications, the Chief conveys his message loud and clear. Though weak in number, his people are strong in heart; though inferior in legal status, his tribe is superior in customs and values. The governor may buy their land, but, Seattle reminds him, he may never buy their pride or their silence.

5

Chief Seattle Passage—Student Sample B

Chief Seattle, one of great speakers for the Native Americans, spoke out against Governor Stevens in an attempt to discourage the buying of more Indian land. His style which includes similes, rhetorical questions, and emotional diction, not only gets his point across, but warns and denounces the whites as well.

1

Right in the beginning, Seattle starts emotionally with "wept tears of compassion" to try to gain a sympathy for his people. Later on in the passage, he exclaims, "Your God is not our God!" and blatantly announces "Your God loves your people and hates mine." These harsh words obviously convey Chief Seattle's anger and disapproval.

2

To further increase the emotional appeal, Seattle employs rhetorical questions in an attempt to make the reader wonder and empathize. He states ". . . he will protect us. But can that ever be?" and "How then can we be brothers? We are two distinct races." Since this was addressed to Governor Isaac, what this did was it made the Governor question himself whether the buying of more Indian land and pushing the Indians west are right and moral. In addition, the rhetorical questions allow Chief Seattle to express his anger better.

3

The use of similes in this piece not only add a poetic touch, but also effectively describe the decrease in Native Americans and the increase in whites. He compares the invasive whites as "grass that covers vast prairies" while describing the disappearing Indians as "scattering trees of a storm-swept plain." The storm that swept through clearly also represents the whites that pushed the Native Americans westward or bought their land. By comparing the whites to grass that grows anywhere they want and as a storm, Chief Seattle subtly establishes the idea that whites are land-hungry and greedy.

4

In addition, the Chief denounces certain cultural aspects of whites through a series of antitheses. As he uses "To us the ashes of our ancestors are sacred . . . You wander . . . from the graves . . . without regret" and "your dead cease to love you . . . Our dead never forget the beautiful world," there seems to be a criticism of whites as loveless people who don't respect the dead. And, as a final warning, Chief Seattle says, "Your time of decay may be distant, but it will surely come . . ." As he tried to tell the whites that what they have done will eventually cause their demise.

5

In all, Chief Seattle's speech to Governor Isaac not only achieves his purpose of discouraging the actions of the whites, but warns and denounces the culture of the whites as well.

6

Rating Student Sample A

This is a high-range essay for the following reasons:

- An immediate and clear indication of Seattle's purpose and attitude
- Understanding and discussion of Seattle's attitude and purpose (paragraph 2)
- Demonstration of a mature voice
- Thorough and effective connection between texts and insights (last two sentences of paragraph 2)
- Superior use of connective tissue—transitions and echo words ("in addition," "despite his calm," "acting respectfully," "winning favor")
- Refers to a variety of rhetorical strategies and devices to support the writer's assertion (paragraph 3: rhetorical questions), (paragraph 3: cause and effect), (paragraph 4: details), (paragraph 4: figurative language)
- Mature perceptions and insights (paragraph 2, sentence 2), (paragraph 4, sentence 2), (paragraph 5, next to last sentence)
- Mature writing style (last sentence)

This high-range essay indicates the clear voice of a mature writer and reader. Once the writer has committed to Seattle's purpose and attitude, the writer develops in each successive paragraph a supporting aspect of the stated purpose and/or attitude.

Rating Student Sample B

This is a mid-range essay for the following reasons:

- Concise, on-target development of prompt
- Indicates an understanding of the oration
- Makes intelligent points, but does not always develop them or defend them (paragraph 3, last sentence)
- Each paragraph deals with a different strategy (paragraph 2: emotional details), (paragraph 3: rhetorical questions), (paragraph 4: simile), (paragraph 5: antithesis)
- Good connective tissue
- A few lapses in syntax and diction (paragraph 3, next to last sentence)

This essay is indicative of a writer who understands both the passage and the prompt. There is an adequate analysis of the rhetorical strategies and devices present in the text, and the student reaches for unique insights (paragraph 4, last sentence). The lack of development of a couple of the cited points places this essay squarely in the mid-range.

Rubric for the Affluenza Synthesis Essay

A **9** essay has all the qualities of an 8 essay, and the <u>writing style</u> is especially <u>impressive</u>, as is the analysis and integration of the specifics related to affluenza and the given sources.

An **8** essay <u>effectively</u> and <u>cohesively</u> addresses the prompt. It clearly takes a position on affluenza and supports the argument using carefully integrated and appropriate evidence, including at least three of the given sources. The essay also shows the writer's <u>ability to control language</u>.

A **7** essay has all the properties of a 6 essay, only with a <u>more complete</u>, well-developed, and integrated argument, or a more mature writing style.

A **6** essay <u>adequately</u> addresses the prompt. The argument centers on affluenza and integrates, as well as makes use of, appropriate evidence, including at least three references from the given sources. These elements are less fully integrated and/or developed than scores in the 7, 8, or 9 range. The writer's ideas are expressed with clarity, but the writing may have a few errors in syntax and/or diction.

A **5** essay demonstrates that the writer <u>understands the prompt</u>. The argument/claim/position about affluenza is generally understandable, but the development and/or integration of appropriate evidence, and at least three of the given sources are limited or uneven. The writer's ideas are expressed clearly with a few errors in syntax or diction.

A **4** essay is <u>not an adequate response</u> to the prompt. The writer's argument indicates a misunderstanding, an oversimplification, or a misrepresentation of the assigned task. The writer may use evidence that is not appropriate or not sufficient to support the argument, or may use fewer than three of the given sources. The writing presents the writer's ideas, but it may indicate immaturity of style and control.

A **3** essay is a lower 4 because it is <u>even less effective</u> in addressing the question. It is also less mature in its syntax and organization.

A **2** essay indicates <u>little success in speaking to the prompt</u>. The writer may misread the question, only summarize the given sources, fail to develop the required argument, or simply ignore the prompt and write about another topic. The writing may also lack organization and control of language and syntax. (***Note:*** **No matter how well written, a summary will never rate more than a 2.**)

A **1** essay is a lower 2 because it is even <u>more simplistic</u>, <u>disorganized</u>, and <u>lacking in control of language</u>.

Student A

Affluenza. This new word created only nine years ago aptly describes the pervasive illness in American society and culture that involves our obsession with wealth and possessions. Symptoms include stress, a hollow feeling of still not having enough to be happy, credit and debt, and depression-ridden withdrawals when the dream becomes a nightmare. 1

The justification for our gluttony is, as some would say in its defense, written into our Declaration of Independence. "We hold these Truths to be self-evident . . . the unalienable right to life, liberty, and the pursuit of happiness" they shout. "We have the unalienable rights of freedom to buy everything to make ourselves happy, and we'll live with it!" The Enlightenment ideals of the 18th century have been tweaked to fit those of Bergdorf-Goodman and eBay. 2

In a country where we have no national religion, we did find something that tied us together. Money quickly became our national religion, with the wealthy as its priests. Rockefeller and Carnegie were our first high priests. Social Darwinists to the core, they lived and preached the power of copper, gold, oil, commerce, and wealth from their glittering towers, and the plebian masses ate the crumbs left over, hoping to become a member of the clergy some day. "This change, however, is . . . welcomed as highly beneficial," cries the high priest Carnegie. "Much better this great irregularity than universal squalor" (Source G). 3

But, is it much better? As pictured in a recent *New Yorker* cartoon, when a rich man and woman lie in bed surrounded by paintings, lamps, sculptures, and other luxurious 4 odds and ends, and say to each other, "Something is missing," it is indicative of the fact that they and we don't begin to realize how deep a truth this is (Source D). What they are missing is a meaning, an intimacy, a happiness in their lives. That can't be found in a four-poster bed with lavish objet d'art encroaching from all sides.

Perhaps the worst thing about affluenza is the way it is taught to the children of today. According to statistics provided by Jesse H. O'Neill's *The Golden Ghetto: The Psychology of Affluence*, most working mothers play with their children forty minutes a week. They SHOP six hours a week (Source E). The family is replaced by shopping bags strewn across the bed. No wonder ninety-three percent of teenage girls list shopping as their favorite hobby. They can't go to the beach without designer bikinis. They can't listen to music without an iPod, and it <u>must</u> be accessorized!

We hold these truths to be self-evident: money buys <u>things</u>, no more, no less. It can't replace people, or love, or nature, or travel to places where they just don't worship <u>things</u> as much as we do. It's time for America to wake up and stop smelling the designer perfume and ink on the greenbacks. There's no cure for affluenza but ourselves.

Student B

In a world in which material possessions are looked upon as treasures to be collected and guarded, the thought of being content with what one has is considered a prehistoric myth. America, the main culprit, has been infected by what PBS calls "affluenza." This "disease" has crept into American homes causing "an epidemic of stress, overwork, waste, and indebtedness." (introduction to prompt) The claim that Americans are never satisfied holds much validity and gains more validity as the economy continues to flourish.

As the economy continues to grow and produce objects in which Americans can become infatuated, one can only see America's affluenza infection worsening. A recent cartoon in which a husband and wife peer over their bed sheets into a vast room ridden with trinkets and stuffed with mere junk, one can only agree with the claim that Americans value "stuff" too much (Source D). The cartoon described ends with a witty comment, "Something is missing." This cartoon is a clear satirical look at what America has become. Although the room is already stuffed with belongings, the couple feels that something is missing, showing that Americans are never happy with what they have.

To be happy is one thing, but to buy happiness is something completely different. Yet, Americans have fallen into the trap of widespread consumerism. O'Neill states that "we have based . . . our entire culture . . . on the belief that 'just a little bit more' will finally buy happiness" (Source E). He, then, continues on to provide statistics showing that "93% of teenage girls list shopping as their favorite pastime." It is a sad reality that what we have is never good enough; that, hopefully, a new pair of shoes will bring happiness for at least a day or two. America's future, its youth, are the ones with the most serious infection of affluenza, and as time ticks on that infection only continues to grow.

Happiness has been a goal of America since its creation, *The Declaration of Independence* states that Americans have the "unalienable" rights: life, liberty, and the pursuit of happiness (Source B). Although we continue to pursue happiness, American's idea of happiness has taken a drastic turn. Our idea of happiness in today's standards is to be rich, and have anything and everything we want. Our days are consumed with the prospect of reaching happiness. Money is what drives us to work extra hours, but what will that money buy us? Not happiness, but simply objects—objects that may bring us happiness for a day or so, but will never satisfy us in the long run.

America's affluenza infection has become a widespread epidemic. Society has become   5 infatuated with purchases and gifts in hopes of finding happiness. Americans are truly never satisfied with what they have. As America continues to buy, the affluenza only roots itself deeper into our society and into our future.

Rating the Student Essays: Affluenza

Student A

This is a high-range essay for the following reasons:

- The essay opens dramatically, immediately catching the reader's attention. It creatively defines the term and implies the argument to follow.
- The writer establishes a tone and voice through diction and allusion: *shout*, *tweaked*, *Bergdorf*, and *eBay*.
- The writer illustrates the argument by presenting an extended analogy.
- Following a rhetorical question that serves as a transitional device, the writer adeptly incorporates and comments on one of the sources.
- Personal examples and strong details and images continue to support and develop the writer's position.
- The writer employs proper citation guidelines.
- The conclusion is especially effective because it enforces the opening, leaves the reader with the essence of the argument, and presents the writer's thesis as a parting comment.

Student B

This is a mid-range essay for the following reasons:

- The writer states a position on Americans being afflicted with affluenza: "The claim that Americans are never satisfied holds much validity and gains more validity as the economy continues to flourish."
- The writer recognizes and addresses the demands of the prompt.
- The writer properly integrates transitions.
- Varied sentence structure is evident in the analysis.
- The development is organized into an orderly presentation.
- The essay presents a clear thesis in the next-to-last paragraph: "Money is what drives us to work extra hours, but what will that money buy us? Not happiness, but simply objects—objects that may bring us happiness for a day or so, but will never satisfy us in the long run."
- The analysis of the writer's sources is brief, leaving the reader looking for more development.

Rubrics for the Stegner Essay

High-Range Essay

- Correctly identifies Stegner's position and attitude regarding the environment *and* wilderness
- Effectively presents a position about Stegner's position *and* attitude
- Clear writer's voice
- Successfully defends his or her position
- Presents carefully reasoned arguments making reference to specific examples from personal experience, knowledge, reading
- Effectively manipulates language
- Few, if any, syntactical errors

Mid-Range Essay

- Correctly identifies Stegner's position and attitude about the environment *and* wilderness
- Understands the demands of the prompt
- Clearly states the position of the writer
- Presents a generally adequate argument that makes use of appropriate examples
- Less well-developed than the high-range essay
- Ideas clearly stated
- A few lapses in diction or syntax

Low-Range Essay

- Inadequate response to the prompt
- Misunderstands, oversimplifies, or misrepresents Stegner's position and attitude
- Insufficient or inappropriate use of examples to develop the writer's position
- Lack of mature control of elements of essay writing

This prompt posed some difficulties for students. Many had a tendency to address only one aspect of it: the loss of wilderness. Often, they did not adequately connect this to the Brave New World concept of a human-controlled environment. The stronger writers included references to and discussions of the "reflection and rest" in their essays. Many student writers opposed Stegner's position by expanding on the concept of wilderness. Those who agreed with Stegner cited pertinent illustrations ranging from the rain forest to gasoline princes to overpopulation and the ozone layer. Contradictory and qualifying essays relied heavily on humankind's "frontier spirit" and artistic endeavors.

Stegner Passage—Student Sample A

Wallace Stegner writes in an essay, "Without any remaining wilderness we are committed wholly, without chance for even momentary reflection and rest, to a headlong drive into our technological termite-life, the Brave New World of a completely man-controlled environment." This excerpt attempts to convey that humankind is on a direct path to a highly mechanical and technological world; one that is ideal in man's quest for scientific and technological dominance over nature. According to Stegner, man has neglected to stop and smell the proverbial patch of roses. The idea that humankind aims at ultimately dominating the earth with its technological advances can be tenable.

1

However, Stegner's argument is fallacious because people DO pause to observe and introspect.

Humans have been in constant search of enlightenment in the world since time immemorial. Like all other organisms, man tends to innovate in order to better adapt to his natural surroundings. As time progresses, man develops more and better ways to survive. From the days of the Enlightenment, to the Scientific Revolution, to the Industrial Revolution, and to the computerized world of today, humankind has persistently been pursuing ways to analyze and control his environment. During the Enlightenment, natural philosopher Francis Bacon developed the scientific method as a set process which experiments ought to follow. His methodology has been adhered to since then in experimentation throughout the world. Using this method, Benjamin Franklin experimented with a kite in a storm and discovered electricity. Other thinkers utilized Franklin's findings and developed ways to use new energy sources. One concept has led to another and another, eventually arriving at our highly evolved world today. 2

These advances serve to benefit man's survival, which is why Stegner sees humans as heading for a man-controlled environment. To relieve nature-related hardships, man seeks ways to make things more comfortable for himself. For instance, air-conditioning was invented to control temperature. Another example of man controlling his environment can be found in the area of transportation: automobiles, trains, airplanes, ships, etc. Man is naturally slow, and to adapt himself to the large world, he creates machines to do the transporting. All of the inventions in the world today demonstrate attempts mankind has made in order to survive and to make life more "livable," and in these efforts, man controls nature. 3

Though Stegner's case that humanity's focus on dominating their environment can be defended, his idea that people ignore the need to rest for reflection is erroneous. While scientific and technological advancement is a commanding aspect of humankind, it is not as if history, art and culture do not exist. These facets of human society contribute to introspection. We create art to express modes of self-examination. Musicians, painters, sculptors, poets, and other artists concentrate on reflecting about man and his world. We study history as a method of introspection, and, in so doing, we essentially examine our past and reflect on it. There exist in this world goals other than the desire to control nature with technology. Humans are not "committed wholly, without chance for even momentary reflection and rest," to dominate the globe. 4

While Stegner's concept of humanity's desire to attain dominance over nature contains truth, his notion that people do not focus on anything else is false. Yes, humans do possess the tendency to explore and conquer. However, humans do not exclude all else in life. We are not always in pursuit of scientific and technological accomplishment. We are also seekers of cultural, artistic and philosophical achievement. 5

Stegner Passage—Student Sample B

Wallace Stegner wrote that, "Without any remaining wilderness we are committed wholly, without chance for even momentary reflection and rest, to a headlong drive into our technological termite-life, the Brave New World of a completely man-controlled environment." It seems that in writing this, Stegner expresses his concern for the receding forests and other wilderness areas, along with the extinction of the species that populate them. His concern is quite justified, for as we use our natural resources, we destroy those species that we now share this planet with.

It has long been known that unlike the other species of the Earth, the one known as Homo Sapiens does not adapt well to its environment. Instead, this species adapts the environment to it, and the Devil take anything that stands in its way. Homo Sapiens cannot bear the fierce winters of New England or the hot summers of the Caribbean, so it chops down trees to build houses. It does this without the slightest concern for the other species that call the forest home. Many terrible injuries have been dealt to the ecosystem of this planet because of the lack of concern Homo Sapiens has shown. Holes in the ozone layer, which let terrible amounts of ultra-violet radiation bombard the earth. The constant growth of the Sahara Desert, and the destruction of the rainforests are painful examples of Homo Sapiens' ignorance, painful not just to other species, but to Homo Sapiens itself. It seems as though Homo Sapiens does not realize that when all the trees are gone, there will be no oxygen left for anyone. Hopefully before that atrocity is carried out, for it is almost sure that it will be, Homo Sapiens will figure out how to adapt very quickly.

When Stegner wrote of a "completely man-controlled environment," he is talking of a world where our species has destroyed the wilderness or at least bent it totally to our will. He writes of a world with cities, inhabited "termite-like" by reflective Homo Sapiens, the size of which no one has ever seen, most likely with rampant air pollution. Let us hope that we are not one day forced, as in "Lost in Space," to seek out other planets to live on because ours is taking its last breath. This is one possibility; Stegner is warning us to change our ignorant ways before it is too late, and he certainly has the right idea. For, if we don't, we will have truly become exactly like our hated enemy, the virus.

Rating Student Sample A

This is a high-range essay for the following reasons:

- Effectively covers the points made by Stegner in his statement
- Clearly takes a position regarding Stegner's statement
- Thoroughly develops the argument with specific examples and historical references (paragraphs 2 and 3)
- Indicates and discusses the fallacy of Stegner's statement (paragraphs 4 and 5)
- Good topic adherence
- Thorough development of the points of the writer's argument
- Mature voice, diction, and syntax

This high-range essay was written by a student who is both confident and well-versed and one who has balanced the presentation with scientific and introspective illustrations in support of the argument.

Rating Student Sample B

This is a mid-range essay for the following reasons:

- Clearly understands Stegner's statement and the demands of the prompt
- Creative voice is present
- An interesting objectification of humanity (paragraph 2—"Homo Sapiens")
- Strong conclusion
- Linkage between man's destruction of the wilderness and its consequences needs further development
- Development of the argument needs further support
- A few syntactical errors
- Lacks needed transitions

This student writer has a definite opinion to which he or she gives a strong voice. Although there is a strong, clear opening and conclusion, the body paragraphs containing the argument need further development.

PRACTICE EXAM 2

ANSWER SHEET FOR MULTIPLE-CHOICE QUESTIONS

1. _____   19. _____   37. _____

2. _____   20. _____   38. _____

3. _____   21. _____   39. _____

4. _____   22. _____   40. _____

5. _____   23. _____   41. _____

6. _____   24. _____   42. _____

7. _____   25. _____   43. _____

8. _____   26. _____   44. _____

9. _____   27. _____   45. _____

10. _____   28. _____   46. _____

11. _____   29. _____   47. _____

12. _____   30. _____   48. _____

13. _____   31. _____   49. _____

14. _____   32. _____   50. _____

15. _____   33. _____   51. _____

16. _____   34. _____   52. _____

17. _____   35. _____   53. _____

18. _____   36. _____   54. _____

I _____ did _____ did not complete this part of the test in the allotted 1 hour.

I had _____ correct answers. I had _____ incorrect answers. I left _____ blank.

I have carefully reviewed the explanations of the answers, and I think I need to work on the following types of questions:

PRACTICE EXAM 2
ADVANCED PLACEMENT ENGLISH LANGUAGE

Section I

Total Time—1 hour

Carefully read the following passages and answer the questions that follow.

Questions 1–10 are based on the following passage from Annie Dillard, *What an Essay Can Do*.

In some ways the essay can deal in both events and ideas better than the short story can, because the essayist—unlike the poet—may introduce the plain, unadorned thought without the contrived entrances of long-winded characters who mouth discourses. This sort of awful evidence killed "the novel of idea." (But eschewing it served to limit fiction's materials a little further, and likely contributed to our being left with the short story of scant idea.) The essayist may reason; he may treat of historical, cultural, or natural events, as well as personal events, for their interest and meaning alone, without resort to fabricated dramatic occasions. So the essay's materials are larger than the story's.

The essay may deal in metaphor better than the poem can, in some ways, because prose may expand what the lyric poem must compress. Instead of confining a metaphor to half a line, the essayist can devote to it a narrative, descriptive, or reflective couple of pages, and bring forth vividly its meanings. Prose welcomes all sorts of figurative language, of course, as well as alliteration, and even rhyme. The range of rhythms in prose is larger and grander than that of poetry. And it can handle discursive idea, and plain fact, as well as character and story.

The essay can do everything a poem can do, and everything a short story can do—everything but fake it. The elements in any nonfiction should be true not only artistically—the connections must hold at base and must be veracious, for that is the convention and the covenant between the nonfiction writer and his reader. Veracity isn't much of a drawback to the writer; there's a lot of truth out there to work with. And veracity isn't much of a drawback to the reader. The real world arguably exerts a greater fascination on people than any fictional one; many people at least spend their whole lives there, apparently by choice. The essayist does what we do with our lives; the essayist thinks about actual things. He can make sense of them analytically or artistically. In either case he renders the real world coherent and meaningful; even if only bits of it, and even if that coherence and meaning reside only inside small texts.

1. Which technique does the author employ to focus the reader's attention on the specific topic of the passage?
   A. use of parallel structure
   B. identifying herself with her audience
   C. beginning each paragraph with the same subject
   D. use of passive voice
   E. use of anecdote

2. Based on a careful reading of the first paragraph, the reader can conclude that the author blames the death of the "novel of idea" on
   A. real life and situations
   B. simplicity
   C. appeal to philosophy
   D. reliance on historical data
   E. artificiality

3. The primary rhetorical strategy the author uses to develop the first paragraph is
   A. process
   B. narration
   C. description
   D. cause and effect
   E. definition

4. Near the end of the third paragraph, Dillard states, "The essayist does what we do with our lives; the essayist thinks about actual things. He can make sense of them analytically or artistically." The most probable reason for the author choosing to write two separate sentences rather than constructing a single, longer sentence using a listing, is
   A. to reinforce cause and effect
   B. both subjects are of equal importance, although separate processes
   C. to create a parallel situation
   D. to contrast the two ideas
   E. to highlight the criticism of fictional writing

5. In paragraph 3, in the sentence beginning with "The real world . . .," the word "there" refers to
   A. the fictional world
   B. novels
   C. poetry
   D. "the real world"
   E. short stories

6. The primary rhetorical strategy the author uses to develop the second paragraph is
   A. contrast and comparison
   B. narration
   C. argument
   D. description
   E. analogy

7. In terms of her position on her subject, the author can best be categorized as
   A. an adversary
   B. a critic
   C. an advocate
   D. an innovator
   E. an artist

8. An example of parallel structure is found in which of the following lines taken from the passage?
   A. "But eschewing it served to limit fiction's materials a little further, and likely contributed to our being left with the short story of scant idea."
   B. "The essay may deal in metaphor better than the poem can, in some ways, because prose may expand what the lyric poem must compress."
   C. "The elements in any nonfiction should be true not only artistically—the connections must hold at base . . ."
   D. ". . . that is the convention and the covenant between the nonfiction writer and his reader."
   E. "In either case he renders the real world coherent and meaningful; even if only bits of it, and even if that coherence and meaning reside only inside small texts."

9. The contrast between the short story writer and the essayist is based on which of the following?
   A. reflection
   B. presentation
   C. fundamental reality
   D. content
   E. clarity of purpose

10. The tone of the passage can best be described as
   A. impartial and critical
   B. condescending and formal
   C. candid and colloquial
   D. clinical and moralistic
   E. confident and informative

Questions 11–21 are based on the following passage in which Henry James responds to a literary critic's ideas about the state of the English novel.

There is one point at which the moral sense and the artistic sense lie very near together; that is in the light of the very obvious truth that the deepest quality of a work of art will always be the quality of the mind of the producer. In proportion as that intelligence is fine will the novel, the picture, the statue partake of the substance of beauty and truth. To be constituted of such elements is, to my vision, to have purpose enough. No good novel will ever proceed from a superficial mind; that seems to me an axiom which for the artist in fiction, will cover all needful moral ground: if the youthful aspirant take it to heart it will illuminate for him many of the mysteries of "purpose." There are many other useful things that might be said to him, but I have come to the end of my article, and can only touch them as I pass. The critic in the Pall Mall Gazette, whom I have already quoted, draws attention to the danger, in speaking of the art of fiction, of generalizing. The danger that he has in mind is rather, I imagine, that of particularizing. I should remind the ingenuous student first of the magnificence of the form that is open to him, which offers to sight so few restrictions and such innumerable opportunities. The other arts, in comparison, appear confined and hampered; the various conditions under which they are exercised are so rigid and definite. But the only condition that I can think of attaching to the composition of the novel is, as I have already said, that it be sincere. This freedom is a splendid privilege, and the first lesson of the young novelist is to learn to be worthy of it. "Enjoy it as it deserves," I should say to him; "take possession of it, explore it to its utmost extent, publish it, rejoice in it. All life belongs to you, and do not listen either to those who would shut you up into corners of it and tell you that it is only here and there that art inhabits, or to those who would persuade you that this heavenly messenger wings her way outside of life altogether, breathing superfine air, and turning away her head from the truth of things. There is no impression of life, no manner of seeing it and feeling it, to which the plan of the novelist may not offer a place; you have only to remember that talents so dissimilar as those of Alexander Dumas and Jane Austen, Charles Dickens and Gustave Flaubert have worked in this field with equal glory. Do not think too much about optimism and pessimism; try and catch the color of life itself. If you must indulge in conclusions, let them have the taste of a wide knowledge. Remember that your first duty is to be as complete as possible—to make as perfect a work. Be generous and delicate and pursue the prize. (1884)

11. James draws a distinction between the purpose of the novel and
A. the moral theme
B. the artistic sense
C. the mind of the producer
D. obvious truth
E. the substance of beauty

12. From the opening of the passage, it is clear that the author's attitude toward the creation of a work of art is
A. democratic
B. indifferent
C. superficial
D. reverent
E. elitist

13. According to James, beauty and truth are directly related to
A. the novel
B. intelligence
C. a picture
D. a statue
E. vision

14. According to the fourth sentence, the word "axiom" can best be defined as
   A. a mystery
   B. an anecdote
   C. a paradox
   D. a rule of thumb
   E. a proverb

15. In the fifth sentence, "There are many other useful things that might be said to him, but I have come to the end of my article, and can only touch them as I pass," the pronoun "him" refers to
   A. "youthful aspirant"
   B. "the critic"
   C. "the producer"
   D. the artist in fiction
   E. the author

16. In the seventh sentence, "The danger that he has in mind is rather, I imagine, that of particularizing," the word "rather" is used to establish
   A. a paradox
   B. an analogy
   C. an ambiguity
   D. a syllogism
   E. an antithesis

17. According to Henry James, the freest form of art is
   A. sculpting
   B. painting
   C. speaking
   D. writing
   E. photography

18. In the middle of the passage, the sentence " 'Enjoy it as it deserves,' I should say to him; 'take possession of it, explore it to its utmost extent, publish it, rejoice in it,' " includes an example of
   A. a complex sentence
   B. parallel structure
   C. an analogy
   D. inversion
   E. passive voice

19. In the second half of the passage, if the student follows the logic and advice of James in the set of sentences beginning with "This freedom is a splendid . . ." and ending with "the truth of things," that student would have to
   A. imitate the great writers
   B. pray for inspiration
   C. recognize that only after death can a writer be assessed properly
   D. ignore James's advice
   E. turn away from writing

20. Also in the middle of the passage is a sentence beginning with "All life belongs . . ." and ending with "the truth of things." The metaphor, "this heavenly messenger," contained in this sentence refers to
   A. freedom
   B. the teacher
   C. sincerity
   D. art
   E. the critic

21. The overall tone of the passage can best be described as
   A. informal and sarcastic
   B. condescending and sardonic
   C. didactic and exhortative
   D. reverential and laudatory
   E. indignant and contemptuous

Questions 22–35 are based on the following passage from Herman Melville's "Moby-Dick."

Nantucket! Take out your map and look at it. See what a real corner of the world   1
it occupies; how it stands there, away off shore, more lonely than the Eddystone
lighthouse. Look at it—a mere hillock, and elbow of sand; all beach, without a background. There is more sand there than you would use in twenty years as a substitute
for blotting paper. Some gamesome wights* will tell you that they have to plant weeds
there, they don't grow naturally; they import Canada thistles; they have to send beyond
seas for a spile† to stop a leak in an oil cask; that pieces of wood in Nantucket are
carried about like bits of the true cross in Rome; that people there plant toadstools
before their houses, to get under the shade in summer time; that one blade of grass
makes an oasis, three blades a day's walk in a prairie; that they wear quicksand shoes,
something like Laplander snowshoes; that they are so shut up, belted about, every way
inclosed, surrounded, and made an utter island of by the ocean, that to their very chairs
and tables small clams will sometimes be found adhering, as to the backs of sea turtles.
But these extravaganzas only show that Nantucket is no Illinois.

Look now at the wondrous traditional story of how this island was settled by the   2
red-men. Thus goes the legend. In olden times an eagle swooped down upon the
New England coast, and carried off an infant Indian in his talons. With loud lament
the parents saw their child borne out of sight over the wide waters. They resolved to
follow in the same direction. Setting out in their canoes, after a perilous passage they
discovered the island, and there they found an empty ivory casket,—the poor little
Indian's skeleton.

What wonder, then, that these Nantucketers, born on a beach, should take to the   3
sea for a livelihood! They first caught crabs and quahogs in the sand; grown bolder,
they waded out with nets for mackerel; more experienced, they pushed off in boats
and captured cod; and at last, launching a navy of great ships on the sea, explored
this watery world; put an incessant belt of circumnavigations round it; peeped in
at Behring's Straits; and in all seasons and all oceans declared everlasting war with
the mightiest animated mass that has survived the flood; most monstrous and most
mountainous! That Himmalehan, salt-sea Mastodon, clothed with such portentousness
of unconscious power, that his very panics are more to be dreaded than his most fearless
and malicious assaults!

And thus have these naked Nantucketers, these sea hermits, issuing from their   4
ant-hill in the sea, overrun and conquered the watery world like so many Alexanders;
parceling out among them the Atlantic, Pacific, and Indian oceans, as the three pirate
powers did Poland. Let America add Mexico to Texas, and pile Cuba upon Canada; let
the English overswarm all India, and hang out their blazing banner from the sun; two
thirds of this terraqueous globe are the Nantucketer's. For the sea is his; he owns it, as
Emperors own empires; other seamen having but a right of way through it. Merchant
ships are but extension bridges; armed ones but floating forts; even pirates and
privateers, though following the sea as highwaymen the road, they but plunder other
ships, other fragments of the land like themselves, without seeking to draw their living
from the bottomless deep itself. The Nantucketer, he alone resides and riots on the sea;
he alone, in Bible language, goes down to it in ships; to and fro ploughing it as his own

* wights: human beings
† spile: a small plug

special plantation. *There* is his home; *there* lies his business, which a Noah's flood would not interrupt, though it overwhelmed all the millions in China. He lives on the sea, as prairie dogs in the prairie; he hides among the waves, he climbs them as mountain goats climb the Alps. For years he knows not the land; so that when he comes to it at last, it smells like another world, more strangely than the moon would to an Earthsman. With the landless gull, that at sunset folds her wings and is rocked to sleep between billows; so at nightfall, the Nantucketer, out of sight of land, furls his sail, and lays him to his rest, while under his very pillow rush herds of walruses and whales.

22. The controlling analogy of the passage is
   A. Nantucket:Illinois
   B. sea:land
   C. Noah:Nantucket
   D. moon:Earthsman
   E. legends:reality

23. Melville describes Nantucketers as all of the following <u>except</u>:
   A. conquerors
   B. natives of the sea
   C. farmers of the sea
   D. strangers to the land
   E. exploiters of the Native American claims

24. The tone of the passage can best be described as
   A. self-congratulatory and confident
   B. formal and pompous
   C. admiring and hyperbolic
   D. informal and cynical
   E. pedantic and objective

25. The most probable reason for repeating and italicizing "*There*" in the middle of paragraph 4 at the beginning of two main clauses in the same sentence is to
   A. force the reader to look for an antecedent
   B. sound poetic
   C. provide a break in a long, complicated sentence
   D. emphasize the sense of place
   E. indicate sympathy for the plight of the Nantucketer

26. The shift in the focus of the piece occurs in which line?
   A. The first sentence of paragraph 2
   B. The first sentence of paragraph 3
   C. The first sentence of paragraph 4
   D. The third sentence in paragraph 4
   E. The last sentence

27. The first paragraph contains an extended example of
   A. parallel structure
   B. anecdote
   C. periodic sentence
   D. generalization
   E. argument

28. Melville retells the Native American legend of how the island was settled in order to
   A. have his audience identify with the Native American population
   B. make the passage seem like a parable
   C. contrast with the reality of the Nantucketers
   D. bring a mythic quality to the subject
   E. highlight the plight of the Nantucketers

29. The development of paragraph 3 is structured around
   A. spatial description
   B. selection of incremental details
   C. central analogy
   D. parallel structure
   E. paradox

30. Based on a careful reading of the passage, complete the following analogy:
   NANTUCKET:ILLINOIS ::
   A. merchant ships:pirate ships
   B. Native American:eagle
   C. ivory casket:skeleton
   D. backs of sea turtles:chairs and tables
   E. walrus:prairie dog

31. One may conclude from the information contained in paragraph 3 that "Himmalehan, salt-sea Mastedon" refers to
   A. the ocean
   B. the whale
   C. the power of nature
   D. Biblical vengeance
   E. emperors

32. The purpose of the passage is most probably to
    A. encourage people to settle on Nantucket
    B. use Nantucket as a model of ecological conservation
    C. honor the indomitable spirit of the Nantucketers
    D. plead for the return of Nantucket to the Native Americans
    E. present a nostalgic reminiscence of the writer's birthplace

33. Melville uses *thus* twice in this passage: once in the second sentence of paragraph 2 to begin the Native American legend about the island being settled. What is the reason for using *thus* a second time in the first sentence of paragraph 4?
    I. to begin a comparative legend with the Nantucketers settling the sea
    II. to balance the first part of the passage with the second part
    III. to reinforce the formality of his presentation
    A. I
    B. II
    C. III
    D. I and II
    E. I, II, and III

34. The subtle humor of the first paragraph is dependent upon
    A. paradox
    B. hyperbole
    C. juxtaposition
    D. irony
    E. ad hominem argument

35. The last sentence of the passage continues the analogy between
    A. reality:illusion
    B. night:day
    C. man:animal
    D. gull:walrus
    E. sea:land

Questions 36–44 are based on the following passage from Lucy Stone, "A Disappointed Woman," a speech she gave to the national women's rights convention in Cincinnati, Ohio, in October, 1855.

The last speaker alluded to this movement as being that of a few disappointed 1
women. From the first years to which my memory stretches, I have been a disappointed
woman. When, with my brothers, I reached forth after the sources of knowledge, I
was reproved with "It isn't fit for you; it doesn't belong to women." Then there was but
one college in the world where women were admitted, and that was in Brazil. I would
have found my way there, but by the time I was prepared to go, one was opened in the
state of Ohio—the first in the United States where women and Negroes could enjoy
opportunities with white men. I was disappointed when I came to seek a profession
worthy an immortal being—every employment was closed to me, except those of a
teacher, the seamstress, and the housekeeper. In education, in marriage, in religion, in
everything, disappointment is the lot of woman. It shall be the business of my life to
deepen this disappointment in every woman's heart until she bows down to it no longer.
I wish that women, instead of being walking show-cases, instead of begging of their
fathers and brothers the latest and finest new bonnet, would ask of them their rights.

The question of Woman's Rights is a practical one. The notion has prevailed that 2
it was only an ephemeral idea; that it was but women claiming their right to smoke
cigars in the streets, and to frequent bar-rooms. Others have supposed it a question of
comparative intellect; others still, of sphere. Too much has already been said and written
about women's sphere. Trace all the doctrines to their source and they will be found to
have no basis except in the usages and prejudices of the age. This is seen in the fact that
what is tolerated in woman in one country is not tolerated in another. In this country
women may hold prayer-meetings, etc., but in other countries it is written upon their
houses of worship, "Women and dogs, and other impure animals, are not permitted
to enter." Wendell Phillips says, "The best and greatest thing one is capable of doing,
that is his sphere." I have confidence in the Father to believe that when He gives us the
capacity to do anything, He does not make a blunder. Leave women, then, to find their
sphere. And do not tell us before we are born even, that our province is to cook dinners,
darn stockings, and sew on buttons. . . ."

36. The tone of the passage can best be described as
   A. pedantic and cynical
   B. flippant and irreverent
   C. reverent and somber
   D. indignant and argumentative
   E. ambivalent and resigned

37. A major hypothesis presented by the speaker is that
   A. religion is the cause of women's position in the United States
   B. women are not as intelligent as men
   C. education is the only way to cure the evils of society
   D. the question of Women's Rights is a philosophical issue
   E. women and African Americans are on the same level

38. What can the reader infer based upon the sentence found in the middle of paragraph 1 that begins with "I was disappointed . . ." and ending with "and the housekeeper"?
   A. Lucy Stone is not a religious person.
   B. Teaching was not considered a worthy profession.
   C. The speaker is an adventurer.
   D. Stone values the opinions of others.
   E. She is married with children.

39. The theme of the passage is best expressed in
   A. paragraph 1, sentence 3 ("When, with my brothers . . .")
   B. paragraph 1, sentence 7 ("In education . . .")

C. paragraph 2, sentence 1
("The question . . .")
D. paragraph 2, sentence 6
("This is seen . . .")
E. paragraph 3, sentence 9
("Wendell Phillips says . . .")

40. Stone develops her speech using all of the
following except:
A. an ad hominem argument
B. an anecdote
C. direct quotations
D. facts
E. an ethical appeal

41. In light of the passage, how can the following
sentence near the end of the first paragraph best
be characterized? "It shall be the business of
my life to deepen this disappointment in every
woman's heart until she bows down to it no
longer."
A. ironic and paradoxical
B. analytical and pedantic
C. formal and detached
D. informal and anecdotal
E. allegorical and ambivalent

42. Based on a careful reading of the passage, one
can assume that the speaker
A. believes that women are superior to men
B. believes that religion is the salvation of
women
C. believes in fate and destiny
D. believes that foreign countries are more
enlightened about women's rights than the
United States
E. is disappointed with her female
contemporaries

43. In the sentence beginning with "Wendell
Phillips says . . ." in the middle of paragraph 2,
Lucy Stone develops her point using
A. an analogy
B. a straw-man argument
C. a syllogism
D. an ad hominem argument
E. sarcasm

44. The speaker's purpose is most probably to
A. explain
B. exhort
C. amuse
D. describe
E. narrate

Questions 45-54 are based on the following excerpt from a review and discussion by Christopher Jencks of *American Dream: Three Women, Ten Kids, and a Nation's Drive to End Welfare*, written by Jason DeParle and published by Viking/Penguin in 2005. The review appeared in the December 15, 2005, edition of *The New York Review of Books*.

[According to the US Census Bureau] The poverty rate for single mothers [who headed their own households and had children under eighteen] was only 36 percent in 2003, compared to 44 percent in 1994, when unemployment was about what it had been in 1996.[4]

The official poverty rate has serious flaws. It omits food stamps, free medical care, housing subsidies, and taxes. So it is important to see whether direct measures of material hardship tell the same story. The Agriculture Department's Food Security Survey (FSS) is a good place to begin. It asks mothers whether money problems forced them to skip meals or cut the size of their meals at any point during the previous twelve months. Between April 1995 and April 2001, as the welfare rolls were being cut in half, the fraction of single mothers who said they had to limit what they ate fell from 17.7 to 12.5 percent.[5] By 2003, with unemployment slightly above its 1995 level, the percentage of mothers who reported cutting back what they ate had risen, but only to 13.8 percent.

The FSS also asked mothers whether there was a time when their children were not getting enough to eat. The proportion who said this was the case fell from 10.6 percent in 1995 to 7.8 percent in 2001 and had only risen to 8.0 percent in 2003.[6] Both of these measures are consistent with the official poverty rate in suggesting that even when unemployment was 6 percent, single mothers did better after welfare reform than before.

The proportion of unmarried mothers living in someone else's home is another indicator of financial stress. Some mothers live in someone else's home by choice, but most get their own place when their income rises. Twenty-two percent of unmarried mothers lived in someone else's home in both 1989 and 2000.[7] When welfare reform passed, its critics also predicted a surge in the number of families living in public shelters. The United States does not collect national data on trends in homelessness, but in Milwaukee, which cut about ten thousand families from its welfare rolls, [Jason] DeParle reports that the number of families in shelters on an average night rose by only forty-one. On December 12, 2004, Boston counted 1,157 homeless children in the city, down from 1,274 a decade earlier.[8] Nationally, the proportion of children not living with either their mother or their father was the same in 2004 as in 1994.

These measures of material well-being can be summarized in two ways. Defenders of welfare reform stress the fact that the proportion of single mothers who cannot afford to rent their own housing is no higher today than in 1996, and that the proportion who report not having enough to eat has fallen significantly. Critics of welfare reform stress

5

10

15

20

25

30

4 US Census Bureau, *Historical Poverty Tables*, www.census.gov/hhes/www/poverty/histpov/hstpov4.html.

5 Scott Winship and Christopher Jencks, "How Did the Social Policy Changes of the 1990s Affect Maternal Hardship Among Single Mothers? Evidence from the CPS Food Security Supplement," Kennedy School of Government, Working Paper RWP04-027, June 2004 (ksgnotes1.harvard.edu/Research/wpaper.nsf/rwp/RWP04027/$File/rwp04-027-Winship-Jencks.pdf). The comparisons between 1995 and 2001 use the common screen.

6 Tabulations by Scott Winship.

7 I am indebted to Joseph Swingle of Wellesley College for all the estimates derived from the Census Bureau's Annual Demographic Survey.

8 Friends of Boston's Homeless, "2004 City of Boston Homeless Census: Homeless Families Increase Dramatically," available at www.fobh.org/census.htm, accessed August 26, 2004. The title of this report refers to an increase between 2003 and 2004.

the fact that millions of single-parent families still have trouble putting food on the
table and that even larger numbers cannot afford an apartment of their own. Welfare   35
reform is clearly a success relative to the dismal situation that prevailed in the United
States before 1996. But the country is still a long way from achieving the goals that
more compassionate societies set for themselves.

45. The essence of the argument presented in this
passage can be found in lines
   A. 5–6
   B. 13–14
   C. 16–17
   D. 26–28
   E. 29–32

46. The organizational pattern of the passage is
   A. general to specific
   B. specific to general
   C. familiar to unfamiliar
   D. most important to least important
   E. cause and effect

47. The reader may infer from lines 35–38 that the
writer
   A. believes welfare is clearly a success
   B. believes welfare is failing to meet dismal
      situations
   C. admires the welfare programs of countries
      other than those of the United States
   D. maintains that there has been little need for
      welfare reform since 1996
   E. believes that the goals of the United States
      are the proper ones

48. The tone of the passage can best be described as
   A. factual
   B. sarcastic
   C. laudatory
   D. ironic
   E. sentimental

49. Which of the given footnotes is a primary
source?
   A. 4
   B. 5
   C. 6
   D. 7
   E. 8

50. A critical reader of this passage should ask all
of the following questions about footnote 7
__except__:

   A. What is the relationship between Swingle
      and the author of this review?
   B. How many estimates were actually
      constructed?
   C. To what does the word *all* refer?
   D. What are Swingle's qualifications as a
      reliable source?
   E. Can I locate an annotated citation about
      Swingle in another section of this review?

51. Another effective means of presenting the
statistical material found in this passage would
most probably be a(n)
   A. personal anecdote
   B. short story
   C. one-act play
   D. chart or graph
   E. interview with a homeless mother

52. The footnote that most likely reflects a specific
bias is found in
   A. 4
   B. 5
   C. 6
   D. 7
   E. 8

53. In lines 35–38, the author's bias/agenda is most
clearly evidenced through
   A. statistical information and interpretation
   B. definition
   C. description
   D. diction and syntax
   E. summarization

54. Based on a careful reading of footnote 5, the
reader can correctly assume that Winship and
Jencks are
   A. recognized authorities in this field
   B. social workers
   C. students
   D. welfare reformers
   E. employees of the federal government

END OF SECTION I

Section II

Question 1

Suggested Writing Time: 40 minutes

Based on the Constitutional First Amendment guarantee of the right to freedom of speech, some citizens and citizen groups have used public burning of the American flag as a means of political expression. A proposed amendment to the *U.S. Constitution* states: "The Congress shall have the power to prohibit the physical desecration of the flag of the United States." Is desecrating the flag a legitimate form of expression guaranteed by the Constitution? Should the Constitution be amended to protect the flag?

Carefully read the following sources (including any introductory information). **Then, in an essay that synthesizes at least three of the sources for support, take a position that defends, challenges, or qualifies the claim that the flag should be protected under a constitutional amendment.**

Make certain that you take a position and that the essay centers on your argument. Use the sources to support your reasoning; avoid simply summarizing the sources. You may refer to the sources by their letters (Source A, Source B, etc.) or by the identifiers in the parentheses below.

> Source A (First Amendment to the *U.S. Constitution*)
> Source B (The Proposed Amendment)
> Source C (*USA Today* Survey)
> Source D (Two Supreme Court Decisions)
> Source E (Rehnquist's Dissenting Opinion)
> Source F (Editorial in the *Los Angeles Times*)
> Source G (Congressional Votes)
> Source H (Political Cartoon by Clay Bennett)
> Source I (Editorial by Todd Lindberg)

Source A
From "The Bill of Rights," *The U.S. Constitution.*

> #### Amendment I
>
> *Congress shall make no law respecting an establishment of religion, or prohibiting the free exercise thereof; or abridging the freedom of speech, or of the press; or the right of the people peaceably to assemble, and to petition the government for a redress of grievances.*

Source B
The Proposed Amendment to the *U.S. Constitution* taken from *The Congressional Record.* Available at http://thomas.loc.gov/cgi-bin/query/F?r109:8:./temp/~r109rrd1VK:e0.

> #### The full text of the amendment:
>
> *The Congress shall have power to prohibit the physical desecration of the flag of the United States.*

Source C

Results of a survey conducted by *USA Today*, June 23–25, 2006, http://www.usatoday
.com/news/washington/2006-06-26-poll-results_x.htm.

> *Some people feel that the U.S. Constitution should be amended to make it illegal to burn or desecrate the American flag as a form of political dissent. Others say that the U.S. Constitution should not be amended to specifically prohibit flag burning or desecration.* Do you think the U.S. Constitution should or should not be amended to prohibit burning or desecrating the American flag?
>
> *Results based on 516 national adults in Form B:*
>
> | Date asked | Yes, amended | No, not | No opinion |
> | --- | --- | --- | --- |
> | June 23–25, 2006 | 45% | 54% | 2% |

Source D

Two Supreme Court Decisions related to the desecration of the flag. Available at
http://www.firstamendmentcenter.org/speech/flagburning/overview.aspx?topic=
flag-burning_overview.

> Texas v. Johnson, *491 U.S. 397 (1989), was a decision by the Supreme Court of the United States. The question the Supreme Court had to answer was: "Is the desecration of an American flag, by burning or otherwise, a form of speech that is protected under the First Amendment?" Justice William Brennan wrote the 5–4 majority decision in holding that the defendant's act of flag burning was protected speech under the First Amendment to the United States Constitution.*
>
> *The court held that the First Amendment prevented Texas from punishing the defendant for burning the flag under the specified circumstances. The court first found that burning of the flag was expressive conduct protected by the First Amendment. The court concluded that Texas could not criminally sanction flag desecration in order to preserve the flag as a symbol of national unity. It also held that the statute did not meet the state's goal of preventing breaches of the peace, since it was not drawn narrowly enough to encompass only those flag burnings that would likely result in a serious disturbance, and since the flag burning in this case did not threaten such a reaction.*
>
> *Subsequently, Congress passed a statute, the 1989 Flag Protection Act, making it a federal crime to desecrate the flag. In the case of* United States v. Eichman, *496 U.S. 310 (1990), that law was struck down by the same five-person majority of justices as in* Texas v. Johnson, *491 U.S. 397 (1989).*

Source E
Chief Justice William Rehnquist's dissenting opinion in the *Texas v. Johnson* (1989) case.
Available at http://www.bc.edu/bc_org/avp/cas/comm/free_speech/texas.html.

In his dissenting opinion in Texas v. Johnson *(1989), regarding Texas law against flag burning, the late Chief Justice William H. Rehnquist wrote,*

The American flag, then, throughout more than 200 years of our history, has come to be the visible symbol embodying our Nation. It does not represent the views of any particular political party, and it does not represent any particular political philosophy. The flag is not simply another 'idea' or "point of view" competing for recognition in the marketplace of ideas. Millions and millions of Americans regard it with an almost mystical reverence regardless of what sort of social, political, or philosophical beliefs they may have. I cannot agree that the First Amendment invalidates the Act of Congress, and the laws of 48 of the 50 States, which make criminal the public burning of the flag.

Rehnquist also argued that flag burning is "no essential part of any exposition of ideas" but, rather "the equivalent of an inarticulate grunt or roar that, it seems fair to say, is most likely to be indulged in not to express any particular idea, but to antagonize others."

Source F
"The case for flag-burning: An amendment banning it would make America less free."
An editorial that appeared in the *Los Angeles Times*, June 27, 2006.

THERE ARE MANY ARGUMENTS AGAINST a proposed constitutional amendment to outlaw "the physical desecration of the flag of the United States." Let us count the ways in which the amendment, which is disturbingly close to the 67 votes required for Senate approval, is unworthy of that body's support:

- *It's a "solution" to a problem that doesn't exist. There has been no epidemic of flag-burning since the Supreme Court ruled in 1989 that destruction of Old Glory as a protest was symbolic speech protected by the 1st Amendment.*
- *As Sen. Mitch McConnell (R-Ky.) pointed out, "The First Amendment has served us well for over 200 years. I don't think it needs to be altered." Placing a no-flag-burning asterisk next to the amendment's sweeping guarantee of free speech is a mischievous idea, and it could invite amendments to ban other sorts of speech Americans find offensive.*

But the best argument against the flag amendment is the one some opponents are reluctant to make for fear of political fallout: It would make America less free.

Rare as flag-burning may be, a nation that allows citizens to denounce even its most sacred symbols is being true to what the Supreme Court in 1964 called the "profound national commitment to the principle that debate on public issues should be uninhibited, robust and wide-open, and that it may well include vehement, caustic, and sometimes unpleasantly sharp attacks on government and public officials."

In that decision, and in 1989, the court interpreted the free-speech protections of the First Amendment generously but correctly. The Senate, including Feinstein and fellow Democrat and Californian Barbara Boxer (who has opposed a flag-burning amendment in the past), should let those decisions be.

Source G

Congressional votes regarding proposed constitutional amendment regarding desecration of the flag. Available at http://en.wikipedia.org/wiki/Flag_Burning_Amendment#Congressional_votes.

The chronology of the House of Representatives' action upon the flag-desecration amendment running over a period of more than ten years:

Congress	Resolution(s)	Vote date	Yeas	Nays
104th Congress	*House Joint Resolution 79*	*June 28, 1995*	*312*	*120*
	Senate Joint Resolution 31	*December 12, 1995*	*63*	*36*
105th Congress	*House Joint Resolution 54*	*June 12, 1997*	*310*	*114*
106th Congress	*House Joint Resolution 33*	*June 24, 1999*	*305*	*124*
	Senate Joint Resolution 14	*March 29, 2000*	*63*	*37*
107th Congress	*House Joint Resolution 36*	*July 17, 2001*	*298*	*125*
108th Congress	*House Joint Resolution 4*	*June 3, 2003*	*300*	*125*
109th Congress	*House Joint Resolution 10*	*June 22, 2005*	*286*	*130*
	Senate Joint Resolution 12	*June 27, 2006*	*66*	*34*

Source H

Political Cartoon by Clay Bennett, the *Christian Science Monitor*, Boston, July 4, 2006. Available at http://www.cagle.com/news/FlagBurning2/2.asp.

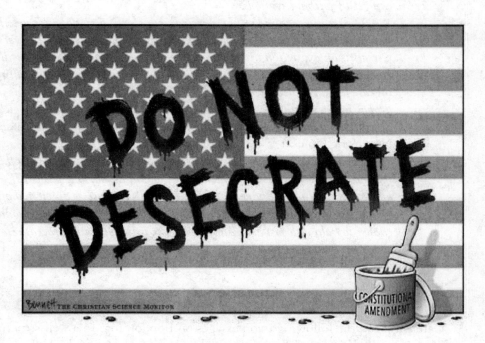

Clay Bennett, *Christian Science Monitor*, Boston 7/4/06

Source I

An excerpt from "The Star-Spangled Banner," an editorial by Todd Lindberg that appeared in the *Washington Times*, July 4, 2006. Available at http://washingtontimes.com/op-ed/20060703-102601-1107r.htm.

. . . the last thing that a constitutional amendment banning flag-burning strikes me as is a slippery slope toward broader restriction on freedom of expression. There are two reasons for this.

First, the flag is the flag; the only reason to accord it special status (if that's what you decide) is that it is, in fact, the singular national symbol. We are not even talking about a ban on burning red, white, and blue things, such as bunting, nor of suppressing the debate over whether banning the burning of the flag is a good thing. It's not hypocrisy but rather a pretty good philosophical point to say that the flag, as the symbol of the freedom to burn, baby, burn, is the one thing you shouldn't burn. For if you burn the freedom to burn, you have no freedom. For more on the danger that lies in this direction, see the collapse of the Weimar Republic in Germany.

On the other hand, the flag is not the freedom itself but its symbol. The freedom continues even if a particular flag is consumed in fire. To burn the flag is not to burn the only flag. There is no "the" flag, only flags; or if there is "the" flag, it is an idea of the flag and therefore beyond the reach of the flames.

Except that a perfectly acceptable way to dispose of a worn-out flag, according to the old Boy Scout manual Dad gave me, is by burning. The ceremony is to be at all times respectful and somber. Here, one reveres "the" flag by seeing to it that "a" flag gets decommissioned properly. So the symbolic content is always present. When someone burns a flag in protest, it's just not about the fire and the piece of cloth. The flag is indeed a symbol of a political community, and I'm not sure that political communities can get by without symbols.

The second reason I'm not worried about a slippery slope constricting expression once you ban flag-burning is that in the current environment, socially enforced restraints on expression are far broader and more important than legal restraints. In the case of flag-burning, if you do it now, most Americans will think you are an ingrate jerk, as noted above. But even if a constitutional amendment passes, no one is proposing the death penalty for flag-burning, nor life in prison. If you get busted, you can probably look forward to a few days in the clink, plus adulatory editorials in the New York Times.

So while I am not a great supporter of an amendment banning flag-burning, neither do I think that such an amendment would do harm if passed. If I were a member of the Senate, I would have voted for it. That's because as an elected officeholder, I would feel more solicitous of the national symbol, as perhaps befits someone who has chosen to hold office in accordance with the principles and procedures of the political community in question.

Question 2

Carefully read the following two passages on London fog. In a well-structured essay, compare the two selections with regard to purpose and style. Consider such elements as diction, figurative language, organization, syntax, and manipulation of language.

London was the first great city in history to be fuelled by coal. The combination of ever greater quantities of coal being burned by an expanding population, and London's naturally misty situation in a marshy river valley, meant London was plagued by regular fogs from Stuart times on. The worst lasted from November 1879 to March 1880 without a break. 1

In 1936–7, 322 tons of solid matter per square mile was deposited on Archbishop's Park, Lambeth, which meant nearly 30,000 tons of matter a year 2 *was deposited on London from smoky atmosphere. At the same time central London received 18 per cent less sunshine than the inner suburbs. In 1934 there was fog from 10 November to 1 December, and deaths from respiratory diseases tripled. The fog of 1952 was estimated to have caused 4000 deaths. The Clean Air Act was passed in 1956, and the last great London fog was in 1962.*

—(Tim Goodwin, 1997)

Fog everywhere. Fog up the river, where it flows among green aits and meadows;   1
*fog down the river, where it rolls defiled among tiers of shipping and waterside pollu-
tions of a great (and dirty) city. Fog on the Essex marshes, fog on the heights, fog creeping into the cabooses of [coal barges]. Fog lying out on the yards, and hovering in the
rigging of great ships; fog drooping on the gunwales of barges and small boats. Fog in
the eyes and throats of ancient Greenwich pensioners, wheezing by the firesides of their
wards; fog in the stem and bowl of the afternoon pipe of the wrathful skipper, down in
his close cabin; fog cruelly pinching the toes and fingers of his shivering little 'prentice
boy on deck. Chance people on the bridges peeping over the parapets into a nether sky
of fog, with fog all round them, as if they were up in a balloon, and hanging in the
misty clouds.*

—(Charles Dickens, *Bleak House*, 1852–53)

Question 3

In one section of *Walden*, Henry David Thoreau ponders the advice offered by elders in a society. Carefully read the following passage from this American classic. Then, in a well-constructed essay argue how your position on advice from elders relates to that of Thoreau. Use appropriate evidence from your own experiences, readings, and observations to explain and support your argument.

> *What everybody echoes or in silence passes by as true today may turn out to be false-
> hood tomorrow, mere smoke of opinion, which some had trusted for a cloud that
> would sprinkle fertilizing rain on their fields. What old people say you cannot do,
> you try and find that you can. Old deeds for old people, and new deeds for new. Old
> people did not know enough once, perchance, to fetch fresh fuel to keep the fire a-going;
> new people put a little dry wood under a pot, and are whirled around the globe with
> the speed of birds, in a way to kill old people, as the phrase is. Age is no better, hardly
> so well, qualified for an instructor as youth, for it has not profited so much as it has
> lost. One may almost doubt if the wisest man has learned anything of absolute value
> by living. Practically, the old have no very important advice to give the young, their
> own experience has been so partial, and their lives have been such miserable failures,
> for private reasons, as they must believe; and it may be that they have some faith left
> which belies that experience, and they are only less young than they were. I have lived
> some thirty years on this planet, and I have yet to hear the first syllable of valuable or
> even earnest advice from my seniors. They have told me nothing, and probably cannot
> tell me anything to the purpose. Here is life, an experiment to a great extent untried by
> me; but it does not avail me that they have tried it. If I have any experience which I
> think valuable, I am sure to reflect that this my Mentors said nothing about . . .*

END OF SECTION II

ANSWER KEY

1. C	19. D	37. E
2. E	20. D	38. B
3. D	21. C	39. B
4. B	22. B	40. A
5. D	23. E	41. A
6. A	24. C	42. E
7. C	25. D	43. C
8. E	26. B	44. B
9. C	27. A	45. E
10. E	28. D	46. B
11. C	29. B	47. C
12. E	30. E	48. A
13. B	31. B	49. A
14. D	32. C	50. B
15. A	33. D	51. D
16. E	34. B	52. E
17. D	35. E	53. D
18. B	36. D	54. C

Explanations of Answers to the Multiple-Choice Section

The Annie Dillard Passage

1. **C.** Each paragraph opens with the words "the essay." With this repetition, Dillard guarantees that the reader's focus does not waver. It also provides the organizational framework of the passage. There is no passive voice present. (By the way, the previous sentence is an example of passive voice.) The author relates no personal narrative and does not identify herself with her audience.

2. **E.** In the first two sentences, the author blames "contrived entrances" for killing "the novel of idea." She supports this in the next to the last sentence in paragraph 1 by criticizing "fabricated dramatic occasions." Both of these examples point to the artificial construct of fiction.

3. **D.** The first paragraph contains two major cause-and-effect situations. The first is found in sentences 1–3, and the second is found in the last two sentences.

4. **B.** The first of the two sentences states what the essayist does: he thinks. The second sentence tells the reader *how* he thinks and writes. By writing two separate sentences, Dillard reinforces the equal importance of each of these points.

5. **D.** A careful reading of the sentence and a knowledge of how to locate antecedents can only lead the reader to choose "the real world." Any other choice negates the correct meaning of antecedent/referent.

6. **A.** The second paragraph clearly develops its point through a contrast and comparison between prose and poetry. None of the other strategies is present in the paragraph.

7. **C.** Dillard's subject is the essay. Her position is one of unswerving allegiance to its form and function. Nowhere does she criticize the essay or the essayist, and nowhere does she discuss innovations or the changing of its form. Dillard **is** an artist. This classification, however, does not reveal her stance on the essay form.

8. **E.** Knowing the definition of parallel structure and being able to recognize it makes the choice of E an easy one. ("Even if . . . even if . . .")

9. **C.** Look carefully at sentences 1–3 of paragraph 3 and notice the author's use of the words "connections," "covenant," "veracity," and "truth." With this specific diction, the only appropriate choice is C.

10. **E.** The only choice that contains two adjectives that are *BOTH* applicable to the author's tone in this passage is E. The purpose of the essay is to inform/explain the function of the essay and the essayist. This, in itself, is the support for choosing E. The confidence is apparent in the writer's discussion of the other forms of literature.

The Henry James Passage

11. **C.** This is located in the first sentence. Here James tells his audience that the quality of the mind of the producer is the key factor in creating high-quality art. The moral and artistic grow out of this quality. "Obvious truth" refers to his premise, and beauty is a by-product of the process.

12. **E.** James's diction is indicative of an elitist attitude. Note phrases such as "No good novel will ever proceed from a superficial mind . . ." He closes out any other possibility for a creative endeavor of quality.

13. **B.** The question demands your close attention to the structure of the sentence. In this instance, beauty as truth is directly proportionate to intelligence. "This" applies to the novel, picture, statue. And, it is James's vision.

14. **D.** A rule of thumb is a generally accepted truth as to how to proceed. In this context, James presents a ground rule for the young writer.

15. **A.** This is a straight question about antecedents. To find the referent, look back at the sentence preceding this one.

16. **E.** One needs to know and recognize examples of the terms used in this question. Here, "rather" opposes "generalizing" with "particularizing."

17. **D.** The sentence in the middle of the passage beginning with "The other arts . . ." will

indicate to the careful reader that James is making a point to the student that art forms other than the novel are "confined and hampered." No other choice is appropriate in this context.

18. **B.** It is easy to see the parallel structure in this sentence. Notice "enjoy it"; "explore it"; "publish it"; "rejoice in it." The other choices are not present.

19. **D.** This question may seem daunting at first, but careful examination of the structure of the lines reveals that James is telling the student not to allow himself to be cornered into following advice that limits his horizons. Ironically, James has already limited the scope of art and the artist.

20. **D.** The pronoun "this" in the middle of the sentence beginning with "All life belongs to you . . ." is your best clue to the answer "This" is referring to the word "art." Therefore, the only appropriate choice is D.

21. **C.** Through both the process of elimination and recognizing that both parts of your answer must be correct, the only appropriate choice is didactic, because the author is attempting to instruct the young novelist and exhortative in his urging the young writer to "catch the color of life itself."

The Herman Melville Passage

22. **B.** Throughout the passage, Melville builds his description on the comparison between items connected to the sea and those related to the land. Choices A and C are examples of this controlling analogy. D is another specific detail provided, and E is an example used by Melville to reinforce his description of the Nantucketer.

23. **E.** Paragraph 4 supports choices A, B, C, and D. The only choice not supported in the text is E.

24. **C.** The diction and selection of detail all support the tone of admiration. The hyperbole can easily be seen in paragraph 1 and the end of paragraph 3.

25. **D.** Italics are used for very definite reasons. The purpose here is for emphasis. Melville wants to draw the reader back to the

only other italicized word in the piece—*Nantucket*—the very first word of the passage.

26. **B.** Here, pronouns are very important. In paragraph 2, *this* refers the reader to paragraph 1, which is about the island. *These* in paragraph 4 refers to the previous paragraph, which is about the inhabitants of Nantucket. The last sentence of the passage, while quite moving, indicates, again, a reference to Nantucketers. However, *these* in the first sentence of paragraph 3 is a definite shift in focus from the island to its inhabitants.

27. **A.** The only choice appearing in the first paragraph is parallel structure, which is used throughout the listing of "extravaganzas" that Melville bestows on Nantucket. Many of the items in the listing begin with the word *that*.

28. **D.** Keeping in mind the central focus of the passage, Melville's retelling of the Native American legend is not to highlight or focus on Native Americans, but to reinforce his attitude toward the Nantucketers, whom he perceives in mythic proportions. He compares them to Noah, to Alexander the Great, and to Emperors.

29. **B.** The question requires the reader to be aware of the consecutive details that build in size and importance: from the clam to the whale.

30. **E.** The analogy established with Nantucket to Illinois is that of an island to a landlocked state. The only choice given that illustrates the same relationship is walrus to prairie dog. Here a walrus lives its life surrounded by the sea; whereas, the prairie dog is surrounded by the land.

31. **B.** The whale is a "mightiest animated mass." This can only refer to the largest creature in the sea. "Himmalehan" and "Mastadon" reinforce the power and size of the creature.

32. **C.** The tone, diction, syntax, and selection of detail all point to Melville's admiration of the fortitude, perseverance, and uniqueness of the Nantucketer.

33. **D.** In this question, the repetition balances the dual focus: the island and its inhabitants. The diction and syntax of this selection are not

formal, but rather a grand folk myth of epic proportions.

34. B. Beginning with "There is more sand" and continuing to the end of the paragraph, Melville presents examples dependent upon extreme exaggeration.

35. E. The paragraph develops an extended analogy that compares the world of the sea to that of the land, such as sea to prairie, sailor to prairie dog. None of the other choices are valid in this context.

The Lucy Stone Passage

36. D. If you chose E, you're out of our class for the day. Seriously, it is obvious that the speaker both is outraged about the treatment of women and demands the right of women to be recognized. No other choice is correct in both descriptions.

37. E. The fifth sentence in paragraph 1 provides the answer to this question. In these two lines, the student should see that Stone makes a case that both women and blacks are not being educated and are by implication being treated in the same way.

38. B. If the student carefully looks at the sixth sentence in paragraph 1, he or she will see that it is valid to conclude that the speaker does not hold teaching in high esteem.

39. B. Each of these lines plays an important role in the speech. However, only one plays the role of controlling the entire thought process. The other choices are subtopics.

40. A. Anecdotal support is found in the first six sentences of paragraph 1. A direct quotation is located in the second half of paragraph 2. Facts are used in the fourth and fifth sentences of paragraph 1, and the appeal to emotion is presented in the seventh sentence of paragraph 2. There is no ad hominem argument in the speech.

41. A. Stone wants women to rise up and stop the oppression of their gender. But, according to this statement, she must actually see to it that women are oppressed until they can no longer bear it. It is only then that Stone sees their being willing to demand their rights.

42. E. If you look carefully at the section of the speech beginning with "I wish that women . . ." and ending with "frequent bar-rooms," you will note that Stone says she is disappointed that women concern themselves only with the superficial. Her remarks about religion, foreign countries, fate, and men are in opposition to the actual choices. Notice the use of the word *ephemeral.*

43. C. The speaker aims for a logical conclusion when she points to Phillips' definition of sphere. She creates an implied syllogism that if God cannot make a mistake, if God created each of us to do our best, this must apply to all—men and women alike.

44. B. To exhort: to urge, to warn earnestly. In her speech, Lucy Stone is urging her audience to begin to stand up for their rights as women. She wants them to understand what is oppressing them and, as a result, to "no longer bow down to it." A careful reading of the passage will indicate that the basis for the speech is *NOT* telling a story, nor is there an attempt to amuse or describe. The last sentence provides the final impetus for her exhortation.

The Poverty Excerpt

45. E. The argument is derived from the examples presented in the other choices.

46. B. Each paragraph provides specific statistics to support the claim that welfare reform is not a complete success. This thesis is presented at the end of the passage, *NOT* at the beginning.

47. C. There is an indictment of the United States for failing to enact the policies and meet the goals that other countries have already put into practice.

48. A. A cursory look at the inclusion and preponderance of statistics and other data with little personal commentary support this choice.

49. A. All other footnotes cite sources, depend on other sources, or are personal commentary.

50. B. It doesn't matter how many estimates there are. What is important is the authority and reliability of Swingle.

51. D. The presentation of so many statistics from various years demands a visual representation for clarity and ease of understanding. The other choices would only address a subjective aspect of the topic.

52. E. This source comes from an organization whose very name states its potential bias and agenda.

53. D. The words *dismal* and *but*, plus the phrases *still a long way from* and *more compassionate* all point to the author's disapproval of the current policies of the United States.

54. C. Within the footnote, *Working Paper* and the Internet address point to a recent research project submitted to an academic institution.

Sample Student Essays

Rubrics for Flag Amendment Synthesis Essay

A **9** essay has all the qualities of an 8 essay, and the writing style is especially impressive, as is the analysis and integration of the specifics related to the proposed flag desecration amendment and the given sources.

An **8** essay effectively and cohesively addresses the prompt. It clearly takes a position on the proposed flag desecration amendment and supports the argument using carefully integrated and appropriate evidence, including at least three of the given sources. The essay will also show the writer's ability to control language.

A **7** essay has all the properties of a 6, only with a more complete, well-developed, and integrated argument or a more mature writing style.

A **6** essay adequately addresses the prompt. The argument is on the proposed flag desecration amendment and integrates, as well as makes use of, appropriate evidence, including at least three references from the given sources. These elements are less fully integrated and/or developed than scores in the 7, 8, 9 range. The writer's ideas are expressed with clarity, but the writing may have a few errors in syntax and/or diction.

A **5** essay demonstrates that the writer understands the prompt. The argument/claim/position about the proposed flag desecration amendment is generally understandable, but the development and/or integration of appropriate evidence and at least three of the given sources is limited or uneven. The writer's ideas are expressed clearly with a few errors in syntax or diction.

A **4** essay is not an adequate response to the prompt. The writer's argument indicates a misunderstanding, an oversimplification, or a misrepresentation of the assigned task. The writer may use evidence that is not appropriate or not sufficient to support the argument, or may use fewer than three of the given sources. The writing presents the writer's ideas, but may indicate immaturity of style and control.

A **3** essay is a lower 4 because it is even less effective in addressing the question. It is also less mature in its syntax and organization.

A **2** essay indicates little success in speaking to the prompt. The writer may misread the question, only summarize the given sources, fail to develop the required argument, or simply ignore the prompt and write about another topic. The writing may also lack organization and control of language and syntax. (***Note:*** **No matter how well written, a summary will never rate more than a 2.**)

A **1** essay is a lower 2 because it is even more simplistic, disorganized, and lacking in control of language.

Student A

Some were shocked. Others were indifferent. Still others were proud. What event   1
could cause such an array of emotions in so many different people? The burning of the
American flag. However, what seems to lead to even more controversy than the actual
burning of the flag is the legal ramifications of flag-burning—specifically, whether or not
it should be banned by the Constitution. Politicians in favor of such a law are proposing a
one-sentence amendment to the First Amendment to target the "desecration" of the flag.
But such an amendment is just not necessary.

Supreme Court Chief Justice William Rehnquist vehemently protested the burning   2
of the flag, stating, "Millions and millions of Americans regard it with an almost
mystical reverence." Indeed, quite true is that declaration, which matches the regard—in
the forms of laws which criminalize public flag-burning—of 48 states to such a symbol
(Source E). And, of course, the ultimate reflection of this point of view exists in the
very amendment causing such ruckus, which states, "The Congress shall have power to
prohibit the physical desecration of the flag of the United States" (Source B).

However, if Americans are in such cohesive opinion of flag-burning, or so it would   3
seem, why are some still setting fire to the beloved stars and stripes? Once again, we
return to the respected Chief Justice Rehnquist, who also states that "[The flag] does not
represent any particular political philosophy" (Source E). In a sense, this makes the flag
mutable enough to represent all things politically American, such as government officials
or even government policy. Such is the reasoning that the *Los Angeles Times* justified the
burning of the flag—as "attacks on government and public officials" (Source F). But,
other than a crowd's "distaste" at the politicians of America, another, more practical
explanation rights the burning of the flag: disposing it. According to Todd Lindberg,
the Boy Scout manual delineates a "ceremony" for getting the flag "decommissioned
properly. So the symbolic content is always present" (Source I). Such a respectful gesture
to a flag that has served its days seems almost shameful to ban.

Then, of course, arises the issue of freedom of speech. An opinion of Senator   4
McConnell of Kentucky finds that, "Placing a no-flag-burning asterisk next to the
amendment's sweeping guarantee of free speech . . . could invite amendments to ban
other sorts of speech" (Source F). Such a thought seems a little flawed in the snowball-
down-a-hill way, but the adage "power corrupts," no matter how trite, might still give
the idea enough fuel to scorch. However, Mr. Lindberg of the *Washington Times* proved
the hypocrisy of such an amendment best. A ban on "the symbol of the freedom to
burn, baby, burn," leaves a paradoxical taste in anyone's mouth. Limiting the freedom to
destroy freedom means, to Mr. Lindberg and many others, "you have no freedom."

But "burn, baby, burn" doesn't exactly sound like a right "of the people peaceably   5
to assemble," as stated in the First Amendment of the Constitution (Source A). Fire is
hardly a symbol of peace, and one could almost make the argument that burning the
flag is equivalent to yelling "fire!" in a crowded theater (almost, but not in the landmark

case of *Texas v. Johnson*). The justices of the Supreme Court ruled that the burning of the flag caused neither "breaches of the peace" nor "a serious disturbance" (Source D). Furthermore, United States v. Eichman voices the same opinion, thus, effectively eliminating the Flag Protection Act of 1989 (Source D). And, finally, to sooth the naysayers voicing opinions of a free-for-all burn, a 2006 *Los Angeles Times* editorial reports that "no epidemic of flag-burning" has occurred since such rulings. Indeed, flag-burning, as a freedom, fulfills all legal qualifications as an act of peaceful expression. No harm, no foul.

Ultimately, the voice of the people clearly decrees that an amendment to rid flag-burning is superfluous. The Supreme Court has already sanctioned flag-burning as a right in the penumbra of the First Amendment, and that Amendment, throughout its decade of existence, hasn't achieved the needed majority of Congress (Source G). But the sovereign of this state, the people, says it all. The 2006 poll in *USA Today* shows a minor, but significant 54 percent majority of the American public believing an amendment against flag-burning is unnecessary (Source C). Mr. Lindberg really did say it best in his own editorial: ". . . most Americans will think you are an ingrate jerk . . . But even if a constitutional amendment passes, no one is proposing the death penalty for flag-burning." Flag-burning is unpatriotic at best, but Americans have enough common sense not to use flag-burning as a favorite pastime without a law on their backs.

6

Student B

Over the course of American history, political freedoms and inalienable rights have been the ultimate treasure of the American people. As a nation, we pride ourselves on our right to express our opinions without threat of punishment. From the Supreme Court ruling against the Alien and Sedition Acts to the current flag burning issue, free speech has been upheld.

1

In the cases of *Texas v. Johnson* and the *U.S. v. Eichman*, the Supreme Court has said that the act of desecrating the American flag is not illegal (Source D). This reliable source states that flag burning does not directly threaten anyone; in fact, a reference to the flag is amorphous. The flag is a symbol that takes billions of forms across the entire country. As stated in Source I, "There is no 'the' flag . . . it is an idea of the flag and therefore beyond the reach of the flames." An anti-flag burning amendment would be nebulous and would be incapable of addressing a specific act of flag desecration.

2

A survey taken by *USA Today* indicated that more than half of those Americans tallied do not want such an amendment added (Source C). The Constitution is a document for the people, by the people, and of the people; therefore, if an opinion is to matter, it should be the viewpoint of the people. They are the ones who need to abide by the laws and should have some say in their construction.

3

However, when Congress voted a series of six times, every single time there were more representatives for the amendment than were against it (Source G). There is a serious discrepancy between the people and their representatives. The author of Source F

4

expresses his opinion on this matter, maintaining that if these representatives passed the amendment, it would severely restrict the freedoms that we as Americans have come to love.

The first amendment to the Constitution has clauses that are contradictory to the 5 proposed anti-flag burning amendment (Source A). The proposed amendment would restrict the provided freedoms and would "prohibit the physical desecration of the flag of the United States." Source F claims that the destruction of Old Glory as a protest was symbolic speech protected by the First Amendment. Though the editorial may be biased, the author makes a provocative argument. This country has been content with the First Amendment. Why change it now? It may even create more of a problem. Telling someone to do something often provokes him to do the opposite. When a child is told to refrain from an action, the typical response is for the child to test the parent. Clay Bennet's ironic political cartoon (Source H) reinforces this idea. It shows an American flag marked with the quote, "do not desecrate." The cartoon mocks the idea of forbidding the desecration of the flag and demonstrates that the amendment may not be taken seriously and may possibly have the opposite effect from what it is trying to enforce.

It is apparent that the government and the people are currently undecided on the 6 issue. When it resurfaces, and it will, the representatives will be faced with a conundrum: "yea" or "nay." Hopefully, the representatives will see the contradictions and turn down the amendment for the good of the American people and their freedom.

Rating the Student Essays: Flag Amendment

Student A
This high-range paper:

- Effectively introduces the argument and indicates the opposition in paragraph 1
- Opens with an interesting example of parallelism
- Clearly establishes the writer's position against the amendment
- Exhibits strong control of language: diction, syntax, transitions, rhetorical questions
- Builds a cohesive and convincing argument against the amendment by effectively introducing, combining, and commenting on appropriate sources
- Employs transition to further the development of the points in the argument: *however, then, but, ultimately*
- Creates mature concluding sentences in each paragraph that drive home the writer's position
- Smoothly integrates and cites sources material
- Presents a coherent, strong voice and tone

Student B
This mid-range essay:

- Opens convincingly by including outside information to indicate the writer's position against the amendment
- Incorporates and properly cites at least three sources to support the argument
- Adequately comments on the synthesized material and includes some relevant outside information to reinforce the sources used
- Indicates an understanding of the process of writing a synthesis essay

- Demonstrates control of language through diction and syntax
- Recognizes the bias in source material
- Adds to the argument by creating an analogous situation: the child testing the parents
- Understands tone and intent

Rubrics for "Fog" Essays

High-Range Essay

- Successfully identifies the purpose of each passage
- Effectively compares the style of each passage
- Refers to appropriate examples from each passage
- Effectively analyzes devices such as diction, organization, syntax, and manipulation of language in a clear voice
- Good connective tissue
- Focused organization and development
- Few, if any, flaws

Mid-Range Essay

- Correctly identifies the purpose of each passage
- Adequately compares the style of each passage
- Uses specifics from each passage to analyze rhetorical devices
- Adequately links examples to the analysis of the style and purpose of each passage
- Less well-developed than the high-range essays
- A few lapses in diction or syntax

Low-Range Essay

- Inadequate response to the prompt
- Misunderstands, oversimplifies, summarizes, or misrepresents the purpose and style of each passage
- Insufficient or inappropriate use of examples to develop the demands of the prompt
- Lack of adequate control of elements of essay writing

"Fog" Passages—Student Sample A

A concept defined in the literal sense can be quite different from that same idea defined in the figurative sense. When comparing the Goodwin and Dickens passages, it becomes evident that different approaches in describing the famous London fogs result in two images at radically opposite ends of the "fog spectrum." Differences in stylistic elements, particularly diction and tone, are critical in creating two distinct and opposing descriptions.

The Goodwin passage could easily be categorized as nothing more than a newspaper or textbook article. Expository in nature, the piece highlights the facts pertaining to the London fogs. He includes such facts as the tons of solid matter per square mile in a section of London in 1937, and how much less sunshine was in London as compared to the inner suburbs. The didactic tone of the passage lends itself to explanation of factual details. Moreover, the diction is marked by technical jargon, such as "solid matter per square mile." This combination of tone and diction is instrumental in presenting a fact-based description of London fog. Because the piece is founded on facts only, it seems that the purpose would be to educate/inform the audience about this unique phenomenon. It also seems the author wants to underline the harmful consequences of the fogs, such as the indicated respiratory disease and excessive pollution.

On the other hand, Dickens implements a style, which personifies the fog. The diction in the piece is critical in giving the fog animate qualities. Figurative language like "creeping" and "lying out on the yards," give London fogs a life-like quality. The fog is also "hovering," "drooping" and "wheezing." These characteristics give the reader the eerie feeling that the fog is human and is going to take over. Moreover, the diction in this passage uses simple, everyday words, and not the technical vocabulary employed in the Goodwin paragraph. The tone of the Dickens description is concerned with the emotional impression that fog gives to the bystander. Because the tone and diction are more figurative in nature, Dickens' purpose appears to be to relate the London fogs emotional qualities to the reader so that the reader feels as if surrounded by this fog. Dickens style leads to a totally opposite impression of the fog, and it also achieves a different purpose.

These two passages employ differing stylistic elements to meet different ends. Goodwin is successful in presenting a factual analysis. Dickens, on the other hand, uses rhetorical devices to create an almost living-breathing image of the fog, one that is all-enveloping.

"Fog" Passages—Student Sample B

These two passages describe fog in England in two completely opposite ways. The first passage, written by Tim Goodwin, gives an objective view of the fog, stating its qualities in a list-like manner. The author of the second passage uses parallel structure and figurative language to give a more impressionistic view of London fog.

The first passage is something one would find in an encyclopedia. It first gives an explanation of why there is so much fog in London. It then goes on to give exact dates and amounts of fog in London. Goodwin gives the reader details and statistics to illustrate the continuing problems related to fog. He connects the effects from 1879 to 1962. For example, in 1936 nearly 30,000 tons of matter were deposited on London. Towards the end of the passage Goodwin uses chronological organization to discuss the last of the great London fogs. This is a detached conclusion to a purely objective piece of writing.

2

The second passage is extremely different from the first passage. Charles Dickens gives an impressionistic description of the London fog. His repetition of the word "fog" makes an imprint on the reader's mind. Dickens also uses parallel structure, beginning almost every sentence or clause with "fog." This constantly reminds the reader that Dickens is describing fog, which is everywhere. Dickens also personifies the fog, writing that it is "cruelly pinching the toes and fingers of his shivering little 'prentice boy." Dickens makes it seem more menacing and powerful. He also uses an analogy towards the end of the passage, saying that the people feel "as if they were up in a balloon, and hanging in the misty clouds." Because the fog is everywhere, there is no distinction between earth and sky. This gives the reader a lasting impression on how the fog is omnipresent.

3

Selection One and Selection Two are two very different passages with two very different purposes. Each passage is well suited for its purpose; the first is straightforward and explanatory, while the second evokes emotions and feelings.

4

Rating Student Sample A

This is a high-ranking essay for the following reasons:

- Effectively presents and discusses the purpose and intent of each passage (end of paragraph 2), (end of paragraph 3)
- Thoroughly addresses the stylistic differences between the two pieces (paragraph 2), (paragraph 3)
- Strongly supports his or her position with appropriate details from the passage (paragraphs 2 and 3)
- Well-focused throughout
- Mature voice and clear style

This high-ranked essay that is both informative and direct is so well-focused that the reader can almost see the writer's mind at work. And, as a result, the audience comes away with a clear understanding of the differences between the style and purpose of the two excerpts.

Rating Student Sample B

This is a mid-range essay for the following reasons:

- Clearly indicates an understanding and an application of the prompt (paragraph 1)
- Good control of sentence structure

- Provides specifics from each text to support the analysis (paragraph 1), (paragraph 3)
- Clear transitions
- Clear topic adherence
- Obvious development lacking connections to insights resulting from a close reading of the texts
- A few syntax and diction errors

This mid-range essay is a concise, "bare-bones" presentation. Its strength lies in its clear focus and appropriateness of support. However, these citations are more like listings rather than serving as the foundation for discussions of their implications.

Rubrics for the Thoreau Passage

High-Range Essay

- Correctly identifies Thoreau's attitude about the value of advice given by elders
- Effectively presents a position about Thoreau's attitude
- Clear writer's voice
- Successfully defends his or her position
- Presents carefully reasoned arguments making reference to specific examples from personal experience, knowledge, reading
- Effectively manipulates language
- Few, if any, syntactical errors

Mid-Range Essay

- Correctly identifies Thoreau's attitude about the value of advice given by elders
- Understands the demands of the prompt
- Clearly states the position of the writer
- Presents a generally adequate argument which makes use of appropriate examples
- Less well-developed than the high-range essay
- Ideas clearly stated
- A few lapses in diction or syntax

Low-Range Essay

- Inadequate response to the prompt
- Misunderstands, oversimplifies or misrepresents Thoreau's attitude
- Insufficient or inappropriate use of examples to develop the writer's position
- Lack of mature control of elements of essay writing

This prompt presented students with the opportunity to sound off about their place in the pecking order. Interestingly enough, the majority of the student writers disagreed with Thoreau or, at least, qualified his remarks. Relatively few chose to speak about parental advice, but they were willing to admit the influence of teachers, scientists/explorers, and grandparents. Often the anecdotal material rambled and needed to be connected back to the ideas of Thoreau. However, even with these shortcomings, the majority of the students obviously found this excerpt and prompt to be easily accessible.

Thoreau Passage—Student Sample A

In this passage, Henry David Thoreau clearly states that progress is made from generation to generation. However, Thoreau discredits his elders, writing "They have told me nothing, and probably cannot tell me anything." Instead, I would like to argue that the knowledge of those who are older and wiser is of great value. To illustrate this thesis, three examples will be used, first, a doctoral student, second, the protagonist of Mary Shelley's <u>Frankenstein</u>, and third, the twentieth-century poet, T. S. Eliot.

The doctoral student in question is studying physics, the science of motion. In order to reach graduate school, the student must first graduate from elementary, middle and high school. During those years, the student learns to read, an ancient art taught him by a teacher—one who is older than he is and can impart knowledge to him. The numerous teachers he will have impart laws of mathematics, science, and nature. He must learn these rules established by scientists like Descartes, Einstein, and Aristotle. Eventually, he will reach college, where professors will continue to introduce the student to fields like calculus and quantum mechanics. Knowledge of all these fields is necessary for the student to pursue his doctoral work; he must obtain information of the past in order to formulate his own ideas in the future.

From another perspective, Victor Frankenstein, the title character in Mary Shelley's chef d'oeuvre spends his childhood reading metaphysical scientists of the Middle Ages. He later attends university, where his professor instructs him in the natural sciences. Victor then spends years assembling the theories of his elders into a new form, one that will let him re-create life. Bringing the monster to life is a collaborative effort of his creativity and the genius of those who live before him.

Finally, T. S. Eliot firmly believed that one must first study literature before creating it. Evidence of this theory is most clearly demonstrated in the opening lines of <u>The Wasteland</u>, which reference the beginning of Chaucer's <u>Canterbury Tales</u>. Other allusions to Shakespeare, Greek tragedy, and far Eastern religions are scattered throughout the text. By recognizing the significant contributions of his elders, Eliot derived his own place in history. These allusions demonstrate that Eliot felt learning from others was crucial to forming his opinion.

In conclusion, all three examples refute Thoreau's statement that "Age is no better, hardly so well-qualified for an instructor of youth." The doctoral student, Victor Frankenstein, and T. S. Eliot all illustrate the importance of learning from the past as a means of promoting the present.

Thoreau Passage—Student Sample B

Do old people offer valuable advice? Why of course they do! Life has not changed so much that old people cannot relate to teenage life today. Experience is key to giving advice. The ability to empathize and understand is very important for an older person to give advice to a younger person. Henry David Thoreau's point of view in "Walden" is that old people are not capable of offering decent advice. He is incorrect in holding this creed because he does not realize that older people once played through childhood, once matured through puberty, and once became adults. If advice is needed, older people are the best source.

It is common for teenagers to find interest in members of the opposite sex. Occasionally, these young couples have trouble getting along. The relationship takes a turn for the worst. Ready to console her teary-eyed granddaughter sits grandma. At age 70, she has been happily married for nearly 45 years. Presenting her shoulder to her granddaughter to cry on, the grandmother talks of her many high school and college relationships. For a moment granddaughter pauses her crying to giggle at grandma's silly stories, but in reality, she is still faced with her own broken heart to deal with. After hours of bonding, the two hug and smile. Grandma's advice on men came from her own experiences. She'd never thought that so many heartaches would ever do her any good. Pleased with life, a husband, children, and grandchildren, this older woman would never worry about those past flings again. But, when her devastated little grandbaby was hurt by a young man, she reached back for those early love stories. She used her bad experiences to her granddaughter's advantage. She showed another woman that there will be plenty of men before "the one." Thoreau, on the other hand, would ask anyone rather than an elder for advice. His past experiences led him to believe that he will never "hear the first syllable of valuable or even earnest advice from [his] seniors." 2

Everything happens for a reason. When people say things, there is a reason behind them. No matter what life tosses at someone, it's had to happen to someone before. If someone has lived life for seventy years, they've got to have plenty of stories to share about experiences life has shared with them. Henry David Thoreau is an unlucky man for not seeing the beauty in the elderly. They are the most respectable people and give superior advice because they have experienced it all. Older people are the buttress of life today. Their actions shaped the way and set precedents for future generations. Older people have lots to say, whether it be on teenage relationships or any topic. You name it, they've lived it! 3

Rating Student Sample A

This is a high-range essay for the following reasons:

- Clearly establishes a position regarding Thoreau's assertion
- Thoroughly develops the argument with hypothetical and literary references
- Good topic adherence
- Excellent connective tissue
- Thorough development of the argument that reveals a well-read writer
- Mature voice, diction, and syntax
- Indicative of a willingness to stretch with regard to manipulation of language (paragraph 3, sentence 1) and support for the writer's position (paragraph 4)

This high-range essay is clear, coherent, cohesive, and compact. It reveals a confident, smooth writing style. There is nothing extraneous contained in this concise, well-organized presentation.

Rating Student Sample B

This is a mid-range essay for the following reasons:

- Establishes a clear voice (paragraph 2)
- Indicates an understanding of the text and the prompt
- Addresses the prompt
- Presents a reasonable argument in support of the writer's assertion
- Demonstrates topic adherence
- Interesting use of parallel structure (paragraph 1)
- Needs transitions (paragraphs 2 and 3)
- Paragraphing errors (paragraphs 2, 3)
- Several syntactical errors

The writer of this mid-range essay chose to develop his or her argument with an extended example. The conversational tone, although simple and straightforward, clearly supports the writer's position.

Appendixes

Glossary
Selected Bibliography
Websites

Abstract refers to language that describes concepts rather than concrete images.

Ad Hominem In an argument, an attack on the person rather than on the opponent's ideas. It comes from the Latin meaning "against the man."

Allegory a work that functions on a symbolic level.

Alliteration the repetition of initial consonant sounds, such as "Peter Piper picked a peck of pickled peppers."

Allusion a reference contained in a work.

Analogy a literary device employed to serve as a basis for comparison. It is assumed that what applies to the parallel situation also applies to the original circumstance. In other words, it is the comparison between two different items.

Anecdote a story or brief episode told by the writer or a character to illustrate a point.

Antecedent the word, phrase, or clause to which a pronoun refers. The AP English Language and Composition exam often expects you to identify the antecedent in a passage.

Antithesis the presentation of two contrasting images. The ideas are balanced by word, phrase, clause, or paragraph. "To be or not to be . . ." "Ask not what your country can do for you, ask what you can do for your country . . ."

Argument a single assertion or a series of assertions presented and defended by the writer.

Attitude the relationship an author has toward his or her subject, and/or his or her audience.

Balance a situation in which all parts of the presentation are equal, whether in sentences or paragraphs or sections of a longer work.

Cacophony harsh and discordant sounds in a line or passage in a literary work.

Character those who carry out the action of the plot in literature. Major, minor, static, and dynamic are types of characters.

Colloquial the use of slang in writing, often to create local color and to provide an informal tone. *Huckleberry Finn* is written in a colloquial style.

Comic Relief the inclusion of a humorous character or scene to contrast with the tragic elements of a work, thereby intensifying the next tragic event.

Conflict a clash between opposing forces in a literary work, such as man vs. man; man vs. nature; man vs. god; man vs. self.

Connective Tissue those elements that help create coherence in a written piece. See Chapter 8.

Connotation the interpretive level of a word based on its associated images rather than its literal meaning.

Deduction the process of moving from a general rule to a specific example.

Denotation the literal or dictionary meaning of a word.

Dialect the re-creation of regional spoken language, such as a Southern dialect. Zora Neale Hurston uses this in such works as *Their Eyes Were Watching God*.

Diction the author's choice of words that creates tone, attitude, and style, as well as meaning.

Didactic writing whose purpose is to instruct or to teach. A didactic work is usually formal and focuses on moral or ethical concerns.

Discourse a discussion on a specific topic.

Ellipsis an indication by a series of three periods that some material has been omitted from a given text. It could be a word, a phrase, a sentence, a paragraph, or a whole section. Be wary of the ellipsis; it could obscure the real meaning of the piece of writing.

Epigraph the use of a quotation at the beginning of a work that hints at its theme. Hemingway begins *The Sun Also Rises* with two epigraphs. One of them is "You are all a lost generation" by Gertrude Stein.

Euphemism a more acceptable and usually more pleasant way of saying something that might be inappropriate or uncomfortable. "He went to his final reward" is a common euphemism for "he died." Euphemisms are also often used to obscure the reality of a situation. The military uses "collateral damage" to indicate civilian deaths in a military operation.

Euphony the pleasant, mellifluous presentation of sounds in a literary work.

Exposition background information presented in a literary work.

Extended Metaphor a sustained comparison, often referred to as a conceit. The extended metaphor is developed throughout a piece of writing.

Figurative Language the body of devices that enables the writer to operate on levels other than the literal one. It includes metaphor, simile, symbol, motif, and hyperbole, etc.

Flashback a device that enables a writer to refer to past thoughts, events, or episodes.

Form the shape or structure of a literary work.

Hyperbole extreme exaggeration, often humorous, it can also be ironic; the opposite of understatement.

Image a verbal approximation of a sensory impression, concept, or emotion.

Imagery the total effect of related sensory images in a work of literature.

Induction the process that moves from a given series of specifics to a generalization.

Inference a conclusion one can draw from the presented details.

Invective a verbally abusive attack.

Irony an unexpected twist or contrast between what happens and what was intended or expected to happen. It involves dialog and situation and can be intentional or unplanned. Dramatic irony centers around the ignorance of those involved; whereas, the audience is aware of the circumstance.

Logic the process of reasoning.

Logical Fallacy a mistake in reasoning (see Chapter 9 for specific examples).

Metaphor a direct comparison between dissimilar things. "Your eyes are stars" is an example.

Metonymy a figure of speech in which a representative term is used for a larger idea (*The pen is mightier than the sword*).

Monologue a speech given by one character (Hamlet's "To be or not to be . . .").

Motif the repetition or variations of an image or idea in a work used to develop theme or characters.

Narrator the speaker of a literary work.

Onomatopoeia words that sound like the sound they represent (hiss, gurgle, pop).

Oxymoron an image of contradictory term (bittersweet, pretty ugly, jumbo shrimp).

Pacing the movement of a literary piece from one point or one section to another.

Parable a story that operates on more than one level and usually teaches a moral lesson. (*The Pearl* by John Steinbeck is a fine example.)

Parody a comic imitation of a work that ridicules the original. It can be utterly mocking or gently humorous. It depends on allusion and exaggerates and distorts the original style and content.

Pathos the aspects of a literary work that elicit pity from the audience. An appeal to emotion that can be used as a means to persuade.

Pedantic a term used to describe writing that borders on lecturing. It is scholarly and academic and often overly difficult and distant.

Periodic Sentence presents its main clause at the end of the sentence for emphasis and sentence variety. Phrases and/or dependent clauses precede the main clause.

Personification the assigning of human qualities to inanimate objects or concepts. (Wordsworth personifies "the sea that bares her bosom to the moon" in the poem "London 1802.")

Persuasion a type of argument that has as its goal an action on the part of the audience.

Plot a sequence of events in a literary work.

Point of View the method of narration in a literary work.

Pun a play on words that often has a comic effect. Associated with wit and cleverness. A writer who speaks of the "grave topic of American funerals" may be employing an intentional or unintentional pun.

Reductio ad Absurdum the Latin for "to reduce to the absurd." This is a technique useful in creating a comic effect (see Twain's "At the Funeral") and is also an argumentative technique. It is considered a rhetorical fallacy, because it reduces an argument to an either/or choice.

Rhetoric refers to the entire process of written communication. Rhetorical strategies and devices are those tools that enable a writer to present ideas to an audience effectively.

Rhetorical Question one that does not expect an explicit answer. It is used to pose an idea to be considered by the speaker or audience. (François Villon [in translation] asks, "Where are the snows of yesteryear?")

Sarcasm a comic technique that ridicules through caustic language. Tone and attitude may both be described as sarcastic in a given text if the writer employs language, irony, and wit to mock or scorn.

Satire a mode of writing based on ridicule, that criticizes the foibles and follies of society without necessarily offering a solution. (Jonathan Swift's *Gulliver's Travels* is a great satire that exposes mankind's condition.)

Setting the time and place of a literary work.

Simile an indirect comparison that uses the word *like* or *as* to link the differing items in the comparison. ("Your eyes are like stars.")

Stage Directions the specific instructions a playwright includes concerning sets, characterization, delivery, etc.

Stanza a unit of a poem, similar in rhyme, meter, and length to other units in the poem.

Structure the organization and form of a work.

Style the unique way an author presents his ideas. Diction, syntax, imagery, structure, and content all contribute to a particular style.

Summary reducing the original text to its essential parts.

Syllogism the format of a formal argument that consists of a major premise, a minor premise, and a conclusion.

Symbol something in a literary work that stands for something else. (Plato has the light of the sun symbolize truth in "The Allegory of the Cave.")

Synecdoche a figure of speech that utilizes a part as representative of the whole. ("All hands on deck" is an example.)

Syntax the grammatical structure of prose and poetry.

Synthesis locating a number of sources and integrating them into the development and support of a writer's thesis/claim.

Theme the underlying ideas the author illustrates through characterization, motifs, language, plot, etc.

Thesis simply, the main idea of a piece of writing. It presents the author's assertion or claim. The effectiveness of a presentation is often based on how well the writer presents, develops, and supports the thesis.

Tone the author's attitude toward his subject.

Transition a word or phrase that links one idea to the next and carries the reader from sentence to sentence, paragraph to paragraph. See the list of transitions in Chapter 8.

Understatement the opposite of exaggeration. It is a technique for developing irony and/or humor where one writes or says less than intended.

Voice can refer to two different areas of writing. The first refers to the relationship between a sentence's subject and verb (active voice and passive voice). The second refers to the total "sound" of a writer's style.

SELECTED BIBLIOGRAPHY

The following is a select listing of both fiction and nonfiction writers, past and present, whose works include: essays, news articles, novels, short stories, journals, biographies, histories, autobiographies, diaries, satire, and political treatises. Each of these writers presents ideas in original, thought-provoking, and enlightening ways. Our recommendation is that you read as many and as much of them as you can. The more you read, discuss, and/or analyze these writers and their work, the better prepared you will be for the AP English Language and Composition exam. And, there is another wondrous benefit. You will become much more aware of the marvelous world of ideas that surrounds you. We invite you to accept our invitation to this complex universe.

Personal Writing: Journals, Autobiographies, Diaries

Maya Angelou
Annie Dillard
Frederick Douglass
Lillian Hellman
Helen Keller
Martin Luther King, Jr.
Maxine Hong Kingston

Mary McCarthy
Samuel Pepys
Richard Rodriguez
May Sarton
Richard Wright
Malcolm X

Biographies and Histories

Walter Jackson Bate
James Boswell
Thomas Carlyle
Bruce Catton

Winston Churchill
Shelby Foote
George Trevelyan
Barbara Tuchman

Journalists and Essayists

Joseph Addison
Michael Arlen
Matthew Arnold
Francis Bacon
Russell Baker
Harold Bloom
G. K. Chesterton
Kenneth Clark
Joan Didion
Maureen Dowd

Ellen Goodman
Pauline Kael
Garrison Keillor
John McPhee
N. Scott Momaday
Anna Quindlen
John Ruskin
Marjorie Sandor
Susan Sontag
Richard Steele

Nora Ephron
Anne Fadiman
William Hazlett
John Holt
Paul Russell

Henry David Thoreau
Calvin Trillin
Eudora Welty
E. B. White
Paul Zimmer

Political Writing and Satire

Hannah Arendt
Simone de Beauvoir
W. E. B. DuBois
William F. Buckley
Thomas Hobbes
Thomas Jefferson
John Locke
Machiavelli

John Stuart Mill
Sir Thomas More
Lincoln Steffens
Jonathan Swift
Alexis de Tocqueville
T. H. White
Tom Wolfe

Writers Known for Their Fiction and Nonfiction

Charlotte Perkins Gilman
Zora Neale Hurston
Norman Mailer

George Orwell
Virginia Woolf

Naturalists, Scientists, Adventurers

Edward Abbey
Rachel Carson
Charles Darwin
Loren Eisley
Stephen Jay Gould
William Least Heat-Moon

Verlyn Klinkenborg
Barry Lopez
Peter Matthiessen
Margaret Mead
Carl Sagan

Literally thousands of websites are, in some way, related to the study of college-level English. We are not attempting to give you a comprehensive list of all these websites. What we want to do is to provide you with a list that is most relevant to your preparation and review for the AP English Language and Composition exam. You can decide which websites may be of interest and/or offer you special benefits.

> *Note:* **These websites were available and online at the time this book was revised. Please be aware that we cannot guarantee that a site you choose to explore will be operating when you go to that URL.**

"After I found an AP chat room on the net, I felt a lot better knowing that there were other AP students out there I could talk to and share ideas and questions with. I know I'm not alone."
—Tyler W.,
　AP student

- Because this is an Advanced Placement exam you are preparing for, why not go to the source as your first choice: http://apcentral.collegeboard.com.
- Comnet: http://webster.comnet.edu/grammar is an all-purpose grammar site.
- Dogpile: www.dogpile.com is a good search engine that finds topics via categories and other search engines.
- Search.com is one of the newest and best search engines that accesses the biggest of the search engines available at www.search.com.
- Bowling Green University Writer's Lab: www.bgsu.edu/offices/acen/writerslab is chock full of information.
- Purdue On-Line Writing Lab (OWL): http://owl.english.purdue.edu is a helpful online writing center with a huge set of links.
- University of Missouri's Online Writery: www.missouri.edu/~writery is user-friendly with terrific graphics.
- Rensselaer Polytechnic Writing Center: www.rpi.edu/web/writing center offers good advice on mechanics and style.
- Syracuse University Writing Center: http://wrt.syr.edu/thewritingcenter.html is good for writing skills across the curriculum.
- A+ Research and Writing: http://ipl.si.umich.edu/div/teen/aplus is a comprehensive guide to writing research papers.
- University of Michigan's Sweetland Writing Center: www.lsa.umich.edu/swc/help/help .html is user-friendly and quite comprehensive.
- A portal site that links to the best of library and research sites is available at www .libraryspot.com. It consists of three sections: libraries (academic, film, government, and so forth), reference desk (almanacs, biographies, dictionaries, and so forth), and reading room (books, journals, newspapers, magazines).
- www.americanrhetoric.com has political speeches and speeches from movies.
- A site that links to many other websites related to AP English Language and Composition is http://www.kn.att.com/wired/fil/pages/listaplitma.html.
- For terms, exercises, tips, and rules from a primate with attitude, go to Grammar Bytes: http://chompchomp.com.

- Three useful sites that provide help with rhetorical and literary terms are: www.uky .edu/AS/Classics/rhetoric.html http://andromeda.rutgers.edu/~jlynch/terms/index.html http://humanities.byu.edu/rhetoric/Silva.htm
- You can compare coverage of major events in newspapers from around the world at www.newseum.org/todaysfrontpages.
- A website that provides access to the world of arts and letters—including newspapers, literary magazines, and blogs—is: http://artsandlettersdaily.com.

Each of these websites will lead you to many more. Take the time to explore the various sites and make your own evaluations about their value to you. You might even decide to set up your own AP Language website, or chat room!

Prepare for Success at Every Step in Your AP* Journey!

AP*

Prepare for Upcoming AP Classes

McGraw-Hill
ONboard™
FOR ADVANCED PLACEMENT*

This online, interactive program builds the skills & background knowledge you'll need to succeed in upcoming AP coursework and beyond.

Prepare for the AP Exam

McGraw-Hill
SCOREboard™
FOR AP* TEST PREP

This online, adaptive, diagnostic AP Test Prep series includes 4 complete AP practice exams and personalized study plans to help you maximize your time leading up to the exam.

Mc Graw Hill Education

To learn more or to purchase, visit
MHEonline.com/advancedplacement

* Advanced Placement program and AP are registered trademarks of the College Board, which was not involved in the production of, and does not endorse, these products.